Toward a Better Worldliness

Toward a Better Worldliness

Ecology, Economy, and the Protestant Tradition

Terra Schwerin Rowe

Fortress Press
Minneapolis

TOWARD A BETTER WORLDLINESS

Ecology, Economy, and the Protestant Tradition

Copyright © 2017 Fortress Press. All rights reserved. Except for brief quotations in critical articles or reviews, no part of this book may be reproduced in any manner without prior written permission from the publisher. Email copyright@1517.media or write to Permissions, Fortress Press, PO Box 1209, Minneapolis, MN 55440-1209.

Cover image: © Thinkstock [ninanaina] [istock 508025024]

Cover design: Joe Reinke

Hardcover ISBN: 9781506423333

Paperback ISBN: 9781506422329

eBook ISBN: 9781506422336

The paper used in this publication meets the minimum requirements of American National Standard for Information Sciences — Permanence of Paper for Printed Library Materials, ANSI Z329.48-1984.

Manufactured in the U.S.A.

This book was produced using Pressbooks.com, and PDF rendering was done by PrinceXML.

To young theologians who will live in the world we leave them,
especially my daughter, Mica Joy,
and goddaughters, Hannah Grace and Emily Mae.

"When I grow up," I tell her, "I too will go to faraway places
and come home to live by the sea."
"That is all very well, little Alice," says my aunt,
"but there is a third thing you must do."
"What is that?" I ask.
"You must do something to make the world more beautiful."
"All right," I say.
But I do not know yet what that can be.

—Miss Rumphius, the "Lupine Lady," by Barbara Cooney

Contents

	Acknowledgments	ix
	Introduction	xi
1.	Protestant Ghosts and the Spirits of Capitalism: Ecology, Economy, and the Protestant Tradition	1
2.	Inheriting the Free Gift: Economic and Ecological Implications	33
3.	Ecology of the Gift: The Ecotheologies of Joseph Sittler and Jürgen Moltmann	67
4.	The Gift Revisited: Unconditioned and Multilateral	89
5.	Communicating Grace	119
6.	Toward a "Better Worldliness"	157
	Bibliography	179
	Index	193

Acknowledgments

A text on the graceful interdependencies of the world would be incomplete without an attempt to acknowledge the ways the project itself has emerged as the nexus of a multitude of gifts. I'm particularly grateful for the guidance of teachers and mentors who have encouraged me along the way: Gwen Saylor for putting the idea of scholarly pursuits in my head, Norma Cook-Everist for empowering me to embrace my voice, Jim Martin-Schramm for initiating my environmental consciousness at Holden Village, and Winston Persaud, Craig Nessan, and Brigitte Kahl for key expressions of encouragement along the way. John Hoffmeyer encouraged the feminist in me before I had vocabulary to express it and Chris Boesel cheered on the project—especially its more confessional moments— from beginning to end. Catherine Keller has consistently provided academic, career, and personal guidance with profound grace while nurturing a unique spirit of collegiality and support among her advisees that, in many ways, embodies the values and aims of her scholarly work. I'm grateful for the conversations and encouragement of many of these colleagues as well, especially Karen Bray, Jake Erickson, Beatrice Marovich, Sara Rosenau, and Natalie Williams. Augsburg Fortress, and Michael Gibson in particular, has graciously supplied expertise and resources, making it possible to share this work more broadly with the audience I had in mind.

I'm especially thankful for gifts my family members have given. I'm not sure I would value education and curiosity as I do without the

TOWARD A BETTER WORLDLINESS

example of my grandfather, Gerald, and his stubborn insistence that his daughters—my mother included—be able to attend the college of their choice along with his sons. And I doubt that *he* would have valued education in this way if his older sister, Dorothy, had not defied her elders by attending high school even when it was deemed a morally suspicious choice for a young woman in rural Minnesota. I am sure I would not be where I am today without the material and emotional support of my parents, Jim and Judi, and my sister, Liesl. I think my dad, who took pleasure in all things financial and arithmetic, would have found it amusing that the daughter who dreaded every moment of the math tutoring he enthusiastically supplied found a way to write a couple hundred pages on economics without employing a single equation. More than anything, though, this work has grown out of the grace, love, inspiration, and support of my partner, Jim. Life with him and Mica Joy, our sparkle of dust, has provided the most profound lessons in the ways that grace-filled interdependency can "test and nurture freedom."[1]

---

1. Catherine Keller, *From a Broken Web: Separation, Sexism and Self* (Boston: Beacon, 1988), 3.

Introduction

And we don't have to do anything to bring about this future.
All we have to do is nothing. . . . All we have to do is
not react as if this is a full-blown crisis.
—Naomi Klein, *This Changes Everything: Capitalism vs. the Climate*

We are given to understand . . . that we can do nothing
of ourselves . . . the latter [is] the grace of God.
—Martin Luther, *On the Bondage of the Will*

In[1] August 2014 an Op-Ed on faith and climate change appeared in the *New York Times.* Frustrated with the prevalent antagonism between science and faith in climate change literature, author Kristin Dombek describes the bridge she constructed between her old Christian beliefs and her current climate concerns. She describes how she became disillusioned with her childhood Christian faith, how she found new faith in the images and insights of Darwin, and how this current belief is helping her find a way to cope with paralyzing climate change–induced anxiety. However, coping also depends, she explains, on a key lesson she learned as a child and still retains from the Lutheran-Reformed Heidelberg Catechism: how to "belong, body and soul" to something bigger than herself.[2]

Like many people today, Dombek lives with the awareness that her

---

1. Parts of this chapter have been previously published as "Grace in Intra-action," in *Entangled Worlds: Science, Religion, Materiality*, ed. Mary-Jane Rubenstein and Catherine Keller (New York: Fordham University Press, 2017).
2. Kristin Dombek, "Swimming Against the Rising Tide: Secular Climate-Change Activist Can Learn from Evangelical Christians," *New York Times*, August 9, 2014.

TOWARD A BETTER WORLDLINESS

apartment and neighborhood in Brooklyn, New York— everything she considers home—remain at risk of drowning in a globally rising sea tide. In order to "stay awake, active, [and] useful," rather than frozen by fear and her own insignificance in the face of an incomprehensibly complex and vast shift, Dombek describes the usefulness of a faith woven on the warp of Darwin's insights and the woof of elements from her childhood faith.[3] Where Darwin taught her to feel in her body the world's "vast and humbling contingency,"[4] her childhood faith taught her to trust in—rather than fear—a sense that her life was "linked to something bigger: that [she] belong[ed], body and soul, to a larger story for which [she was] responsible."[5] She compares these overlapping journeys of faith to learning to float in the ocean. One might easily feel overwhelmed by the power and breadth of the sea, but in order to learn buoyancy, she had to develop a sense that her body was part of something bigger and trust that this vast and humbling contingency would hold up in the face of rising tides.

I propose this might be a compelling parable of grace for today: a profound and agentially empowering sense of gratitude that acknowledges we belong, body and soul, to a vast and humbling contingency "outside ourselves" as much as this contingency constitutes, for us, a singular sense of self. Even as we learn to release ourselves in trust to this oceanic inside/outside, we become liberated from fear and anxiety to accept responsibility for a story larger than ourselves. The theological viability of this parable is not immediately apparent from a Protestant perspective. The Reformation has bequeathed to us a heritage of doctrinally driven definitions of grace as a mode of gifting that depends on a strict separation of inside from outside as well as an opposition of grace to reciprocity and action— even responsible action. Where doctrinal commitments have pressed toward defining grace in terms of an inside/outside binary and the rejection of reciprocity, we will find an unfortunate resurgence of a formative grace-versus-nature dynamic. And this binary, as we will

3. Ibid.
4. Ibid.
5. Ibid.

xii

see, is met by the particular tendency to unwittingly bolster concepts foundational for the global economic system currently mass-producing climate change.

Yet, we will also find viable resources within the tradition, particularly in articulating the value of an unconditioned gift embedded in a web of multilateral interdependencies, for developing the kind of buoyant trust Dombek suggests. Rather than reading gift as the opposite of exchange, I will argue that this gift, as grace, is free to empower a wider circulation of gifts. Such conceptual shifts might—just might—open toward a better worldliness saturated and sustained by communicating grace.

All We Have to Do Is Nothing: Grace and Climate Change

Dombek's reference to the Heidelberg Catechism may be surprising given the Protestant tradition's ambiguous history when it comes to environmental issues. As the dust of the Reformation upheaval settled and solidified into a new orthodoxy, the concept of grace, in particular, congealed into an exclusive articulation of forensic justification. Here God's redeeming activity appeared as an external power over and against humanity's passive receptivity. The reformers emphasized a radically Augustinian sense of sinfulness whereby humans were so deprived of any natural inclination for goodness that we could "do nothing of saving significance, whether we wish to or not."[6] On account of the complete lack of human righteousness, God's presence and redeeming work could only be conceptualized *extra nos*, outside of us creatures.

The reformers emphasized that the radical depravity of humanity was answered by God's willing self-denial. By entering into created life God bridges the gulf between God's righteousness and human sin. According to Luther, the key message of the incarnation of God in Christ is that God is not against us, but for us.[7] So, along with the

6. Martin Luther, "The Bondage of the Will," in *The Annotated Luther, Volume 2: Word and Faith*, ed. Kirsi I. Stjerna (Minneapolis: Fortress Press, 2015), 180.
7. Paul Althaus, *The Theology of Martin Luther*, trans. Robert C. Schultz (Minneapolis: Fortress Press, 1966), 185.

emphasis of God's redeeming work, *extra nos,* believers were encouraged to find solace in the realization that God and God's redemptive work in the world is, first and foremost, for me—*pro me.*

Today, a confluence of events and conceptual shifts call into question the value of articulating God's primary redemptive activity in terms of external relations (*extra nos*) aimed primarily at isolated individuals abstracted from the rest of creation (*pro me*). Among these changes are the emerging awareness of dynamic, complex, and internally related systems such as global economics and climate change. Raised consciousness of these systems and the way they function has led to increasing skepticism and condemnation of Cartesian-Newtonian worldviews. Many of these concerns have been highlighted for decades in feminist and ecotheological critical analyses of the Protestant tradition. In briefly sketching such investigations of this influential tradition, a recurrent theme emerges around questions of grace and selfhood. As we will see, concerns consistently arise around the ways our understanding of grace shapes our anthropologies and our relations to others—both created and divine.

The Annihilated Self: Feminist Responses to Protestant Grace

Critical analysis of the kind of self Protestant grace constructs has received relatively broad attention in feminist theologies—many of which came to influence and be influenced by ecotheology. Daphne Hampson's 1988 essay, "Luther on the Self: A Feminist Critique," remains a classic example of early-wave feminist theological critique. Although self-denial has been a consistent theme in Christian thought throughout its history, for Luther, a sense of the loss of self to God and neighbor becomes even more emphatically expressed. Hampson writes, "'We know that our theology is certain,' says Luther, 'because it sets us outside ourselves.' The Christian lives *extra se.*"[8] This external

---

8. Daphne Hampson, "Luther on the Self: A Feminist Critique," *Word and World* 8 (1988): 214. For a Christian to shift the locus of the self to a god who is only *extra se,* she explains, "I must transfer my centre of gravity to one who lives outside myself." Hampson substantiates this point by quoting the following passage from Luther's "Freedom of a Christian": "A Christian lives not in himself, but in Christ and in his neighbor. Otherwise he is not a Christian. He lives in Christ through faith,

emphasis poses a particular danger for women who are already expected by society to deny themselves and put the desires and goals of their husbands and children before their own. Consequently, Hampson argues that Luther's theology cultivates insecurity for women because, in grace, the self is de-centered—found only outside itself, leaving a void or a certain lack in the proper place of an organizing sense of self that contributes to women's agency. Hampson concludes her analysis with the following summary: "Within the tradition, then there is no sense that the self, secure in itself, can freely exist, in easy intercourse with others. We cannot maintain ourselves; we are insecure."[9]

In short, the profound challenge posed to Protestantism by Hampson and other feminists is whether its theology merely glorifies an unhealthy and death-dealing pattern of relationships, particularly for women, by placing the whole weight of the human's relation to God on the loss of self. For some men, this de-centering of self may be a necessary word, but for women whose sense of self is often already found outside itself identifying with another, this may be dangerous.

What's more, Luther's relational dynamic between an active God and receptive human came to signify a particularly abusive model of love. German scholar Karl Holl, whose work on Luther remains influential to this day, describes this divine action on the human passive soul as an ideal model of love: "'Love is now understood as a power that does not hesitate to inflict hurt in order to liberate its object from itself and to raise it above itself.' It is this love that is the 'innermost, the deepest reality in God' (55)."[10] Feminists have consistently pointed to the danger of idealizing such abusive relations when an active/passive binary, implying domination and control, is functioning. As Catherine Keller explains, referring to this tendency more broadly in the tradition, for these theologians, "love is a matter of acting *upon*, the action of a controlling, unilateral will."[11]

---

in his neighbor through love. By faith he is caught up beyond himself into God. To have this new self-understanding is what it means to be Christian" (ibid., 216).

9. Ibid., 218.

10. Karl Holl, "What Did Luther Understand by Religion?," cited in H. Gaylon Barker, *The Cross of Reality: Luther's Theologia Crucis and Bonhoeffer's Christology* (Minneapolis: Fortress Press, 2015), 61. It seems important to note that Barker quotes Holl here uncritically—even approvingly.

TOWARD A BETTER WORLDLINESS

Rejecting the insecure self, found only outside itself, Hampson does not return to an interior ego but affirms, instead, the self "achieved in and through relationship."[12] However, in Deanna Thompson's more recent feminist reading of Luther's theology of the cross, she offers a crucial counter-question to Hampson's emphasis on the redemptive power of relationship for women: Is it any better to articulate an understanding of women's redemption that lies solely in relationship when society's oppressive expectations of women have been primarily relational? In a society where women are expected to prioritize relational commitments over career opportunities or limit themselves to roles of relational care-taking, relationships may appear as further self-evacuation rather than redemption.[13]

What these tensions in feminist analysis bring to light is a basic contradiction at the heart of Lutheran thought regarding the self. On the one hand (what Luther would consider proper to God's right-handed work in the world), we have the passive self—the feminized passive soul, annihilated by the masculine deity, *extra nos.* By emphasizing God's activity as pure exteriority, the Christian self is, as Hampson points out, always insecure since it can only secure a self outside itself. Here, women's traditional roles and postures of passivity are reinforced, even sanctified. On the other hand (aligning with God's left-handed work in the world according to Luther), and corresponding with Thompson's concerns, our acts of service to one another actively evacuate the self, giving it over to fulfill the needs of others. Here, women's overly active modes, self-depleting in their total orientation toward the needs of others, are also encouraged. At the center of the self in both right- and left-hand cases is a void—either passively receiving to fill an inherent lack with a masculinized exteriority or actively emptying the self for others.

---

11. Catherine Keller, *From a Broken Web: Separation, Sexism and Self* (Boston: Beacon, 1988), 37.
12. Hampson, "Luther on the Self," 222.
13. See Deanna Thompson, *Crossing the Divide: Luther, Feminism, and the Cross* (Minneapolis: Fortress Press, 2004), 105–12.

INTRODUCTION

The Modern Subject: Ecotheological Responses to Protestant Conceptions of Grace

Ironically, rather than the radical uncertainty one might expect from this passive yet actively annihilated self, ecotheologians suggest that the Protestant self unfolded toward and contributed to the modern substantial subject.[14] As modernity advanced, the strong binaries of the Protestant doctrine of grace—Creator and creature, giver and receiver, active and passive, self and other—became enmeshed with Cartesian-Newtonian thought and unfolded toward a modern preoccupation with the sovereign self defined over and against every human and other-than-human object. Where the reformers envisioned that the human lay passive before the saving, exterior activity of God, it is more than merely coincidental that the modern human took on an image dominating activity working on the nonhuman passive and inert world toward the purportedly redemptive aims of scientific/technological progress and economic growth.

Among ecologically minded theologians, Sallie McFague and John Cobb stand out as exemplary for their early insistence that we engage economic systems as well as ecological concerns. The importance of their insight has only grown with increased awareness of the key connections between global capitalism and climate change. Both also focus their attention on models of selfhood inspired by the Protestant tradition that are functioning in current economic systems.

McFague, for example, explains that in the "neoclassical economic worldview, two values predominate—the individual and growth."[15] The basic assumption of neoclassical economics is that "human beings are self-interested individuals who, acting on this basis, will create a syndicate or machine, even a global one, capable of benefiting all eventually. Hence, as long as the economy grows, all individuals in

---

14. These critiques come from within the Protestant tradition as well as from without. See Moltmann and Sittler on the self (chapter three), but also McFague and Cobb (below), H. Paul Santmire, *The Travail of Nature: The Ambiguous Ecological Promise of Christian Theology* (Minneapolis: Fortress Press, 1985), and Elizabeth Johnson (below), among others.

15. Sallie McFague, *Life Abundant: Theology and Economy for a Planet in Peril* (Minneapolis: Fortress Press, 2001), 81.

xvii

TOWARD A BETTER WORLDLINESS

a society will sooner or later participate in prosperity."[16] Famously, Adam Smith secured the place of self-interest as fuel for the capitalist engine, explaining, "It is not from the benevolence of the butcher, the brewer, or the baker, that we can expect our dinner, but from their regard to their own interest."[17] Through self-interest, the "invisible hand" of capitalism will work out the greatest good for society: "By pursuing his own interest [the laborer] frequently promotes that of the society more effectually than when he really intends to promote it."[18] McFague analyzes influences contributing to the anthropology functioning in Smith's economics. She lists "the Enlightenment's central insight: the importance of the individual,"[19] the Newtonian view of the world as an inert machine "with all its parts connected only in external ways,"[20] and the Protestant definition of human sinfulness. Smith took the Protestant understanding of sin as the heart turned in on itself, transformed it into the economic concept of human self-interest and harnessed this as an inexhaustible resource to fuel the capitalist machine. Once put to use in the right system, this basic tendency of humanity could be transformed from our downfall to our collective redemption—a growing economy that would eventually lead to better economic conditions for all.

Along with McFague, Cobb also emphasizes the fact that Smith was merely assuming a Protestant anthropology when he placed self-interest at the heart of the capitalist machine. In *Sustaining the Common Good*, Cobb describes the capitalist anthropology as the *homo economicus*.[21] This economic human is "the picture of extreme individualism,"[22] where all relations (not just with God) are purely external. What's more, everything other than humanity becomes

16. Ibid., 77.
17. Adam Smith, *The Wealth of Nations*, ed. Kathryn Sutherland (New York: Oxford University Press, 2008), Book IV, chapter 2.
18. Smith, *The Wealth of Nations*, Book I, chapter 2.
19. McFague, *Life Abundant*, 78.
20. Ibid., 79.
21. John B. Cobb Jr., *Sustaining the Common Good: A Christian Perspective on the Global Economy* (Cleveland: Pilgrim Press, 1994). Developed first in Cobb and Daly, Daly, *For the Common Good: Redirecting the Economy Toward Community, the Environment, and a Sustainable Future* (Boston: Beacon, 1994). See sections starting on 85 and 91 of the latter, for example.
22. Cobb, *Sustaining the Common Good*, 87.

defined solely by its use value, as potential resource. Only commodities exchanged in the market are of interest so that "the gifts of nature are of no importance, nor is the morale of the community of which *Homo economicus* is a part."[23]

In addition to McFague's and Cobb's critical analysis of Protestant and Smithian anthropologies, other ecotheologians emphasize the related cosmological dualism that became popularized with the Reformation. Elizabeth Johnson, for example, explains that where early Christian tradition integrated God, humanity, and creation in a hierarchical cosmology, this ancient relational cosmology was set aside during the Reformation for a dualism between God and world. Combined with an intensified interest in God's relation to the individual human person, Protestant thought emerges, according to Johnson, as "intensely anthropocentric."[24]

For Protestant concepts of selfhood, ecotheological and feminist critiques converge most clearly on the Protestant doctrine of grace. Both perspectives emphasize the detrimental effects of idealized divine relations as external, unilateral, uncooperative, nonreciprocal, and lacking participation. The idealization of external and dualistic relations unfolds in human economic systems and relations to the other-than-human world as well as between men and women. In Catherine Keller's early text, *From a Broken Web: Separation, Sexism and Self,* she argues that the independent self defined over and against others, existing in separative and external relations, is inherently patriarchal in that it idealizes unilateral and external relations of control and power. Describing the conception of God readily associated with the doctrine of grace, Keller argues that God's action on passive subjects from the outside "is the supreme case of external relatedness. Indeed this is the ultimate separate subject, eternally self-sufficient, immune to the influence of those others whom he has created."[25]

---

23. Ibid.
24. Elizabeth Johnson, "Losing and Finding Creation in the Christian Tradition," in *Christianity and Ecology: Seeking the Well-Being of Earth and Humans,* ed. Dieter T. Hessel and Rosemary Radford Ruether (Cambridge, MA: Center for the Study of World Religions, 2000), 8–9.
25. Keller, *From a Broken Web*, 37.

TOWARD A BETTER WORLDLINESS

Similarly, McFague emphasizes that the predominant economic worldview depends on disconnection, where "humans are pictured as separate from one another and isolated from the earth; that is, they are only externally related to both."[26] Finally, Cobb and economist Hermann Daly point out how this mode of relation is explicitly engaged in the predominant practice among economists of identifying other-than-human creatures and matter as "externalities."[27]

Cartesian-Newtonian Legacy

The economic systems and anthropologies implicit in global neoliberal capitalism also arise from particularly modern concepts. The Reformation initiated remarkable shifts in religious practices, a Catholic Counter-Reformation, major upheavals of war, social reorganization, and political shifts such as state segmentation along religious lines, as well as increasing challenges to divinely ordained and exclusive authority. Less than a century later, René Descartes sparked similarly massive shifts in human anthropology, reason, authority, and conceptions of the natural world. Where the reformers had emphasized grace in terms of purely external relations, Descartes refigured the human as only externally related to the other-than-human world. The Cartesian worldview has been a normative characteristic of modern life, but today some of Descartes's most basic assumptions about reality and what it means to be human are being called into question.

The most troubling Cartesian assumptions place humanity outside of nature in a "proper" position of ruling, ordering, and controlling. In creating the modern human, Descartes divorced human creatureliness from other-than-human nature.[28] Before Descartes, Aristotle's

---

26. McFague, *Life Abundant*, 81.
27. Cobb and Daly, *For the Common Good*; see, for example, 53 and on.
28. Indeed, many argue that before Descartes, there were no humans and animals as we understand them in modernity, but creatures ranging from lower-level organisms to humans to heavenly creatures. As biblical scholar Stephen Moore explains, "Prior to the Cartesian revolution in philosophy, there were no 'animals' in the modern sense. There were 'creatures,' 'beasts,' and 'living things,' an arrangement reflected in, and reinforced by, the early vernacular Bibles. As Laurie Shannon notes, '*animal* never appears in the benchmark English of the Great Bible (1539), the Geneva Bible (1560), or the King James Version (1611).' Moreover, the continuum evoked

xx

INTRODUCTION

definition of humanity still held sway. Aristotle defined the human as a rational animal, implying humanity shares in the animality of other creatures, but maintains a special ability for rational thought that distinguishes the human species.[29] This implied a hierarchical, but continuous, relationship between humanity and other living beings.[30] For Aristotle, humanity shares in animality, with a little something special on top: the ability for reason.

While the human was prioritized in Aristotle's worldview, it was fundamentally part of the natural and animal world. Descartes questioned all of this. In his famous *Discourse on Method* (1637), he questioned everything: How do I know God exists?; How do I know what I am sensing/experiencing is real?; How do I know I exist? While the questioning remains courageous, his answers have had unpredictable consequences for modern Western thought. In the end, Descartes concluded that the only logical foundation could be that I know I am here, that I exist, because I am thinking. I am the one questioning. If there is such a thought, there must be a being behind this thought. Consequently, he concludes with the famous phrase, *cogito, ergo sum*, "I think, therefore I am" (*Discourse on Method*). With this move Descartes redefined the human by a unique ability for self-reflection or consciousness.

In defining human Being in terms of an ability for self-consciousness, Descartes contrasts this unique human characteristic with the rest of material reality, thus shifting from a cosmic hierarchy of creatures to a binary between human and nonhuman. In this sense,

by a term such as 'creature' also included angels and demons, so that premodern humans were part of a complex, multilayered cosmology. Missing was 'the fundamentally modern sense of the animal or animals as humanity's persistent, solitary opposite" (Stephen Moore, "Why There Are No Humans or Animals in the Gospel of Mark," in *Mark as Story: Retrospect and Prospect*, ed. Kelly R. Iverson and Christopher W. Skinner [Atlanta: Society of Biblical Literature, 2011], 80–81, citing Laurie Shannon, "The Eight Animals in Shakespeare; or, Before the Human," *Publications of the Modern Language Association of America* 124 [2009]: 476).

29. Aristotle, "The History of Animals," in *The Animals Reader: The Essential Classical and Contemporary Writings*, ed. Linda Kalof and Amy Fitzgerald (New York: Berg, 2007), 5–7.

30. Derrida explains, "Descartes will, with all due rigor, do without his definition of the human in the combined terms of animality and rationality, of man as rational animal. There is in his gesture a moment of rupture with respect to the tradition, a rupture for which Descartes is not given credit often enough" (*The Animal That Therefore I Am*, ed. Marie-Louise Mallet, trans. David Wood [New York: Fordham University Press, 2008], 71).

xxi

TOWARD A BETTER WORLDLINESS

Descartes created the modern animal as well as the modern human.[31] Where humans were associated with thinking, conscious reflection, and response rather than innate reaction, all nonhuman creatures and matter became associated with machines. This became known as the *bête-machine* (beast-machine) doctrine because it associated non-humans with automated mechanization.[32] Where humans responded to external stimuli with consciousness, the other-than-human world simply reacted with innate, machine-like impulses.

Isaac Newton built on the understanding of the material world functioning in automated, unconscious, machine-like—thus predictable—reactions to external stimuli. Newton's physics reinforced the idea that humanity was fundamentally different from the material world because, unlike humans, matter was inert, unconscious, and only controlled externally by human will. The problems with this Cartesian-Newtonian worldview have been discussed for at least as long as the environmental movement has been around. Indeed, one could argue that all along, even from the beginnings of modernity, there have always been dissenting voices insisting that humanity is in a fully interdependent relationship with nature and that nature exceeds or transcends machine-like characteristics so readily associated with their use value. Romantic thinkers, nature poets, and Darwinians have long insisted that the Cartesian-Newtonian characterization of the other-than-human world as inert, merely awaiting human definition and use, is severely limited.[33] They have long noted that the view of humanity as the crowning achievement of the material world or conceptually divorced from it has deleterious effects on the human spirit as well as the material wellbeing of other-than-humans.

---

31. Moore, "Why There Are No Animals or Humans in the Gospel of Mark," 80.
32. Ibid. "This radical reconception of the nonhuman animal," Stephen Moore notes, "was subsequently termed the *bête-machine* ('beast-machine') doctrine for its equation of animals with clocks and other machines with automatic moving parts."
33. See Alfred North Whitehead, *Science and the Modern World* (New York: Free Press, 1967) on Romantics and nature poets, 93 and on. See also Keller on Anne Conway, "Be a Multiplicity: Ancestral Anticipations," in *Polydoxy: Theology of Multiplicity and Relation*, ed. Catherine Keller and Laurel Schneider (New York: Routledge, 2011), especially 83 and on.

INTRODUCTION

Alternative Views of Reality and the Self

In the present, these persistent critiques of modernity are sharpened on the whetstone of social, ecological, and economic crises. Today, climate change is evidence for the fact that, as physicist Karen Barad writes, "We are part of the nature we seek to understand."[34] In addition, economic turmoil seems to have heightened awareness of the growing gap between rich and poor. Along with increasing consciousness of a direct correlation between fossil fuel dependence, global capitalism, and climate change, conversation around these concerns has created space for more serious criticisms of an increasingly unregulated global neoliberal economy. These concerns are intimately related to views of reality, materiality, humanity, and creatureliness that have emerged as responses to harmful aspects of modern thought. Particularly with the advent of the science of ecology and the discoveries of quantum physics, conceptions of material reality have shifted from being conceived as structured by isolated atoms or individuals that only bounce off one another in external relations to a view of reality emerging through relational, internal interactions of interdependence.

In a recent collection of essays addressing concerns relating to Cartesian-Newtonian assumptions and proposing constructive alternatives, Diana Coole and Samantha Frost explain that new materialisms and ontologies reject old binaries between subject and object that render matter inert and relations external. In these models, matter and reality are conceptualized in ways "that compel us to think of causation in far more complex terms; to recognize that phenomena are caught in a multitude of interlocking systems."[35] Coole and Frost explain that "forces, charges, waves, virtual particles, and empty space suggest an ontology that is very different from the substantialist Cartesian or mechanistic Newtonian accounts of matter."[36] Where

---

34. Karen Barad, "Posthumanist Performativity: Toward an Understanding of How Matter Comes to Matter," *Signs: Journal of Women in Culture and Society* 28, no. 3 (2003): 828.
35. Diana Coole and Samantha Frost, eds., *New Materialisms: Ontology, Agency, and Politics* (Durham, NC: Duke University Press, 2010), 9.
36. Ibid., 13.

xxiii

Newton's cause and effect assumed linear time and the inert nature of matter, these are fundamentally called into question in relational, ecological, and quantum accounts of reality because they assume separative substances—and thus external relations. Here, an isolated substance may affect another by bumping into it, causing it to react or move in a certain way, but, significantly, the interacting partners remain substantially and ontologically the same before and after the meeting.

Substantial consistency and mere external relations allow for predictable outcomes. Newton's insights, for example, make it possible to predict with impressive accuracy the damage a marble will cause on a car windshield on street level when dropped from a fifth-story window. There are phenomena at the microcosmic as well as the macrosystemic level, however, that linear causality cannot account for. In cases of dynamic systems such as global economics and climate change, for example, we cannot simply add up causes and predict the effects. This is not simply a matter of a lack of information, an inability as yet to account for all variables. Nor is it simply a case where "the sum is greater than the parts" because "there are system effects that are different from their parts."[37] Coole and Frost explain, "Because innumerable interactions between manifold elements that produce patterns of organization successively *transform* those elements, it is impossible either to predict outcomes in advance or to repeat an event. Since, moreover, determination within dynamic systems is nonlinear, terminal effects cannot be construed as possibilities that were already latent in some initial moment."[38] In other words, dynamic systems such as global economies, ecologies, and climate change cannot be explained in terms of external relations.

As quantum physicist Karen Barad explains, we are not just talking about the difference between classical causality and complex systems theory. In order to account for a kind of reality that is not simply more complex with more variables than we previously imagined, Barad

37. John Urry in Coole and Frost, *New Materialisms*, 14.
38. Ibid.

INTRODUCTION

argues we need a different account of reality: "an alternative meta/physics that entails a reworking of the notions of causality and agency."[39] Building on the philosophical physics of Niels Bohr, Barad suggests a profoundly relational ontology where matter itself emerges in what she calls "intra-action." Barad's neologism is closely related to more commonly familiar concepts of quantum entanglement and complementarity. As Bohr noted in his famous complementarity theory, in taking measurements of an atomic object it is impossible to mark any absolute separation between the object of observation and the measuring tool. Rather than remaining distinct and "objective" in the traditional sense of external relations, the measuring apparatus and the object of observation become entangled so that the measurement is a phenomenon of their intra-action, rather than an objectively exterior measurement. In other words, in the mere act of measurement, the object being measured and the measuring apparatus intra-act and are both ontologically altered by the encounter.

Barad differentiates intra-action from the more familiar description of relations as *interaction*. She points out that interaction implies originally isolated substances that secondarily enter into relationships that can have an effect on their behavior. These relations, however, are still external. Barad's intra-action suggests that we—and all matter—are constituted in and through our engagements. Barad explains,

> The point is not merely that there is a web of causal relations that we are implicated in and that there are consequences to our actions. We are a much more intimate part of the universe than any such statement implies.... There is no discrete "I" that precedes its actions. Our (intra)actions matter—each one reconfigures the world in its becoming, they become us. And yet even in our becoming there is no "I" separate from the intra-active becoming of the world.[40]

The same, she demonstrates, holds true for matter itself, thus pushing

---

39. Karen Barad, *Meeting the Universe Halfway: Quantum Physics and the Entanglement of Matter and Meaning* (Durham, NC: Duke University Press, 2007), 393.
40. Ibid., 394.

XXV

TOWARD A BETTER WORLDLINESS

us to think beyond mere social ontologies to *material relational* ontologies.

In addition to material causality, the intra-active, interdependent, and dynamic view of reality has a profound effect on some basic assumptions of what it means to be human, to have a self, and to be responsible. Modern life allows for the illusion of self-possession, self-awareness, and self-sufficiency. For many of us, nature feels distant, or at least, "outside." In our homes, cities, and grocery stores, the nature we depend on is carefully packaged, removing any trace of earth and the ecological systems on which they depend.[41] We easily forget the many hands that have toiled, the lives that have been given, and the beings who have flourished through symbiotic relationships.

It is easy to lose track of the fact that the boundaries that seem separated by impervious windows, empty space, or creaturely difference are actually permeable, interrelated, and interdependent. We perceive the end of our selves and the beginning of the "other" through the boundary of skin, but these boundaries are anything but sealed. Biologists remind us that our bodies, what we think of as securely "me" and "mine," are actually riddled with others: bacteria, fungi, and other microorganisms. Biologist Donna Haraway reminds us that a mere 10 percent of what I consider "my" body's cells actually contain human DNA.[42] The rest is made up of communities of microbial "others" who help my body function in a human way. Political science scholar Jane Bennett similarly reminds us that even the crook of an elbow is not merely mine, but a community.[43] Suddenly, our bodies emerge less as isolated humans where the eco-redemptive goal is to reach across the moat surrounding our fortress-like humanity to connect with an outside world, and more as ecosystems themselves, as communities within communities, within communities.

---

41. See, for example, Michael Pollan, *The Omnivore's Dilemma: A Natural History of Four Meals* (New York: Penguin, 2006).

42. Donna J. Haraway, *When Species Meet* (Minneapolis: University of Minnesota Press, 2008), 3–4.

43. "My 'own' body is material, and yet this vital materiality is not fully or exclusively human. My flesh is populated and constituted by different swarms of foreigners. The crook of my elbow, for example, is 'a special ecosystem, a bountiful home to no fewer than six tribes of bacteria" (Jane Bennett, *Vibrant Matter: A Political Ecology of Things* [Durham, NC: Duke University Press, 2010], 112).

xxvi

INTRODUCTION

We find that even more than being permeable or porous, we depend on these communities of others and are constituted in (or intra-act), with, and through them. Recent studies of the microbiome demonstrate that bacteria living in the ecological system of human bodies but lacking our genes make possible basic human functions such as digestion and brain function.[44] As it turns out, that unique Cartesian characteristic—consciousness, the *ego cogito*—that delineated humanity from the other-than-human world in modernity fundamentally depends on something other-than-human. As religious scholar Whitney Bauman explains, "At the very center of the self are multiple earth others. At the very core of what it means to be human is the multitude of nonhuman earth others."[45] We quite literally would not be—let alone be human—without the presence, assistance, and gifts of multiple human, other-than-human, and divine "others."

Given that our emotional states, thought processes, bodies, and material reality rely so fundamentally on the gifts of a multitude of others, it seems a shame that our theologies of grace would not account for these gifts as well. So, we wonder: What would grace look like if we took a Copernican-like shift and removed humanity from its isolated and central location in the universe? What would it mean for our theological concepts of grace to account for the ways our lives and our beings are profoundly gifted to us by both creaturely and divine others? What would grace look like if we could no longer assume we were isolated individuals or that an individual could essentially be extracted from the web of relations that not only supports them but also constitutes them? What does *extra nos* mean in an ecological universe where no thing can be said to be absolutely separate or outside relation with others? Or what does *pro me* mean when there is no "me" apart from a community of others? Rather than diminishing

---

44. See the American Natural History Museum exhibit on the micro-biome: "The Secret World Inside You," http://www.amnh.org/exhibitions/the-secret-world-inside-you; also, Rob DeSalle and Susan Perkins, *Welcome to the Microbiome: Getting to Know the Trillions of Bacteria and Other Microbes In, On, and Around You* (New Haven: Yale University Press, 2015).

45. Whitney Bauman, *Religion and Ecology: Developing a Planetary Ethic* (New York: Columbia University Press, 2014), 116.

TOWARD A BETTER WORLDLINESS

the importance of grace, might such questions lead us to a radical appreciation of the nature of reality as fundamentally graced?

Eco/nomy

Common disagreements voiced in American politics around ecological concerns often revolve around a central and competing distinction between economics and ecology. Voices supporting ecological care are often charged with prioritizing the health of the natural world over the economic wellbeing of hardworking families, while those supporting economic sustainability are often accused of shortsightedly prioritizing human wellbeing at the expense of the natural world. But economy and ecology are falsely separated inasmuch as they are divided along the Cartesian line that is also seen to divide the human from the nonhuman: agency, choice, will, self-consciousness, rationality, and so on. Where this dualistic divide can no longer be said to hold, we need to start talking in terms of eco/nomy and see economy and ecology as an interconnected whole where one is not prioritized over the other.

Where does the category of economy end and ecology begin? Both are systems of exchange that, at their most basic level, are meant to support life. So does economy simply end and ecology begin where humans no longer are considered central? Does economy end and ecology begin when the actors are not willfully organizing or managing? Does such a dividing line not assume the Cartesian-Newtonian binary between humans and nonhumans, culture and nature? It is not enough to simply reverse the hierarchy. Where economy is typically prioritized, many eco-conscious voices suggest we reverse the dualism and prioritize ecology, thereby putting economy in a place of secondary importance. But by simply reversing the hierarchy, the argument may still be read as assuming a basic dualism between economy and ecology—and thereby, between humanity and nature. We cannot say, on the one hand, that the separation of the human from the natural world is a main contributing factor to ecological degradation, and then, on the other, proceed to talk about

xxviii

INTRODUCTION

economy and ecology as if they were two separate realms. When we do so, we fail to recognize that the line separating economy and ecology falls on the Cartesian line separating the human from the nonhuman world.

This logical inconsistency is similarly not yet acknowledged among many theologians critical of capitalism's socially and ecologically destructive effects. Among these scholars, a common argument against the pervasive power of capitalism is that economy presents a meaning-making force in competition with religion. Gordon Lathrop, for example, argues that "when that economy presents itself as a global system—and when monetary values are seen as primary values, the 'bottom line' as the most basic knowledge about anything—then we have arrived at something like a cosmology."[46] This approach is also taken by Douglas Meeks, Paul Chung, and Ulrich Duchrow in their texts on religion and economics.[47] These scholars contrast the idolatrous meaning-making structures of economy with true religious belief. This does make for a particularly potent religious argument. I worry, though, that by pitting religion against economics, we villainize economy and place it in opposition to God's work in the world. In acknowledging the damaging effects of certain expressions of capitalism, we must distinguish our protests of a certain *kind* of economy from the condemnation of economic exchange in general.

Instead of condemning economy *tout court* for its world-ordering power in competition with God's world-ordering power, we must pause and ask: Why do we raise up and sanctify ecology and villainize economy? Again, my hunch is that we assume economy and ecology are divided along the same line as culture and nature—the line between the human and the other-than-human. Does the line between ecology and economy just reinscribe the human/other-than-human boundary, thus continuing to place humanity outside of "nature"? How would

46. Gordon Lathrop, *Holy Ground: A Liturgical Cosmology* (Minneapolis: Fortress Press, 2003), 11.
47. Douglas Meeks, *God the Economist: The Doctrine of God and Political Economy* (Minneapolis: Augsburg Fortress, 1989); Paul Chung, *Church and Ethical Responsibility in the Midst of World Economy: Greed, Dominion, and Justice* (Eugene, OR: Cascade, 2013); and Ulrich Duchrow, *Alternatives to Global Capitalism: Drawn from Biblical History, Designed for Political Action*, trans. Elizabeth Hickes et al. (Utrecht, The Netherlands: International Books, 1995).

xxix

TOWARD A BETTER WORLDLINESS

our analyses of the deleterious effects of capitalism change if, in the spirit of getting to the root of the human/nature divide, we refuse to oppose ecology and economy? In acknowledging the damaging effects of capitalism, we must surely make clear that we are protesting a certain *kind* of economy and not economic exchange in general.

The question of a dividing line between economy and ecology is more than just semantics. There are material consequences to this common assumption. Global environmental advocate Vandana Shiva, for example, argues that "This total disconnect between ecology and economics is threatening to bring down our *oikos*, our home on this planet."[48] What holds economy and ecology together is that they are both systems of interdependent exchange. Both are conceptualized as systems of exchange that either support, create, and sustain life or orient toward death and destruction. At their best, both remain systems of exchange that can support the flourishing of the world. In this sense, eco/nomy points to the fact that, as biologist Donna Haraway insists, "the one fundamental thing about the world [is] relationality."[49]

In the spirit of analyzing the relationality of the world in a nondual manner—and so, protesting forces in the world that lead toward unsustainable relations—several theologians propose that we retrieve the ancient concept of the world as *oikonomia*. *Oikos*, as Shiva explains, means home, and also serves as the root for economy, ecology, and ecumenism. Theologian Marion Grau suggests a return to this concept which, "points toward the inseparability and irreducibility of creation beyond any binary opposition between the human and the natural in which nature would be designated as an 'environment.'"[50] Theologian John Cobb and economist Herman Daly share Grau's concerns and also recommend we think of economics in a more integral way, along the lines of Wendell Berry's "Great Economy" that "sustains the total web of life and everything that depends on the land."[51] This integral

---

48. Vandana Shiva, *Soil Not Oil: Environmental Justice in an Age of Climate Crisis* (Brooklyn, NY: South End Press, 2008), 104.
49. Cited in Marion Grau, *Of Divine Economy: Refinancing Redemption* (New York: T&T Clark, 2004), 8.
50. Ibid., 10.

perspective—whether *oikos* or Great Economy—resists a recurrent relapse into a nature/culture and nonhuman/human divide where ultimately the other-than-human world is relegated to resources or "externalities."[52] Cobb and Daly insist that we view "human communities . . . [as] part of a larger community that includes the other creatures with whom human beings share the world."[53] As such, the "Great Economy" becomes the all-inclusive system of exchange that "sustain[s] the total web of life and everything that depends on the land."[54]

Where economy and ecology are merged, conveying the basic interdependence and relationality of life in the world, we also see that eco-justice and social justice can be seen as one and the same, rather than in competition with one another. For over half a century now, ecotheologians have insisted that Christian theology take seriously the interconnected mode of the natural world in our doctrines and theological reflections. More recently, inspired by the interconnected nature of reality, influential voices are resisting the persistent assumption that ecological concern means one must choose between trees and people—between social justice and ecojustice. Pope Francis's powerful encyclical on climate change, for example, urges a perspective he calls "integral ecology."[55] Pope Francis's integral ecology calls for an expansion even of the scope of ecological interconnections. "We are not faced with two separate crises, one environmental and the other social," he writes, "but rather one complex crisis which is both social and environmental."[56] The encyclical highlights the ways that our most pressing issues of human injustice (racism, colonialism, income disparity, etc.) are also deeply intertwined with ecological injustice.

Pope Francis's argument converges with the case Lutheran ethicist

---

51. Cobb and Daly, *For the Common Good*, 18.
52. See Cobb and Daly's analysis of economic externalities, cited above.
53. Cobb and Daly, *For the Common Good*, 18.
54. Ibid.
55. Pope Francis, *Laudato Si': On Care for Our Common Home* (Vatican City: Libreria Editrice Vaticana, 2015).
56. Ibid., 94.

Cynthia Moe-Lobeda has been building for seeing the interconnections of ecological and social justice. She emphasizes the injustice of the fact that those who contribute the least to global warming are likely to suffer first and most profoundly from it. Such injustice is compounded by the fact that these populations are also most likely to be colonized, economically and politically marginalized, and non-European. Moe-Lobeda highlights the racialized effects of climate change as well as the symptoms of systemic racism evident in a persistent lack of political will to address climate change. She describes the slippery nature of systemic violence that allows for it to persist, remaining generally invisible and ignored by those who benefit from the system and have the power to change it. Structural violence like climate change and racism, she explains, involves systems, rather than individuals. Many people are involved and most may even remain wholly unaware of the violence or bias of the systems in which they participate. "To illustrate," she explains, "my driving a gas-fueled car to work is legal, happens over time, and is connected to the countless people who work in the automotive and oil industries or drive cars, yet are not responsible for the decisions that have created a culture and infrastructure of automobile dependence."[57] Such structural violence transgresses perceived boundaries between human and nonhuman, the social and the ecological, economy and ecology.

Mere weeks before the largest climate march in history—"The People's Climate March," in New York City on September 21, 2014—journalist Naomi Klein published *This Changes Everything: Capitalism vs. the Climate*.[58] Her persuasive book anticipates Pope Francis's integration of ecological, economic, and social concerns, and parallels Moe-Lobeda's argument that in addressing the causes of climate change, we will also need to address social, political, and economic structures.[59] For Klein, addressing the causes of climate

---

57. Cynthia Moe-Lobeda, "Climate Change as Climate Debt: Forging a Just Future," *Journal of the Society of Christian Ethics* 36, no. 1 (Spring/Summer 2016): 11–12.

58. Naomi Klein, *This Changes Everything: Capitalism vs. the Climate* (New York: Simon & Schuster, 2014).

59. Indeed, Klein has been invited to advise Pope Francis on issues of climate change (see Naomi Klein, "A Radical Vatican?," *The New Yorker*, July 10, 2015, http://www.newyorker.com/news/news-desk/a-visit-to-the-vatican).

INTRODUCTION

change means critically addressing systems that prevent basic democratic principles that would allow for more socially just and egalitarian relations. She argues that if we are to confront the ecological crisis of climate change, we will also need to address the fundamentally undemocratic nature of our current global economy.

In order to account for the ways that our mundane daily acts contribute—not just individually, directly, or with linear causality—to ecological and economic, social and other-than-human injustices, a more integrated perspective is in order. But if being human means being part of communities within communities of humans and other-than-humans, how do we account for human responsibility and agency? What kind of shifts in our anthropologies might better account for our interdependent relationships with one another and the other-than-human world? Where it becomes apparent that we need an integrated perspective resisting an economy/ecology and human/non-human divide, twentieth-century gift theory emerges as a potentially fruitful way of integrating these formerly divided concepts because it can account for a view of reality of continually exchanging gifts between humans and other-than-humans.

Gift Theory

While the three main foci of this project—ecology, economy, and the Protestant theological tradition—represent divergent and diverse discourses, theories of the gift provide a methodological bridge of shared vocabulary and analytical tools that can be applied to these diverse systems of exchange. Significantly, gift theory explicitly brings us back to our main theological concerns regarding grace and self-construction since gift theorists emphasize that the kinds of gift models we engage in and idealize play a key role in shaping our concepts of the human in relation to society, the other-than-human world, and reality in general.

With the 1924 publication of *The Gift: The Form and Reason for Exchange in Archaic Societies,* socio-anthropologist Marcel Mauss initiated twentieth-century interest in the gift as a symbolic economic, moral,

xxxiii

TOWARD A BETTER WORLDLINESS

religious, and social trope.[60] Mauss's socio-anthropological research was a meta-analysis of field studies in locations where premodern social and economic practices were retained. Sociologist Mary Douglas explains that Mauss was motivated to analyze premodern gift economies as a way to critique modern utilitarianism and individualism.[61] As John Milbank explains, for Mauss gift-exchange in premodern societies was not merely an early form of barter economics, "a highly rational, purely material, and economic process . . . which smoothly gives way to the higher convenience of money."[62] Rather, these systems of gift exchange encompassed all aspects of social life, including those we would now distinguish from the private, social sphere as public and economic. Mauss's analysis of premodern societies demonstrates that the reasons for exchange in these societies were not simply utilitarian.[63] Consequently, Mauss concludes that forms and reasons for exchange other than those limited to capitalism, utilitarianism, and individualism are possible.

In demonstrating the ways premodern gift-exchange societies were not simply less developed utilitarian economies, Mary Douglas argues that Mauss's gift economy provides a unique alternative to both capitalism and Marxism.[64] For this reason, Mauss's work continues to spark conversation and interest today. In particular, his resistance to the utilitarianism and individualism characteristic of capitalism has caught the attention of theologians engaged in issues of economic concern. In addition, his rejection of the idealization of the gift as free of reciprocity or exchange has interested theologians engaged in theological debates about the ideal forms of gift in our theological systems. Often, Protestant grace is associated with the free gift exclusive of reciprocity, thus leading to grace versus economy-and-exchange binaries. As we will see, however, the question of whether

---

60. 1924 was the first publication in French as *Essay sur le don*. The first English translation was in 1954.
61. Mary Douglas, forward to Marcel Mauss, *The Gift: The Form and Reason for Exchange in Archaic Societies* (New York: W. W. Norton, 1990).
62. John Milbank, "Can a Gift Be Given?: Prolegomena to a Future Trinitarian Metaphysic," *Modern Theology* 11 (1995): 126.
63. Ibid.
64. Quoted in J. Todd Billings, "John Milbank's Theology of the 'Gift' and Calvin's Theology of Grace: A Critical Comparison," *Modern Theology* 21 (2005): 88.

grace as articulated by the reformers is most accurately defined as free gift has become increasingly complex as the social, economic, ontological and—as argued here—ecological implications of gift concepts become more clear.

Both critiques of concepts foundational to capitalism and the idealization of the free gift have attracted Anglo-Catholic theologian and instigator of Radical Orthodoxy John Milbank to Mauss's work. Along with others also associated with Radical Orthodoxy such as William Cavanaugh and Stephen Long, Milbank has developed a forceful critique of capitalism based on theological and gift categories. For Milbank, different gift structures assume different ontologies since a reciprocal gift does not just indicate the return of a gift object but the return of relation. Where we are concerned not just with the exchange of gift objects but of relation, we will see that the reciprocal gift also indicates a shift to a relational and interconnected ontology. Since neither the gift nor relation is returned in the case of the free gift, this gift structure indicates a separative and individualist ontology. In place of an individualist ontology and the sacred/secular, public/private dualisms that he argues are uniquely modern and foundational for capitalism, Milbank has constructed an ontology of Trinitarian gift-exchange in which the world participates in divine exchange.

Even before Mauss's gift economy caught the attention of theologians interested in economic and soteriological exchanges, his work had already evoked French philosopher Jacques Derrida's critical response. In 1992, Derrida published *Given Time,* where he counters Mauss's rejection of the free gift, arguing that what Mauss describes is not gift, but exchange. For anything to emerge as gift, Derrida insists, there must be no reciprocity or return. For Derrida, the danger is that a "gift" given with expectation of a return "puts the other in debt [appearing] to poison the relationship, so that 'giving amounts to hurting, to doing harm.'"[65] Even a word of thanks or simple recognition turns the gift to exchange. Where Mauss insists on a definition of gift

---

65. Jacques Derrida, *Given Time: I. Counterfeit Money,* trans. Peggy Kamuf (Chicago: University of Chicago Press, 1994), 12.

TOWARD A BETTER WORLDLINESS

that can only be given with interest, with the expectation of a return, Derrida suggests that a gift that returns to its origin is annulled. As we will see, like many Protestant theologies of grace, such opposition to exchange leaves Derrida's gift vulnerable to emerging as a transcendent exteriority in relation to the exchanges of the world. And yet, I will also argue that when read within Derrida's broader project and concerns, certain insights will remain key as we seek to construct a counter-capitalist concept of the gift.

In the case of Milbank and Derrida, as well as in gift theory more broadly, the focus tends to remain on social and divine gift-exchange. But, as I have suggested, gift theory can account for systems of exchange whether they remain between humans or encompass exchange between humans and other-than-humans. This particular insight is the gift of ecotheologian Anne Primavesi. Primavesi engages the lively debates around gift theory in a way that anticipates the aims of this project. Moving beyond the discourse's anthropocentric orientation, she applies it to ecological systems and human/other-than-human interactions. Here, fundamental and life-sustaining ecological exchanges emerge as eco/nomic systems. Take, for example, the exchange between humans and trees that happens continually. With every breath, humans are in exchange relations with trees: we trade our carbon dioxide for their oxygen. Systems of eco/nomic gift-exchange can be seen intimately, as in the exchanges between me and a tree, or they can be seen more globally. Think here of the carbon cycle. In addition to monetary and ecological economies, environmental activist Vandana Shiva suggests we also consider the nature of our carbon economies.

Shiva reminds us that climate change does not indicate a problem with carbon itself. With Shiva's 2009 book, *Soil Not Oil,* the author began to raise awareness about the ways our food production and distribution systems contribute to climate change. In doing so, she reminded us that carbon is not the enemy. "We forget that the cellulose of plants is primarily carbon," she explains. "Humus in the soil is mostly carbon. Vegetation in the forests is mostly carbon. It is living carbon. It is

INTRODUCTION

part of the life cycle."[66] Rather than carbon itself, the problem is an unbalanced, unreciprocal, carbon cycle. "Fossil fuel-based industrial agriculture moves carbon from the soil to the atmosphere. Ecological agriculture takes carbon from the atmosphere and puts it back in the soil."[67] In the shift from organic to industrial farming, we have fundamentally shifted the carbon cycle on earth. Ancient methods of crop rotation, cover crops, and manure use kept a balance in carbon exchanges between the atmosphere and carbon in the ground. Climate change, then, can be seen as the result of a shift from dependence on "renewable carbon economies to a fossil fuel-based non-renewable carbon economy."[68] In order to address climate change, we need to restore a balance through reciprocal gift-exchange between the carbon we send into the atmosphere and the carbon that is absorbed into the soil. I suggest we need a paradigm shift from a unilateral fossil fuel carbon economy where "free gifts" are given from the earth without expectation of a responsible return of carbon reabsorbed into the soil. Closing the carbon cycle by returning carbon to the soil and promoting biodiversity rather than synthetic fertilizers will be key.[69] "To move beyond oil," Shiva explains, "we must reestablish partnerships with other species. To move beyond oil, we must reestablish the other carbon economy, a renewable economy based on biodiversity."[70] Rather than seeing soil as "dead matter, assembled like a machine," Shiva calls for us to see it as a diverse community in reciprocal relation with human communities.[71]

---

66. Shiva, *Soil Not Oil*, 129.
67. Ibid., 111.
68. Ibid., 130.
69. A key characteristic of industrial farming is synthetic fertilizer use. Synthetic fertilizers not only take an enormous amount of fossil fuels to produce, they also contribute directly to global warming when they produce nitrous oxide. Synthetic fertilizers are composed of nitrogen taken from the atmosphere and "fixed" or combined with hydrogen (see Michael Pollan's lucid description of this process in *The Omnivore's Dilemma*, 41–47). When synthetic nitrogen is applied to plants, not all of it is absorbed. Some runs off into rivers, some seeps into groundwater, and some evaporates, combining with O_2 to form nitrous oxide. Nitrous oxide is a greenhouse gas 300 times more potent than carbon dioxide ("Overview of Greenhouse Gases," http://www3.epa.gov/climatechange/ghgemissions/gases/n2o.html).
70. Shiva, *Soil Not Oil*, 131.
71. Shiva, "Soil Papered Over," speech given at the Seizing the Alternative Conference, Claremont, CA, June 2015.

TOWARD A BETTER WORLDLINESS

With Primavesi's shift beyond anthropocentric gift-exchange, economic and ecological issues, such as the carbon cycle, can be integrated where they are typically divided discourses. Such integrations, as we shall see, pose a particular challenge to traditional Protestant concepts of grace that are commonly understood in terms of a free or nonreciprocal gift. Where the reciprocal gift assumes a return of relation, and thus a relational ontology, rather than separative individualism, the reciprocal gift will be a key part of this project. But where grace is maintained as a free or unreciprocal gift, it can only emerge in contrast or opposition to a cycle of gift-exchange as well as a relational ontology.

The Task Before Us: Conceptualizing Alternative Eco/nomies

> I suggest that if we hope to contest effectively the manifold destructive
> effects of capitalist structures of power, we need to begin by taking an
> inventory of the location and embodiment of the formations of
> knowledge and faith that shape theological economies.
> —Marion Grau, *Of Divine Economy*

In rejecting capitalism, Milbank promotes a turn to socialism. Indeed, many economically engaged theologians either propose the rejection of capitalism in favor of socialism, or, like Kathryn Tanner, a radical reformation within capitalism. By contrast, John Cobb and Herman Daly stress that the major task facing us today is to come up with alternatives to the binary of either capitalism or socialism. John Cobb and Herman Daly's study of economics and ecology in *For the Common Good: Redirecting the Economy toward Community, the Environment, and a Sustainable Future* is unique among theological works dealing with economics in that it is the result of a partnership between theologian John Cobb and economist (and former member of the World Bank) Herman Daly. Cobb and Daly reject both economic systems on the grounds that they are growth-based economies that take for granted the possibility and desirability of industrialism.[72] Both systems "are

---

72. Cobb and Daly, *For the Common Good*, 2. Miroslav Volf echoes this sentiment, emphasizing that "Marx held firmly to human independence so it almost seemed to him a value that lies at

xxxviii

INTRODUCTION

fully committed to large-scale, factory-style energy and capital-intensive, specialized production units that are hierarchically managed."[73] As much as theorists and the general public like to polarize socialism and capitalism, Daly and Cobb stress that when it comes to ecological implications, the two systems simply disagree on which one can better produce and spread the benefits of industrialism.

I suggest there is no more important task before humanity in the twenty-first century than to rethink models of relationship and exchange among humans and between humans and other-than-human matter. This task is also an opportunity for religions to draw on our expansive imaginative resources to construct alternate economies, communicate different modes of relational exchange, and articulate a compelling vision of what redemptive, sustaining, and life-giving—indeed, grace-filled—relations look like.

With this task in mind, this project will proceed in the following manner. The first chapter will analyze arguments about the relationship between Protestantism and capitalism, starting with Max Weber's famous *Protestant Ethic and the Spirit of Capitalism.* I will outline the reasons for current skepticism among Protestant scholars toward Weber's thesis. However, I will argue that where he may have gotten Luther and Calvin wrong, his argument resonates strongly with the ways the tradition unfolded. We will also take particular note of a lesser-known connection that Weber presciently makes, already in 1905, between the Protestant tradition, capitalism, and fossil fuel consumption.

Several current scholars point out that capitalist practices were

---

the bottom of all values. Because the reality of God as creator is 'incompatible with human independence' he denied the existence of God." Volf continues, "In a text that remained unpublished during his lifetime, 'Economic and Philosophical Manuscripts,' [Marx] gave an expression to the heart to this rebellion against God: 'A being only counts itself as independent when it stands on its own feet and it stands on its own feet as long as it owes its existence to itself. A man who lives by grace of another considers himself a dependent being. But I live completely by grace of another when I owe him not only the maintenance of my life but when he has also created my life, when he is the source of my life. And my life necessarily has such a ground outside itself if it is not my own creation'" (Marx, "Economic and Philosophical Manuscripts," in *Karl Marx: Selected Writings,* ed. David McLellan, 2nd ed. [Oxford: Oxford University Press, 2000], 94 in Volf, *Free of Charge: Giving and Forgiving in a Culture Stripped of Grace* [Grand Rapids, MI: Zondervan, 2005], 34–35).

73. Cobb and Daly, *For the Common Good,* 13.

xxxix

already emerging by the time the Reformation came around. Consequently, rather than unsuspecting forefathers of capitalism, these scholars suggest early reformers such as Luther and Calvin were actually some of its earliest critics. While valuing the important correctives to a traditional Protestant tendency to avoid issues of economic and social justice, I argue that interpretations that seemingly purify the reformers of responsibility for the emergence of capitalism fail to acknowledge the ways the tradition may have supported (and unintentionally *may still* support) a global and oppressive economic system. A more nuanced interpretation of the tradition is needed that can account both for a sense of responsibility with appropriate theological shifts as well as conceptual and historical strengths.

While Weber's argument may be dismissed for historical and theological inaccuracies, I argue in chapter two that a similar argument is currently being compellingly articulated by proponents of Radical Orthodoxy, building off of Marcel Mauss's gift theory. John Milbank, in particular, argues that the Protestant concept of grace as a gift free of reciprocity and exchange popularized a dualism between gift and exchange that then made way for foundational concepts of capitalism, specifically: individualism, commodification, and the public/private dualism. While I find Milbank's critique of the Protestant concept of grace persuasive, I will also demonstrate that Milbank falls into capitalizing traps of his own.

Chapter three shifts from a primary economic focus to ecological exchange with the ecotheologies of Joseph Sittler and Jürgen Moltmann. Lutheran Pastor Joseph Sittler is widely regarded as one of the earliest ecotheologians, already writing and speaking on the subject in the 1950s—before Rachel Carson's *Silent Spring* (1962), widely credited with initiating the environmental movement, or Lynn White's "The Historical Roots of Our Ecological Crisis" (1976), commonly acknowledged as a text that sparked Christian religious interest in ecological concerns. While discussing Sittler's work, I emphasize his early criticism of the Protestant doctrine of grace as anthropocentric and individualistic. His later works (especially *Essays on Nature and*

xl

INTRODUCTION

Grace, 1972) emerge with insights, still relevant and remarkable today, regarding shifts in grace and corresponding concepts of selfhood. Sittler rejects the separative individual receiving God's forgiveness as pure exteriority. Instead, he constructs an ecological selfhood upheld by a radical sense of gifts given by both God and nature. In this way, from within the Protestant theological heritage, Sittler both demonstrates the important interconnections of grace and selfhood while constructing alternatives to both as fundamentally relational, nonlocal, and ecological. Where Sittler's work stopped short of fully integrating a similarly ecological doctrine of God, Jürgen Moltmann takes these steps by articulating a Trinitarian, interpenetrating, and ecological doctrine of God. Where the Protestant tradition has consistently emphasized the doctrine of redemption over creation, Moltmann creatively reinterprets creation as an act of redemption and redemption on the cross as an act of new creation, thus fully integrating and equally emphasizing each doctrine. The ecotheologies of Sittler and Moltmann made significant contributions toward addressing consistent concerns with key aspects of Protestant theology. However, I will emphasize that when we analyze these theologies from the perspective of Anne Primavesi's suggestion that ecological reality be conceptualized as gift-exchange, we find that both Sittler and Moltmann revert to the free and unilateral gift in key places.

While chapters one through three articulate the problems facing the Protestant doctrine of grace in relation to an exchangist eco/nomic reality, chapter four opens this project's constructive move in articulating a theology of grace that remains recognizably Protestant but does not revert to or idealize the free, unilateral gift. Chapter four will approach this task with key support from other Protestant theologies engaged in and responding to gift theory. There have been many and various responses to John Milbank's gift-exchange and condemnation of the free gift. In introducing some of these responses we will note a consistent tendency again among Protestant theologians to revert to the gift as a unilateral gesture—even among those who

xli

TOWARD A BETTER WORLDLINESS

emphasize that some kind of exchange is central to a Protestant theology of grace. However, we will also build off of important insights from these theologians in order to construct a sense of gift that is unconditioned in that it does not circle back to the giver and, yet, does not exclude continual exchange.

A key insight will emerge in Finnish Lutheran Risto Saarinen's and Danish Lutheran Niels Henrick Gregersen's differentiation between unilateral, bilateral, and multilateral gifting. Building on this distinction, I will argue that despite their opposing concepts of gift, Mauss, Milbank, and Derrida all assume a bilateral gift structure—that is, a model of gifting between a giver and receiver. I suggest that this gifting structure, and not necessarily the noncircular or unconditioned gift itself, creates an opposition between the noncircular gift and exchange. It also assumes a Newtonian sense of linear causality. The ecologically multilateral gift that Primavesi's and Sittler's models seem to intuit, however, can account for nonlinear causality while providing a way for the gift to not necessarily return to the giver and thus continue to circulate and spread more broadly. I argue, therefore, that the multilateral gift would have allowed both Derrida and Protestant theologians concerned with economic justice to avoid the gift/exchange dualism while maintaining there insistence on the counter-capitalist potential of a gift that may not be returned with capital gains for the giver. Consequently, rather than rejecting exchange in order to protest the capitalizing gift, I suggest economically concerned Protestant theologians turn their protest to accounts of the world and gifting that exclusively maintain Newtonian linear causality.

Continuing the constructive work, chapter five will deal with the key question of the place of exchange within a Reformation articulation of grace. Some gift theologians emphasize a clear sense of gift exchange between Christ and the sinner in Luther's soteriological notion of the "happy exchange." I argue that while this language does open the door to a fresh notion of exchange, this interchange still reverts to an active/passive binary since it articulates the model in terms of traditional gender relations: Christ the husband/giver and the

Christian soul as wife/receiver. Such active/passive binaries indicate a return to a unilateral gift structure. Rather than the happy exchange, I suggest that Luther's particularly scandalous interpretation of the *communicatio idiomatum* offers a remarkable sense of exchange between God and creation such that God is not only giver, but also profoundly receives from the world as well. Luther's interpretation of the *communicatio idiomatum*—particularly the extent to which Luther was willing to allow God's nature to receive human characteristics like suffering—is currently being debated.[74] This chapter will outline the ecological and economic implications of this debate, finally demonstrating how Luther's christological understanding of the mutual exchange of properties shaped his economic ethics as demonstrated especially in the establishment of community chests.

This chapter will also highlight the ways that an exclusive sense of grace as an alienable or free gift is—and has been—challenged from marginal voices within the tradition who insist that Luther has always maintained an important sense of union between giver and gift. The current Finnish interpretation of Luther, in particular, will be highlighted for its insistence that Christ is not just means of grace, the giver of divine gifts, but the ontological presence of Christ united with us as gift itself. Beyond the Finns, though, I will suggest that Luther extends the *communicatio idiomatum* to ethical relations so that a sense of communing relationality emerges between Christ, the self, and the neighbor. Here, Christ, self, and neighbor communicate so intimately that they change into one another. This interpretation disrupts the modern sovereign, self-possessed, isolated individual that Luther is purported to inspire. Consequently, I will argue that Luther's *communicatio idiomatum* is also a multilateral gift where nonlinear gifts are given in a network of relations and a wider circulation of gifts is facilitated.

---

74. See, for example, David J. Luy, *Dominus Mortis: Martin Luther on the Incorruptibility of God in Christ* (Minneapolis: Fortress Press, 2014), who argues that modern theologians have overstated Luther's willingness to see God as accepting human characteristics, especially suffering, in their interpretations of his articulation of the *communicatio idiomatum*. On the other side of the debate, for example, see Oswald Bayer and Benjamin Gleede, eds., *Creator est Creatura: Luthers Christologie als Lehre von der Idiomenkommunikation* (Berlin: Walter de Gruyter, 2007).

TOWARD A BETTER WORLDLINESS

In the conclusion, I will demonstrate that German Lutheran theologian Dietrich Bonhoeffer extended Luther's *communicatio idiomatum* once more. In Bonhoeffer's extension, both a relational ontology and doctrine of God emerge as being-with-others. As such, God is only ever Godself beside Godself in relation to the world. So too, we are only ever ourselves through the communicating grace of divine and creaturely others. Here, a kind of better worldliness begins to emerge where God and world, self and other, economy and ecology communicate in graceful interplay.

My hope is that this project might contribute to a creative reimagining of divine and worldly Protestant eco/nomies. Where grace can be articulated as a sense of being opened to an awareness of the many and various gifts that sustain and constitute my daily life, this gratitude may also empower a profound sense of responsibility for a vast ocean of insider/outsiders. Rather than burden or obligation, this sense of responsibility emerges as profoundly freeing since it entails a shift from the isolated self, vulnerable to fear and insignificance in the face of vast and complex concerns, to a graced self, trusting that I belong, body and soul, to a divine and creaturely ocean of inside/outsiders, just as the reformers intuited.

1

Protestant Ghosts and the Spirits of Capitalism: Ecology, Economy, and the Protestant Tradition

Come[1] to me all you that are weary and are carrying heavy burdens,
and I will give you rest. Take my yoke upon you, and learn from me;
for I am gentle and humble in heart, and you will find rest for your souls.
For my yoke is easy, and my burden light.
—Matthew 11:28–30

To address the past (and future), to speak with ghosts, is not to entertain
or reconstruct some narrative of the way it was, but to respond,
to be responsible, *to take responsibility for that which we inherit*
(from the past and the future), for the entangled relationalities
of inheritance that "we" are.
—Karen Barad[2]

---

1. Parts of this chapter were previously published in "Protestant Ghosts and Spirits of Capitalism: Ecology, Economy, and the Reformation Tradition," *Dialog: A Journal of Theology* 55 (2016): 50–61.
2. Karen Barad, "Quantum Entanglements and Hauntological Relations of Inheritance: Dis/continuities, SpaceTime Enfoldings, and Justice-to-Come," *Derrida Today* 3, no. 2 (2010): 264, emphasis added.

TOWARD A BETTER WORLDLINESS

What does responsibility entail when it becomes clear our most mundane actions—commuting to work, buying food for our tables, or saving for retirement—contribute to unfathomable economic injustice?[3] What does responsibility involve when it becomes evident that on account of a globalized economic system, every purchase I make, every mode of transportation, and every electronic device I rely on may be tied to the injustice of drought, increasingly extreme weather causing loss of life and livelihood, the rise of oceans and loss of a homeland, and the endangerment of entire species of creatures given life by God?[4] Little wonder we, as a global community, have not been able to look global climate change in the face—its yoke is unbearable.

This chapter will deal with questions of responsibility—but not yet face-to-face with climate change. To begin with, we will only look out of the corner of our eye, starting with responsibility for a tradition entangled with both the rise of global capitalism and the modern environmental movement. Theologian Kathryn Tanner opens her analysis of Christian theologies and social justice in *The Politics of God* with reflections on what it means to claim a theological tradition implicated in histories of oppression, enslavement, and land appropriation. In the face of such injustice, several options regarding one's relationship to the tradition present themselves, ranging from absolute rejection to carrying on as if nothing ever happened. Tanner communicates the experience of many people who today retain affection for and devotion to a particular religious tradition in spite of the fact that they may no longer be able to claim that theirs is the most true, the most ethical, or the most influential. Regardless, the tradition remains mysteriously, but undeniably, *theirs*. Most cannot

---

3. See Albino Barrera, *Market Complicity and Christian Ethics* (New York: Cambridge University Press, 2011).
4. Cynthia D. Moe-Lobeda: "The pernicious power of structural violence is its ability to remain invisible or ignored by those who perpetuate it or benefit from it. Three factors render it so readily ignored. In contrast to direct violence, structural violence is: generally not criminalized, a process not an event, cannot be traced back to an individual, but rather involves many people, disconnected from each other, who may be unaware of the systemic impact of their actions and who may not be responsible for the decisions that shape their actions. ("Climate Change as Climate Debt: Forging a Just Future," *Journal of the Society of Christian Ethics* 36, no. 1 [Spring/Summer 2016]: 11–12. See also her *Resisting Structural Evil: Love as Economic-Ecological Vocation* [Minneapolis: Fortress Press, 2013]).

PROTESTANT GHOSTS AND THE SPIRITS OF CAPITALISM

speak of clear rational reasons for their continued allegiance but may articulate a powerful sense of being claimed or grasped by a tradition, inexplicably captivated by the tradition's ghosts. When, as Tanner writes, "one simply finds oneself believing as one does despite the horrible history of actions perpetuated in the name of those beliefs," one need not choose between either rejection of the tradition or blindness to the counter-ghosts of the oppressed, marginalized, raped, impoverished, and underrepresented who cry out for justice. One may also feel compelled, propelled by hope, to find alternate ways to embody the tradition so that these are not the "necessary effects" of one's inheritance.[5]

Physicist Karen Barad's use of the verb "entangle" also suggests that even beyond any inexplicable sense of regard for a tradition, one may remain yoked with a sense of responsibility to a tradition that—whether or not we accept it—remains our inheritance. Regarding a tradition as an inheritance might also suggest that one way to be faithful *to* a tradition might be working out a way to take responsibility *for* it. On the one hand, a tradition commonly calls for faithfulness to a central message, revered leaders, and original texts. On the other hand, for a tradition to retain the igniting spark of a movement, it seems we must strive just as ardently to be responsible *for* it as we do to remain faithful *to* it.

Here—in the entanglements of inheritance and responsibility—we open into a conversation already over a century in the making about the Reformation tradition and the rise, perpetuation, and explosive growth of industrialization and global economic systems. Beginning with the famous Weberian thesis on the spirit of capitalism and the Protestant tradition, we will find a contrast between Weber's interpretation and a recent proliferation of Reformation scholars who argue that Luther and Calvin offer liberating alternatives—particularly for the poor and econo-mically oppressed—to capitalistic practices. Such critiques of consumer culture and capitalism are not uncommon

---

5. Kathryn Tanner, *Politics of God: Christian Theologies and Social Justice* (Minneapolis: Augsburg Fortress, 1992), ix.

TOWARD A BETTER WORLDLINESS

in Christian theological circles. And yet, they frequently do not adequately examine or acknowledge the ways the tradition has shaped—and may be continuing to support—the values and ideals on which globalized neoliberal capitalism depends. I will argue that Christians must *both* account for unwelcome ghosts reminding us of the tradition's (often unwitting) contributions to the rise of global capital *and* receive or seek out ghosts in the tradition with a certain prophetic ability to propose alternatives. We live in complex times and the scale of the challenges facing us in both income disparity and climate change compel us to recognize that no one—and no one tradition—can be purified of responsibility for creating the conditions we now face and, thereby, be excused from putting the weight of the protesting movement behind a push toward sustainable eco/nomies.

A Light Cloak Turned Iron Yoke

The Puritans *wanted* to be men of the calling—we, on the other hand, *must* be. For when asceticism moved out of the monastic cells and into working life, and began to dominate innerworldly morality, it helped to build that mighty cosmos of the modern economic order (which is bound to the technical and economic conditions of mechanical and machine production). Today this mighty cosmos determines with overwhelming coercion, the style of life *not only* of those directly involved in business but of every individual who is born into this mechanism, *and may well continue to do so until the day that the last ton of fossil fuel has been consumed* ... [C]oncern for outward possessions should sit lightly on the shoulders of [the] saints "like a thin cloak which can be thrown off at any time." But fate decreed that the cloak should become a shell as hard as steel.
—Max Weber, *The Protestant Ethic and the Spirit of Capitalism*[6]

The legacy of *The Protestant Ethic and the Spirit of Capitalism* indefatigably endures. Toward the end of the twentieth century, nearly a hundred years after it was first published in 1905, the International Sociological Association and New York's Public Library included it in their lists of the most significant books of the century[7]—remarkable, given the

---

6. Emphasis added. Max Weber, *The Protestant Ethic and the 'Spirit' of Capitalism and Other Writings*, trans. and ed. Peter Baehr and Gordon C. Wells (New York: Penguin, 2002), 120–21.
7. Lutz Kaelber, "Max Weber's Protestant Ethic in the 21st Century," *International Journal of Politics, Culture, and Society* 16, no. 1 (2002): 133–46.

4

PROTESTANT GHOSTS AND THE SPIRITS OF CAPITALISM

original publication of the book was met with criticism over historical arguments, while it continues to be followed by many alternative and more current theories about the beginnings of capitalism. The fact remains, however, that Weber seems to have tapped into an uncomfortable but nonetheless resonant truth—still today referenced in common parlance as "the Protestant work ethic"—to describe something unique about the Protestant inheritance and its now global economic impact.

Raised with a dominating, nominally Lutheran, father and a devout Calvinist mother, Weber's academic talents were recognized early in his life and he had a number of years of impressive academic productivity before penning his most famous work. At the height of his career in 1897, however, his productivity broke down, along with his mental health. In letters to his wife Marianne, he describes what many today would recognize as the all-too-familiar symptoms of "the Protestant work ethic": an unrelenting drive to produce, like an inner treadmill, so consuming that he had trouble getting peace.[8] In her biography of her husband, Marianne Weber confirms that his illness was the result of long-term incessant overwork.[9] After several attempts, year after year, to find rest from his driving work ethic in tranquil travel destinations during academic breaks, his condition worsened until his productive drive broke down. Eventually, he lost the ability to sleep, read, write, teach, or generally, work.

After about five years and time in a sanitarium, Weber regained health. When he returned to his academic work, however, his research showed a marked shift. Sociologist Ivan Szelenyi notes that "[b]efore the nervous breakdown, Weber is an [enthusiastic] pro-capitalist and pro-liberal. His major concern before 1897 is what blocks the

---

8. Marianne Weber, *Max Weber: A Biography by Marianne Weber*, trans. Harry Zohn (New York: John Wiley & Sons, 1975).

9. In spite of Marianne Weber's comments correlating Max's illness with overwork, Ivan Szelenyi attributes his mental breakdown to his complicated relationship with his father, an explosive fight between the two, and his father's death shortly after their fight and before any reconciliation. Ivan Szelenyi, "Weber on Protestantism and Capitalism," Yale University Open Courses, SOCY-151: Foundations of Modern Social Theory, Lecture 16 (Oct. 27, 2009), http://oyc.yale.edu/sociology/socy-151/lecture-16, accessed, 6/23/15. In life, though, it seems these kinds of variables are not easily separated.

TOWARD A BETTER WORLDLINESS

development in the eastern part of Germany, and how those forces which block the development of capitalism can be overcome. He's very much a liberal in the sense of Adam Smith and John Stuart Mill."[10] After his breakdown, his first major work, *Protestant Ethic and the Spirit of Capitalism,* reveals a new ambiguity in his fascination with capitalism.[11] His interest in the question of what prohibited or supported the proliferation and productivity of capitalism remains, but after the driving force of his work ethic led to a break in his ability to remain productive—or even present—in society, his work reflects the ambiguity of the light cloak-turned-steel yoke.

Weber's preoccupation with capitalism was not unique or original in his time, but should be situated among a mass of contemporary scholars theorizing about the beginnings of capitalism.[12] Even a historical link between capitalism and Protestantism was not new. The original aspect of Weber's thesis was that capitalism functions as anything but a bloodless or sterile set of official policies. Where Marx argued material economic conditions led to capitalism, Weber argued it owed its genesis not only to economic conditions but to social and religious conditions as well.[13] He was not seeking to substitute an idealist for a materialist interpretation of history, but argued material economic factors were just one of many other independent factors that interacted to create capitalism.[14] Another unique aspect of Weber's thesis was that where other scholars placed the burden (or privilege) of initiating capitalism with the Lutheran tradition, Weber argued that this tradition was too socially conservative to inspire such a societal shift. Capitalism needed a religion that could transform society—this ambiguous honor he grants to Calvinism.

Rather than historical causation connecting capitalism and the Reformation tradition, Weber writes of unintended consequences.

---

10. Ibid.
11. Szelenyi reminds us, "He would always say that capitalism is the only viable system we can live in; modernity has no alternative. But he's beginning increasingly to show the downside of this modernity" (ibid).
12. Gianfranco Poggi, *Weber: A Short Introduction* (Malden, MA: Polity Press, 2006), 64.
13. See Rosemary Crompton, *Class and Stratification*, 3rd ed. (Malden, MA: Polity Press, 2008), 34.
14. Both Szelenyi and Poggi emphasize these points regarding interpretation.

PROTESTANT GHOSTS AND THE SPIRITS OF CAPITALISM

Noting the conditions for capitalism were not explicit in or even consistent with key Reformation values, he suggests certain theological ideals added to a certain spirit, ideology, or worldview that contributed to capitalism. Weber describes the relation between the material and ideal conditions as an "elective affinity."[15] One did not originate in the other, but their interaction—or what Barad might call their entangled relationality—prepared the necessary conditions for capitalism.

Weber also differed from other similarly situated theorists by proposing that the answer to such questions lay not with certain influential or forward-thinking individuals, but with a group or community ethos created by religious morals and ideals.[16] He intuited that religious views, values, and practices could make and unmake worlds, shaping reality and the way we live, especially our economic practices. Tracing the influences of these values on economic systems became his particular interest. Sociologist and Weber specialist Gianfranco Poggi explains that the German scholar "attends to the ways in which each religion describes and prescribes the individual's position and role in the cosmos, relates her to the Deity, orients her conduct in this world and inspires her perception of her destiny in the afterlife."[17] One's religiously influenced, perceived view of themselves, the cosmos, and their relation to the world and God not only informs religious practices and beliefs but social and economic practices as well.

Over the course of the text, Weber lays out basic features of the rise of capitalism. For example, he argues an important shift was necessary in attitudes about acquisition; for capitalism to thrive, wealth accumulation could not be a moral liability. The significance of the Protestant tradition for Weber was that it not only allowed one to regard accumulation of wealth as morally justified, but morally *compelled*. When wealth became morally compelled, it no longer remained simply a means to sustain the daily material needs of a

---

15. A likely reference to Goethe's 1809 novel, *Elective Affinities.*
16. Poggi, *Weber*, 65.
17. Ibid., 62.

person's life, but became the ultimate purpose of one's life. In other words, Protestantism provided a necessary link between the ability to gain wealth and a person's moral standing.

Weber explains that the accumulation of wealth also needed to be combined with a shift from monastic to worldly asceticism so that people did not just make money to spend money. The purpose of accumulating wealth could not be for creating lavish or enjoyable lifestyles. Instead, "the strict earning of more and more money, combined with the strict avoidance of all spontaneous enjoyment of life . . . is thought of . . . purely as an end in itself. . . . Man is dominated by the making of money, by acquisition as the ultimate purpose of his life."[18] Corresponding to this ascetic attitude, Weber noted that capitalism needed a new sense of rationalism, calculation, and control over every aspect of life. A cost-benefit analysis needed to be applied to every decision to meet the goal of maximizing acquisition.

The Lutheran tradition contributed the necessary shift from monastic to worldly asceticism by emphasizing the importance of day-to-day work, or *Beruf* (calling, vocation). Daily life, not just religious life, needed to be saturated with spiritual significance. This would lead to "the valuation of the fulfillment of duty in worldly affairs as the highest form which the moral activity of the individual could assume. This inevitably gave everyday worldly activity a religious significance, and which first created the conception of a calling in this sense."[19] Again, articulating a connection between capitalism and the Lutheran shift from monastic vocation for the few to holy vocation for all in daily life was not a new argument. Many other contemporary theories about the beginnings of capitalism emphasized the role of the Lutheran Reformation and held it to be the decisive turning point. For example, Poggi reminds us that Marx's *Capital* notes the significance of the dissolution of the monasteries for transforming all believers into monks who would dedicate their lives to their worldly vocations with religious verve.[20] However, Weber shifts this common contemporary

18. Max Weber, *The Protestant Ethic and the Spirit of Capitalism*, trans. Talcott Parsons (New York: Charles Scribner's Sons, 1958), 53.
19. Ibid., 31.

argument, noting the significance of Lutheran vocation, but ultimately arguing it could not have been the decisive shift. Capitalism could not have risen from Lutheranism itself because it was incapable of promoting the kind of social change Weber believed necessary for the rise of a new economic system. According to Weber's reading, where capitalism demands economic innovation and the opportunity for socioeconomic status elevation, Lutheranism promotes tradition and the status quo. The faithful were called to see their daily work as holy, but for Luther, this was also a divine sanction of people's given economic and political station in society: they were called to serve God in their place—regardless of whether one was a prince or penniless peasant. Since Lutheranism did not encourage this important aspect of the entrepreneurial spirit, it alone could not have contributed the definitive shift to capitalism. For this, Calvinism was necessary.

For Weber, Calvin's doctrine of predestination set Calvinism apart from Lutheranism and Roman Catholicism and completed the alchemic formula for capitalism. According to Calvin, Weber explains, humanity is split into just two groups: the damned and the saved.[21] No one can know whether they are condemned or redeemed and nothing can be done to sway or influence one's eternal destiny. According to Weber, for Lutherans (and even more for Roman Catholics) the question of one's salvation was not set in stone. There was still room for repentance, forgiveness, and the soteriological effect of the sacraments. Calvinism, by contrast, so disenchanted the world that these acts had absolutely no sway over one's ultimate salvation or damnation since the matter was entirely pre-decided.

Beyond what the reformers anticipated or envisioned, this lack of personal power regarding one's ultimate fate inspired a heightened emphasis on agency in matters of daily life. For example, Calvinist pastors responded to their parishioners' insecurity and anxiety about

---

20. Poggi, Weber, 69.
21. Weber does not articulate this difference clearly and one might point out that Luther also held onto a doctrine of predestination. For the sake of clarity, we might add that Weber is here noting the difference between Calvin's "double predestination" (some are damned, some are saved) and Luther's "single predestination" (some are saved, and we would not dare speculate on the rest because this is God's dominion).

TOWARD A BETTER WORLDLINESS

their eternally predestined place by suggesting that it was "an absolute duty to consider oneself chosen, and to combat all doubts as temptations of the devil, since lack of self-confidence is the result of insufficient faith."[22] Parishioners' confidence could be bolstered by engaging in intense worldly activity leading to accumulation of wealth: "It and it alone disperses religious doubts and gives the certainty of grace."[23] In other words, people were encouraged to take their worldly success as assurance of God's care for them—ultimately, that they were among the saved. While Lutheranism inspired a shift to holiness in worldly activity, Calvinism added "the necessity of *proving one's faith* in worldly activity."[24]

In addition, Calvinist disenchantment of the world made way for rational calculation. Where decisions were once made under the influence of tradition, religion, or magic, they were now made by an objective, distant, rational calculation so that every decision involved a cost-benefit analysis to guarantee the best returns and greatest acquisition. Such rational accounting spread its influence over every single aspect of the person's life so that all decisions were united under the common goal of increasing profit and minimizing loss. This rational calculation combined with and contributed to a new kind of asceticism focused on worldly activity. Inevitably, those who carefully watched and calculated their profits also spent very little of their income. As Weber notes, the "inevitable practical result is obvious: accumulation of capital through ascetic compulsion to save."[25]

The confluence of these factors—disenchantment of the world, an accounting logic of gains and losses over all of life, worldly asceticism, spiritual emphasis on worldly vocation, and the fusion of morality and accumulation—make up the spirit of capitalism. Weber carefully demonstrates that the emphasis on economic acquisition was not explicit, intended, or even entirely consistent with official Protestant doctrine. In Poggi's words, these are "largely paradoxical (or indeed

22. Weber, *Protestant Ethic*, Parsons's translation, 111.
23. Ibid., 112.
24. Ibid., 121. Emphasis added.
25. Weber, *Protestant Ethic*, Parsons's translation, 85.

PROTESTANT GHOSTS AND THE SPIRITS OF CAPITALISM

perverse) effects, for they had a negative impact on the vitality of that [religious] sphere."[26] Weber notes, for example, that John Wesley grasped the precise contradiction of this spirit and its danger to the religious movement that had a hand in inspiring it. Weber cites this quote from Wesley as a concise summary of his argument regarding the relation of the religious values and economic acquisition:

> "I do not see how it is possible, in the nature of things, for any revival of true religion to continue long. For religion must necessarily produce both industry and frugality, and these cannot but produce riches. But as riches increase, so will pride, anger, and love of the world in all its branches. . . . Is there no way to prevent this continual decay of pure religion? We ought not to prevent people from being diligent and frugal; we must exhort Christians to gain all they can, and to save all they can; that is, in effect, to grow rich."[27]

Rather than an argument of direct causation, Weber proposed that the Protestant religious influences created a snowball effect so that, eventually, the theological and religious factors were not needed—in fact, could even be contradicted as Wesley's quote demonstrates—as the system continued to gain mass and speed. Famously, Weber describes how the Puritan concern for material goods "should only lie on the shoulders of the 'saint like a light cloak, which can be thrown aside at any moment,'" but instead, became an "iron cage" imposing a driving work ethic whether one ascribed to the religious views or not. Where "[t]he Puritans *wanted* to be men of the calling," Weber laments, "we, on the other hand, *must be.*"[28]

Weber's remarkable reference to fossil fuels in this famous "iron cage" quote has been generally overlooked.[29] But when one begins to examine economic issues from an ecological and not just social point of view, the reference seems plainly and stunningly prescient. Not only does Weber tie together the Protestant tradition and the spirit of capitalism, but he notes—at the opening of the twentieth century—the

---

26. Poggi, *Weber*, 73.
27. Cited in Weber, *Protestant Ethic*, Parsons's translation, 175.
28. Weber, *Protestant Ethic*, Baehr and Wells's translation, 120.
29. Larry Rasmussen is an exception, noting Weber's early connection, in *Earth-Honoring Faith: Religious Ethics in a New Key* (New York: Oxford University Press, 2013).

significant and ominous role fossil fuels play in this religio-economic dynamic. Reference to the unrelenting character of the spirit of capitalism and the Protestant work ethic seems visionary now even as our fears have shifted from running out of fossil fuels to fears that our planet's reserves provide more than enough fuel to ignite global destruction.[30]

Luther and Economic Ethics: Responses to the Weber-Troeltschian Interpretive Tradition

Even today, while the "Protestant work ethic" remains widely acknowledged, a link between the Protestant tradition, capitalism, fossil fuel consumption, and climate change requires a good deal of persuasion and explanation for most people. While this key link has simply not penetrated our collective consciousness, it is not for lack of effort or compelling arguments. Indeed, John Cobb was making this argument in the 1970s and Sallie McFague in the 1980s.[31] Lutheran ethicists Larry Rasmussen and Cynthia Moe-Lobeda also persuasively address climate change,[32] but the message seems not to have landed broadly enough for institutional reformation. While self-critical connections between fossil fuels, capitalism, and Protestantism have not been widely explored, a growing number of scholars are drawing attention to the economic writings of Luther and Calvin, emphasizing their liberating message for those on the underside of global capitalism today.

In branding the tradition "socially conservative," Weber essentially wrote Lutheranism out of a history of transformative economic practices. However, today a growing wave of Lutheran theologians and ethicists claim the authority of Luther in their condemnation of global oppressive capitalist systems while Weber's thesis is only minimally

---

30. See Bill McKibben's essay, "Global Warming's Terrifying New Math," *Rolling Stone*, July 19, 2012.
31. See Cobb and Daly, *For the Common Good*, and Cobb, *Sustaining the Common Good: A Christian Perspective on the Global Economy* (Cleveland: Pilgrim Press, 1994), and McFague, *Life Abundant*.
32. Rasmussen, *Earth-Honoring Faith* and Moe-Lobeda, *Resisting Structural Evil*. Rasmussen and Moe-Lobeda do not make the argument of a key link between Protestantism, capitalism, and fossil fuels quite as strongly as do Cobb and McFague, or as strongly as I do here.

engaged.[33] Much of this scholarship has been an extension of related twentieth-century debates about the role and content of Lutheran ethics after World War II. Conscious of the ways Protestant—particularly Lutheran—theology was abused to promote or passively condone Nazi ideals, conversations in Lutheran ethics since the 1970s have focused on challenging misinterpretations of Lutheran doctrine. Countering such misinterpretations, theo-ethicists Ulrich Duchrow, Craig Nessan, and Paul Chung, along with Reformation church historians Samuel Torvend and Carter Lindberg, argue that the Protestant tradition—particularly Luther in their cases (but Duchrow also discusses Calvin)—offers a fundamental critique of exploitative capitalistic practices and a message of economic liberation for the poor and oppressed. This work has highlighted significant oversights in the interpretation of the Reformation corpus and mobilized late twentieth-century Lutheran ethics in remarkably transformed ways.[34]

In asserting the liberating economic message of the Reformers, these scholars have focused their attention on the work of Protestant theologian and sociologist of religion, Ernst Troeltsch.[35] Troeltsch was critical of Luther, reading him as a socially conservative and dualistic thinker who prioritized the spiritual over the material. Rather than the initiator of the beginnings of modernity, Troeltsch interpreted the Reformer as fundamentally medieval.[36] This reading of Luther became highly influential in Germany. Historian Carter Lindberg explains that "The all too common portrayal of Luther as a conservative ethicist who separated public and private morality, advocated an 'ethic of disposition' and dualistically decreed 'an inward morality for the individual and an external "official" morality' indifferent to social

33. Much of this work has inspired and been inspired by the leadership of ecumenical and international councils such as the World Council of Churches and Lutheran World Federation, which have taken strong, decisive positions on issues of economic and political oppression.

34. William Lazareth, for example, emphasizes the significance of social statements created by the Lutheran Church in America. William Lazareth, *Christians in Society: Luther, the Bible and Social Ethics* (Minneapolis: Augsburg Fortress, 2001), 29.

35. See Lazareth, *Christians in Society*, 6.

36. Mark D. Chapman, *Ernst Troeltsch and Liberal Theology: Religion and Cultural Synthesis in Wilhelmine Germany* (New York: Oxford University Press, 2001), 28. Troeltsch disagreed with Albrecht Ritschl's interpretation of the Reformation as the beginning of modernity.

structures and institutions stems from Troeltsch's famous work, *The Social Teaching of the Christian Churches.*"[37] Significantly, Troeltsch and Weber were close friends and the latter relied primarily on the former for his portrayal of Luther in *The Protestant Ethic and the Spirit of Capitalism.*[38] Consequently, understanding critical responses to Troeltsch also lends insight to the more recent lack of attention Weber's argument has been given among Lutheran scholars engaging economics.

In the late nineteenth and early twentieth century, Karl Holl (1866-1926) defended Luther against Troeltsch's interpretation, igniting a "Luther Renaissance" in Germany. Unfortunately, since Holl's work had not yet been published in English during the Social Gospel movement, American readings of Luther remained influenced by Troeltsch through the writings of Reinhold Niebuhr.[39] Indeed, Niebuhr writes of Luther's "quietistic tendencies" and asserts that, for Luther, "no obligation rests upon the Christian to change social structures so that they might conform more perfectly to the requirements of brotherhood."[40] But Holl challenged Troeltsch's representation, based on lack of textual evidence to support the interpretation that Luther was a religious privatist, social conservative, and spiritual/material dualist.[41] Holl's work inspired a movement in Germany to go back to the writings of Luther himself, distinguishing between Luther and the later Lutheran tradition, including the Lutheran orthodox movement, Lutheran Confessions, and even Luther's successor, Philipp Melanchthon.[42] However, theo-ethicist William Lazareth also notes the "fatal blindspot" of Holl's supporters. For many Germans frustrated at having lost a position of world power and influence due to late industrialization and foreign colonialism, the figure of Luther was lifted up through Holl's influence during the

---

37. Carter Lindberg, *Beyond Charity: Reformation Initiatives for the Poor* (Minneapolis: Fortress Press, 1993), 161.
38. Lazareth, *Christians in Society*, 6.
39. Ibid., 25.
40. Reinhold Niebuhr, *The Nature and Destiny of Man*, 2 vols. (New York: Scribner's, 1964), vol. 2, 192–93, cited in Lindberg, *Beyond Charity*, 161.
41. Lazareth, *Christians in Society*, 6.
42. Ibid.

PROTESTANT GHOSTS AND THE SPIRITS OF CAPITALISM

crucial years leading to WWII as "a heroic figure . . . [and] national liberator of the German Volk."[43] Consequently, the "Luther Renaissance" only added fuel to German nationalistic fervor.[44]

In the years of Lutheran ethical identity crisis following WWII, evidence mounted to demonstrate that Troeltsch's reading of Luther was not textually well supported and that this spurious interpretation—and not Luther's own teachings—led to crucial and quietistic-leaning dualisms between religion and ethics/politics. Much of this post-WWII scholarship has focused on Luther's "two kingdoms teaching." Some of the major moments in this mass of scholarly work are worth highlighting since this scholarship has directly influenced and flowed into contemporary approaches to Luther and economy.

Influenced by both Paul and Augustine's *City of God,* Luther's two kingdoms teaching dealt with the proper relationship between God and the world, religious and state authority, and the church's relation to the world or secular culture. Although the two kingdoms teaching became a defining aspect of the Lutheran tradition, Brazilian-American theologian Vitor Westhelle notes that this was a minor—even marginal—element of Luther's thought. What is more accurately a "two kingdoms teaching" only became interpreted as a "doctrine" in the 1930s when dualistic interpretations of the teaching became resources to authorize the church's uncritical support of the state.[45] The prevailing interpretation of the two kingdoms in and leading up to Nazi Germany was a dualism between God/religion/church and world/politics/ethics. Each authority was "God ordained," which was interpreted to mean that the state's power and actions were authorized by God. Since the church and the state represented two separate

---

43. Ibid., 7.

44. Henrich Assel notes that Holl's interpretation inspired two very different movements in Germany during this time. While one interpretative trajectory—led by Emanuel Hirsch—settled into support of German Christians, another trajectory—characterized by Dietrich Bonhoeffer and Hans Joachim Iwand—inspired resistance to the German Christians and National Socialism. Heinrich Assel, *Der andere Aufbruch: Die Lutherrenaissance—Ursprunge, Aporien und Wege: Karl Holl, Emanuel Hirsch, Rudolf Hermann (1910-1935)* (Göttingen: Vandenhoeck & Ruprecht, 1994).

45. Vitor Westhelle, "God and Justice: The Word and the Mask," *Journal of Lutheran Ethics* 3, no. 1 (January 2003). Cited in Nessan, "Reappropriating Luther's Two Kingdoms," *Lutheran Quarterly* 29 (2005).

kingdoms, the church was to keep to its own private and personal "religious" world and not interfere in politics. This framework contributed to the largely passive response of German citizens to Hitler's authority and actions.

In the 1970s, German theologian Ulrich Duchrow contributed to a major shift in interpreting the two kingdoms teaching. Lazareth describes Duchrow's work as an "impressive multivolume project that provides an array of documentary evidence," to show how nineteenth-century German Lutheran theology and ethics became "dualistically distorted" both by liberal critics such as Troeltsch and Weber and by scholars who sought to continue the tradition.[46] Like Holl, Duchrow distinguishes between Luther's writings and later interpretations of the Lutheran tradition, insisting that if there is a dualism in Luther's work itself, it is an apocalyptic dualism between good and evil, God and the devil, and not between God and world or church and politics.

Building off of Duchrow's work, American Lutheran ethicist Craig Nessan's reinterpretation of the two kingdoms makes evident the importance of Duchrow's insight. Nessan suggests a translation of *Zweireichen* as "two strategies," rather than two kingdoms because it more faithfully communicates Luther's worldview and intention.[47] Rather than upholding two separate realms (God and world), Nessan suggests that in engaging ethical issues in the world today, we envision one realm or world with God working through two strategies: one through the church, and the other through civil society. Where the

---

46. Ulrich Duchrow et al., eds., *Umdeutengen der Zweireichen Lehre Luthers* in 19. Jahrhundert (*Novel Interpretations of Luther's Doctrine of the Two Kingsdoms in the Nineteenth Century*, 1975). "The pre–World Wars' extension and subsequent repudiation of this dangerously quietistic legacy is then extensively documented in both Germany and the United States by Ulrich Duchrow et al., eds., *Die Ambivalenz der Zweireichelehre in Lutherischen Kirchen* des 20. Jahrhundert (*The Ambivalence of the Doctrine of the Two Kingdoms in Lutheran Churches of the Twentieth Century*, 1976), and further internationally expanded in scope in Ulrich Duchrow, ed., *Zwei Reiche und Regimente: Ideologie oder Evangelische Orientierung?* (*Lutheran Churches: Salt or Mirror of Society? Case Studies on the Theory and Practice of the Two Kingdoms Doctrine*, trans. 1977). The parallel volume of the project is geared to English readers and discerningly presents the 'American Reformation of Lutheran Political Responsibility in the Twentieth Century,' in *Two Kingdoms and One World*, ed. Karl H. Hertz, 1976" (Lazareth, *Christians in Society*, 19).
47. Nessan explains that "'Strategy' is a constructive and dynamic translation of the German word, *Regimente*, just as the English term 'regimen' suggests a strategy" (Nessan, "Reappropriating Luther's Two Kingdoms," 311).

previous dualistic model gave divine authority and autonomy to civil orders, and thus tended toward political passivity and quietism, Duchrow and Nessan's model emphasizes one world where God is working for the good of all creation. Just as God is working in the world for good through two different strategies, the people of God are also encouraged and inspired to work toward issues of justice and the common good, both in the church and through political processes. Rather than withdrawing from the world of politics, Nessan and Duchrow's reinterpretation of the two kingdoms calls for rich engagement in advocacy and political processes, even challenging civil and religious structures when they promote inequality and injustice that work against God's strategic work in the world.

For Duchrow, this dual strategic work in the world has more recently taken the form of an intense concern and interest in economic justice, challenging the authority of neoliberal capitalism. In Duchrow's 1994 *Alternatives to Global Capitalism,* he challenges the belief, all the more prevalent since the demise of socialism, that there is no alternative to global capitalism.[48] Based on a biblical model of communities of God in the world, Duchrow concludes that the church today should be a source of resistance and alternative models to political and economic systems of oppression.

Addressing the role of the Reformation in the emergence of global capitalism, Duchrow explains that more recent research on the development of capitalism shows it could not have developed solely on account of the Reformation since the "elements of early capitalism were all there before the Reformation."[49] Understanding that capitalism was already an emerging economic system by the time of the Reformation becomes key as Duchrow and others argue, contra Weber, that Luther and Calvin were remarkably early critics of emerging capitalistic practices. Duchrow focuses particularly on Luther and Calvin's writings against usury, Luther's exposition of the Ten Commandments, and his criticism of emerging monopolist trading

---

48. Made famous by Margaret Thatcher's slogan, TINA: "There is no alternative."
49. Ulrich Duchrow, *Alternatives to Global Capitalism: Drawn from Biblical History, Designed for Political Action,* trans. Elizabeth Hickes et al. (Utrecht, The Netherlands: International Books, 1995), 124.

TOWARD A BETTER WORLDLINESS

and banking companies (Fugger, Wesler, etc.) as evidence that the Reformers were indeed already living in and reacting against oppressive capitalistic practices.[50]

Taking cues from Luther's definition of idolatry, which includes explicit denunciation of capital accumulation, Duchrow argues that global economics has become a theological issue not only because of the massive injustices that the system creates, but because capitalism has become a competing religion.[51] He maintains that when the sole goal of an ideology is the accumulation of wealth, it has become idolatrous. In his explanation of the first commandment, Luther writes, "What does 'to have a god' mean, or what is God? . . . A 'god' is the term for that to which we are to look for all good and in which we are to find refuge in all need. Therefore, to have a god is nothing else than to trust and believe in that one with your whole heart. . . . Anything on which your heart relies and depends, I say, that is really your God."[52] Duchrow highlights the way Luther connects his discussion of idolatry primarily to economic matters: "Many a person thinks he has God and everything he needs when he has money and property, in them he trusts and of them he boasts so stubbornly and securely that he cares for no one. Surely such a man also has a god—mammon by name, that is, money and possessions—on which he fixes his whole heart. It is the most common idol on earth."[53] For Duchrow, the ethical and theological implications are immediately applicable to an oppressive capitalist system today. He suggests that in his usury texts, Luther was primarily aiming at the emergence of oppressive practices among

---

50. Ibid., 217. Duchrow's reading of the usury writings as anticapitalist is a departure from previous interpretations that classify these writings as primarily anti-Jewish.

51. Cobb and Daly, *For the Common Good: Redirecting the Economy Toward Community, the Environment, and a Sustainable Future* (Boston: Beacon, 1994), along with Douglas Meeks, *God the Economist: The Doctrine of God and Political Economy* (Minneapolis: Fortress Press, 1989) and Scott W. Gustafson, *At the Altar of Wall Street: The Rituals, Myths, Theologies, Sacraments, and Mission of the Religion Known as the Modern Global Economy* (Grand Rapids, MI: Eerdmans, 2015) make similar arguments about capitalism and Christianity.

52. From Martin Luther's exposition of the Ten Commandments in the Large Catechism, cited in Duchrow, *Alternatives to Global Capitalism*, 218. Duchrow credits F. M. Marquardt for highlighting the economic implications of Luther here. See also Martin Luther, "The Large Catechism," in *The Book of Concord: The Confessions of the Evangelical Lutheran Church*, ed. Robert Kolb and Timothy J. Wengert, trans. Charles Arand (Minneapolis: Fortress Press, 2000), 386.

53. Ibid.

PROTESTANT GHOSTS AND THE SPIRITS OF CAPITALISM

"big banking and trading companies."[54] On account of Luther's condemnation of these early capitalist practices, Duchrow concludes that Luther was an early critic, rather than instigator, of capitalism.

In 2011, Duchrow and Nessan joined with Korean-American Lutheran theologian Paul Chung to co-author *Liberating Lutheran Theology: Freedom for Justice and Solidarity in a Global Context.* United by their appreciation of German-Protestant counter-cultural voices such as Dietrich Bonhoeffer and F. M. Marquardt as well as Liberation theology, the three scholars move to resolve tension between a tradition of Protestant passivity and Liberation theology's praxis orientation. In continued efforts to counteract the long history of Troeltsch's influence, not only among scholars but among the many faithful who still today believe that their religious views have no bearing on political and economic structures, the author of the introduction, Karen Bloomquist, explains that the three scholars, "inspired by Luther and others, [provide] strong bases for resisting and developing alternatives to the forces that so massively oppress and exploit human beings and creation."[55] Chung, in particular, states that his hermeneutical strategy is "to consider Martin Luther as a theologian of economic justice."[56] Here, Luther begins to shed the form of a quietistic, spiritual/material dualist, emerging instead as a heroic and prophetic anticapitalist figure fighting for the poor and oppressed. This is a bold move with admirable strategic motivations. However, we might also begin to wonder about those unwelcome Protestant ghosts who would render such unambiguous portrayals suspect.

A Historical Example: Community Chests

Complementing the approach of Duchrow, Chung, and Nessan, American Reformation church historians Carter Lindberg and Samuel

---

54. Ibid., 219.
55. Paul S. Chung, Ulrich Duchrow, and Craig L. Nessan, *Liberating Lutheran Theology: Freedom for Justice and Solidarity with Others in a Global Context* (Minneapolis: Fortress Press, 2011), vi.
56. Ibid., 71. Chung's argument here is expanded upon in his more recent publication, *Church and Ethical Responsibility in the Midst of World Economy: Greed, Dominion, and Justice* (Eugene, OR: Cascade, 2013).

TOWARD A BETTER WORLDLINESS

Torvend have similarly worked to revise interpretations of Luther with regard to social and economic justice implications. While Lindberg responds only indirectly to the trajectory of the two kingdoms doctrine, both authors maintain an emphasis on responding to the hermeneutical trajectory influentially launched by Troeltsch.[57]

Particularly in *Beyond Charity: Reformation Initiatives for the Poor*, Lindberg focuses on widely overlooked Reformation sources that demonstrate an unrecognized emphasis on social transformation during the Reformation. In stark contrast to the reading of Luther as one maintaining a "nearly monomaniacal concentration upon the cardinal problem of the individual-personal gaining of grace," focusing on the "inner" and the "religious" and ignoring the material and social,[58] Lindberg argues that the beginnings of modern state welfare were rooted in the theological, ecclesial, and liturgical shifts of the Reformation.

Lindberg begins by analyzing the theological landscape Luther found himself in, reconstructing the medieval theology of poverty. He argues that in medieval theology acts of charity were encouraged not for social change or even genuine concern to alter the conditions of the recipient, but for the spiritual wellbeing of the benefactor.[59] In the twelfth century, for example, most authors considered poverty to be a God-ordained position necessary for the salvation of the rich. Since wealth was dangerous to one's salvation, such a person could atone for their affluence through charitable acts toward the poor. Poverty was thereby justified as a virtue because the poor retained a position necessary for the salvation of the rich.[60]

Lindberg paints a portrait of Luther entering the medieval scene as a warrior fighting an economic war on two fronts: against the medieval

---

57. Lindberg emphasizes the impact of Troeltsch's interpretation just as Lazareth does. See footnote 35 above.
58. Ibid., 162, citing Heinz Schiller.
59. Lindberg does not mention, but it should be noted, that St. Francis of Assisi would be a clear exception during the medieval period.
60. Lindberg cites Giordano da Pisa's 1303/4 sermon as he articulates this understanding of poverty and charity: "God has ordered that there be rich and poor so that the rich may be served by the poor and the poor may be taken care of by the rich. . . . Why are the poor given their station? So that the rich man might earn eternal life through them" (ibid., 30).

spiritual economy that kept people in poverty on the one front, and against capitalistic practices growing in urban environments on the other. By attacking both the theology of virtuous poverty and growing capitalistic practices, Luther provided an important link between "religious and economic mentalities of achievement."[61] Socioeconomic shifts came as a direct result of Luther's doctrine of justification by grace through faith, since "[p]overty and suffering make no one acceptable to God."[62] Appropriately, the refrain "Nobody ought to go begging among Christians" became common among the reformers.[63] Since poverty retained no spiritual value, Luther advocated a shift beyond charity that maintained and reinforced poverty to social welfare legislation in the form of community chests that sought to eradicate poverty and the need for begging.

Similarly, in *Luther and the Hungry Poor: Gathered Fragments*, Torvend lays an economic lens over a story usually told as purely religious and spiritual, both by drawing attention to the economic factors influencing the reformers and by narrating the economic impact of the Reformation. Torvend emphasizes that Luther's unintentional break from the Roman church came not only as a result of spiritual or psychological angst but because he started to ask economic and social justice questions about ecclesial structures and theological doctrine. He cites a Luther one has rarely heard: "Why doesn't the pope, whose wealth today is greater than the richest of the rich, build this one basilica of St. Peter with his own money rather than with money of the poor?"[64] Luther criticized what he saw as an unjust spiritual economy in which believers were encouraged to gain spiritual capital for themselves rather than pour economic resources into the community

---

61. Ibid., 93.

62. Ibid., 106. Lindberg credits Gerhard Uhlhorn's work, dating back to 1895, with the basic thesis that Lindberg expands on here that "Luther's rejection of the salvatory merit of good works cut the nerve of indiscriminate medieval almsgiving designed to spiritually benefit the giver, and thereby made possible the development of rational, communal welfare policies that were far more effective in serving the poor" (10).

63. Ibid., 105.

64. Samuel Torvend, "Those Little Pieces of White Bread: Early Lutheran Initiatives among the Hungry Poor," *Dialog* 52, no. 1 (2003): 19. Citing Martin Luther, *Luther's Works*, 55 vols., ed. Jaroslav Pelikan (St. Louis: Concordia, 1955–1986), 31–33.

TOWARD A BETTER WORLDLINESS

where the need was great. The reformers sought to dismantle these destructive intersections between spiritual and material economies.

Both Lindberg and Torvend highlight the significance—generally overlooked by Reformation historians—of the widespread Reformation practice of addressing social welfare concerns through the creation of common chests in communities. Both scholars highlight one in particular: the Leisnig Community Chest. This community chest is significant because it was the result of Luther's own vision and the first to supplement its initial funding (medieval church sources and the sale of church properties) with a community tax when the other sources became insufficient.[65] The ordinance, with preface written by Luther himself, demonstrates how the church institution was to reflect the transformation of the justified person. Just as a person's justification freed them from putting spiritual and material energies toward maintaining their standing before God, freeing them for service to others, so too the economic resources once collected to maintain the church institution itself were now to be collected, stored in the chest, and distributed to meet the needs of the community.

The needs of the community were many. Specifically, the Leisnig chest funded services such as the "maintenance and construction of common buildings such as the church, school, and hospital as well as storing grain and peas for use during lean times."[66] The order also "regulated disbursement of loans and gifts to newcomers to help them get settled; to the house poor to help them become established in a trade or occupation; and to orphans, dependents, the infirm, and the aged for daily support."[67] Wittenberg's parallel social welfare legislation, the "Order of the Communal Purse," provided funds for a doctor with the purpose of providing free health care for those who could not afford it.[68] Here also, direct relief was provided to the poor

65. Torvend lists these sources of income as: "hereditary lands, supplementary rents, toll income from church-owned bridges, cash, silver, jewels, rents from chapels, benefices, revenues, stores, income from masses for the dead, perpetual memorials, income from indulgence sales, alms, income from annuities from brotherhoods, and contributions, penances, or fines paid by craft guilds and peasant farmers to the church" ("Those Little Pieces of White Bread," 22).
66. Lindberg, *Beyond Charity*, 126.
67. Ibid.
68. Ibid., 120. The first town doctor in Wittenberg was installed in 1527.

PROTESTANT GHOSTS AND THE SPIRITS OF CAPITALISM

and vulnerable through loans or grants, including resources for the sick and mentally ill.[69]

The management of the chest was remarkably egalitarian for its time. To prevent corruption, a council of ten people was put in charge of stewarding the contents of this chest. This council was to include members from every group of society: two nobles, two city council members, three town citizens, and three peasants. Each group of directors was given a key, and four keys were required to open the chest. Consequently, at least one director from each group—noble, city council, common town citizen, and peasant—needed to be present in order to open the chest and distribute goods.[70]

With these community chests, sacramental vision informed and flowed into civic responsibility, inextricably linking the two:[71] "Every Sunday, *at the end of Holy Communion and flowing from it,* the directors [of the community chest] were to distribute the congregation's charity from the common chest to all in need."[72] Lindberg and Torvend illustrate how the Reformers maintained a dynamic relationship between the spiritual and material by integrating social/economic justice into worship. Rather than translating *ecclesia* as "church," Luther translated it as "assembly," "congregation," or "community" to emphasize a shift from a hierarchical to a community-oriented ecclesiastical structure. When Luther reformed worship life, it was to highlight clear connections between religious and social life, making worship the foundation and catalyst for social justice. To do this, Luther recalled patristic sources linking worship and welfare, reinterpreting traditional parts of worship for social action. For example, Lindberg points out that "in interpreting the origin of the 'collect' as a general collection and fund gathered to be given to the poor, Luther may have been aware of patristic sources that linked worship and welfare. If so, these sources may have served as

---

69. Ibid.
70. Ibid., 124.
71. Torvend, "Those Little Pieces of White Bread: Early Lutheran Initiatives among the Hungry Poor," 25.
72. Ibid., 23.

23

TOWARD A BETTER WORLDLINESS

rudimentary models for his development of the common chest concept of social welfare."[73] By linking the liturgical "collect" (typically, the prayers of the church) with a collection for a community chest, Luther consciously linked liturgical and social reforms.

Beyond the prayers, Luther explicitly aimed to connect the Eucharist and social welfare, exhorting:

> When you have partaken of this sacrament [of the altar], you must in turn share the misfortunes of the fellowship. . . . Here your heart must go out in love and learn that this is a sacrament of love. As love and support are given you, you in turn must render love and support to Christ in his needy ones. You must feel with sorrow all the misery of Christendom, all the unjust suffering of the innocent, with which the world is everywhere filled to overflowing. You must fight, work, pray and . . . have heartfelt sympathy. . . . For here the saying of Paul is fulfilled, "Bear one another's burdens, and so fulfill the law of Christ" (Gal 6:2).[74]

Resisting theologies where the Eucharist had been turned into a "mere merchandise, a market, and a profit-making business"[75] where one could obtain "more 'graces,'" Luther shifted sacramental practice and Christian theology from one chest to another: from the indulgence chest to the common chest.[76] For Luther, this was not merely an individual responsibility, but involved a new form of being in community that was intimately tied to liturgical communion: "You must take to heart the infirmities and needs of others as if they were your own. Then offer to others your strength, as if it were their own, just as Christ does for you in the sacrament. This is what it means to change into one another through love to lose one's own form and take on that which is common to all."[77] For the most part, interpretations of the Lutheran tradition have not recognized the remarkable

---

73. Lindberg, *Beyond Charity*, 103.
74. Torvend, "Little Pieces," 25, citing *LW* 35:54.
75. Torvend, *Luther and the Hungry Poor: Gathered Fragments* (Minneapolis: Fortress Press, 2008), 102.
76. "Indeed, if Luther's initial alarm over the sale of indulgences by 'indulgence preachers' focused on the 'coin ringing in the [indulgence] chest,' his often treacherous path to reform focused on another chest, this 'common' chest, in which money and goods would be collected through taxation and donation, for the good of the most needy here on earth. The shift between the two 'chests' would be decisive in theology, sacramental practice, and social ethics" (Torvend, "Those Little Pieces of White Bread," 23).
77. Luther (*LW* 35:61) in Torvend, *Luther and the Hungry Poor*, 126.

24

implications of this porous sense of self: one self flowing into another through love, and likewise, justification flowing into justice. Despite being "an indispensable resource for evaluating the social effect of Reformation theology,"[78] and a widespread practice during that period, church orders instituting community chests and liturgical reforms have been generally overlooked by historians to the detriment of the reputation and development of the Reformation tradition. By reclaiming these founding documents as important sources for understanding the Reformation movement, the disjunction between the social economic vision articulated in these documents and Weber-Troeltschian interpretations of the Reformer maintaining a "nearly monomaniacal concentration upon . . . individual-personal gaining of grace" becomes clear.[79]

Inheriting the Yoke of the Past and the Future

These Lutheran ethicists, theologians, and historians all highlight consistent and tragic misinterpretations and misrepresentations of the Protestant tradition. More than an issue of perception from outside the tradition, these readings have fundamentally influenced the ways the tradition has come to be embodied in the world. Following Karl Holl in going back to reread Luther himself and drawing upon new or overlooked sources to reexamine the extent to which Luther and other reformers attempted and were successful at transforming society, they persuasively demonstrate that a focus on individualism and personal gaining of grace with disregard for social, economic, and political systems of injustice cannot be maintained.

In reframing the Reformation story—pulling away from personalism and individualism toward the social, communal, political, and economic—the value of this scholarship is not to be underestimated. In the face of global income inequality and climate change, these scholars disrupt a certain determinism from within a tradition stuck in codified conceptions of what it means to be Protestant by demonstrating that

78. Lindberg, *Beyond Charity*, 161.
79. Ibid., 162, citing Heins Schilling.

TOWARD A BETTER WORLDLINESS

viable alternatives from within the tradition exist so other ways of embodying the tradition are possible.

Yet, I fear the portrait of Martin Luther emerging in the midst of defensive counters to a dominant Troeltschian reading echo Holl's work in another way: Luther has become a rather unambiguous heroic liberator of the socially, economically, and spiritually oppressed. William Lazareth noted the historical ways the heroic Luther figure has, in the past, turned ugly. Luther's ungraceful reaction to the peasants in the Peasant War that led to the death of around 100,000 of the poorest members of society, no matter his motivation, should at least be cause for an acknowledgment of the ambiguity of Luther and his tradition's socioeconomic implications. And while we need not worry in the American context about the joining of nationalistic zeal and Lutheran pride (the influence of the Lutheran Church is not nearly so broad in twenty-first-century USA as in twentieth-century Germany), I fear that by portraying Luther purely as a liberative and heroic figure we may also blind ourselves to the perilous possibility that we perpetuate the very practices we condemn. If we are critically analyzing solely economic systems and practices (as the above scholars mainly do), it is easier to maintain morally pure ground because the Reformer's rhetoric is aimed at greed, which is easily relegated to the sin of the wealthy—the "one percent." But adding ecological concerns—particularly global climate change—to our economic critiques dramatically shifts the question of responsibility since almost everyone depends, in basic ways, on fossil fuel-based energy production—the extent to which the Reformers could never have conceived. This is not to say all bear equal responsibility, but I would argue that climate change is a sufficiently urgent and complex problem to call for a significant shift in the way issues of economic and ecological justice are dealt with in the Protestant tradition. The urgency and complexity of factors around climate change make portraying Luther as a social justice anticapitalist hero problematic. If we do not also take note of the ways the Protestant tradition has contributed—even unintentionally or in a distorted form—to the

PROTESTANT GHOSTS AND THE SPIRITS OF CAPITALISM

conditions we now face, we may find that our narratives of the Protestant tradition absolve us of responsibility by allowing us to claim that we have been blameless—outside the circle of liability—from the beginning.

In the next chapter I will fill out this argument by demonstrating that the Protestant tradition today finds itself in an ambiguous position with regard to connections between its doctrine of grace and the rise and perpetuation of global neoliberal capitalism. For now, it is important to emphasize that when defensiveness and arguing from positions of purity become problematic, a more subtle and complex approach becomes necessary. Here, we can build off the ambiguities Weber maintains to develop a nuanced approach to questions of the Protestant tradition, economy, and ecology.

The strength in Weber's argument and its persuasive potential for today lies in his avoidance of a direct or linear causal argument, pointing instead to the power of religious ideals to make and unmake worlds that may endure to shape economic practices even after the religious characteristics have been "secularized." Duchrow and others do well to point out their interpretation of Calvin and Luther as early capitalist critics. These points are indeed an important inspiration for Protestant practices of resistance today. But in the push to overturn Troeltsch's misinterpretations, Weber's insight into a certain affinity between the Protestant tradition, capitalism, and fossil fuels has been disregarded as well.[80] Weber rejected the common thesis of the day that Lutheranism led to capitalism because the tradition did not allow for social transformation: Luther essentially preserved the *status quo* in his emphasis on Christian vocation in the world. This was the key characteristic lacking in Lutheranism that Calvinism could supply. In

---

80. Duchrow does concede what we have above identified as Weber's more explicit argument that the effects of the Reformation on capitalism were not causal but unintended. Echoing Weber, Duchrow adds, "it is in the dimension of anthropology that the Reformation had unintended effects, supporting capitalist developments. While Luther intentionally rejected early capitalism . . . his early concentration on the justification of the individual person by faith led to an unintentional reinforcement of bourgeois individualism" (Duchrow, "Property, Money, Economics and Empires," in *Liberating Lutheran Theology*, 167). In light of the urgency of climate change, however, in my estimation, even these unintentional effects need to be given more attention than Duchrow does as vulnerabilities within the Reformation tradition.

27

the larger scope of Weber's argument, rejecting his thesis because it misinterprets Luther is short-sighted for any Lutheran scholar critical of capitalism. In the context of Weber's argument, arguing that Luther's theology *does,* in fact, allow for social transformation turns into a double-edged sword. If Lutheranism is *not* quietist and *can* lead to social change as the ethical and historical scholars above have argued, this only means that Lutheranism contributed to the rise of capitalism just as much as Calvinism. Whether we agree with Weber's historical interpretation or not, the thesis demands attention.

Rather than dismissing Weber, I would argue that William Lazareth's approach to the legacy of Troeltsch also applies to Weber. "Troeltsch is still a force to be reckoned with, and rightly so," he argues. "Even many of those who have shown him to be completely mistaken about Luther's ethics have had to admit that he was often absolutely right about the reaction ethics of nineteenth-century German Lutheranism."[81] Weber, like Troeltsch, may not have gotten Luther right, but he is often absolutely right about Lutheranism and the ways the Lutheran tradition has come to be embodied in the world.

Responsibility to and for a Tradition

In spite of widespread decline in US mainline Protestant churches, the Protestant ethic still has sway over American social consciousness. At the turn of the twentieth century, Weber's link between the idealization of wealth accumulation and the mass consumption of fossil fuels can only be called prophetic. His narrative of unintended consequences and elective affinities retains a compelling and even prescient edge because it points to vulnerabilities in the Protestant theological tradition that have found resonance with what have become ecologically and socially oppressive forces.[82]

---

81. Lazareth, *Christians in Society,* 4.
82. My reading of Weber, above, has been influenced by William Connolly's own thesis on the present-day "resonance" between capitalism and Protestant (Evangelical) ideologies ("The Evangelical-Capitalist Resonance Machine," *Political Theory* 33, no. 6 [2005]). The differences between the ethos Connolly identifies and that of Weber is also described: "the spirituality [Weber] charts differs in tone from that discerned here. And he believes that once the appropriate institutional structures were installed, a spirituality no longer played such a prominent role in

PROTESTANT GHOSTS AND THE SPIRITS OF CAPITALISM

Such intense ambiguities call for a more complex account of the relation between the Reformation trajectory and current eco/nomic concerns. Political theorist William Connolly, for example, also takes a nonlinear causal approach to the question of Protestantism and capitalism. Focusing particularly on Evangelical Protestantism in American economics, politics, and media, Connolly argues that their complex interactions cannot be explained by arguments of causation but by a certain "resonance" among them. Where causality implies "relations of dependence between separate factors," resonance, by contrast, suggests "energized complexities of mutual imbrication and inter involvement in which heretofore unconnected or loosely associated elements fold, bend, blend, emulsify, and dissolve into each other, forging a qualitative assemblage resistant to classical models of explanation."[83] In other words, especially in the USA, the Protestant tradition remains today inextricably entangled with current economic values and policy, and so demands an approach capable of recognizing ambiguity in the tradition.

There are theological voices too of those who articulate a more ambiguous trajectory of the Protestant tradition. Jürgen Moltmann, for example, notes both the responsibility and liberating potential that heirs of the Protestant tradition today face. In *Theology of Play*, a little-known early text, issued before his famous ecotheological work (*God in Creation*, addressed more fully in chapter three), the theologian laments the fact that "the history of life's reformations and revolutions has up to now revealed an irritating paradoxical nature."[84] Where the Protestant Reformation fought justification by works and sought to issue in a new kind of human freedom, the same movement "abolished the holidays, games, and safety valves of that society. This led to the establishment of the Puritan society of penny pinchers and to the industrial workday world among the very people who had at first insisted on believing that [humans] are justified by faith alone."[85] While

---

the system" (ibid., 877). See also Connolly's *Capitalism and Christianity, American Style* (Durham, NC: Duke University Press, 2008).

83. Connolly, "The Evangelical-Capitalist Resonance Machine," 870.

84. Jürgen Moltmann, *Theology of Play*, trans. Reinhard Ulrich (New York: Harper & Row, 1972), 10.

TOWARD A BETTER WORLDLINESS

the Reformation moved society away from a constraining aristocracy, it was replaced with a "meritocracy" that no longer constrains people to social hierarchies but enslaves them to dependence on consumption, growth, and personal achievement.[86] In this society, people's worth is determined by what they are able to produce and can afford to consume. According to Moltmann, the irony of the Reformation legacy is regrettable: "The [current] exploiting society to achievement [itself a consequence of Reformation shifts] is a form of institutionalized justification by works. Its objective compulsion to worship the idols of its own achievements is nothing but organized blasphemy. *Justification by works as practiced by the medieval ecclesiastical society was child's play in comparison.*"[87] Moltmann's work also emphasizes that we cannot be prophets purified of responsibility, standing on the outside of the system looking in. We are in the system and whether Luther and Calvin preceded capitalism or were in it and already responded to it, either way, we must account for the fact that key aspects of the traditions we maintain today contribute to the system. If we paint Luther and Calvin as heroic figures, it may end up diluting our own sense of responsibility, crucial for mobilizing the tradition through playful, constructive reinterpretation in order to contribute to the economic, ecological, and social alternatives we desperately need.

If we are yoked to responsibility through unintended consequences of the Reformation, and thus maintain no blameless ethical ground to start from, one might reasonably wonder about leaving space for the Christian tradition to retain a prophetic voice. Philosopher of Religion Mary-Jane Rubenstein urges the conversation forward in spite of a lack of pure and blameless prophetic ground. In her essay, "Capital Shares: The Way Back into the With of Christianity," Rubenstein addresses the "profound split" at the heart of the Christian tradition: the fact that Christianity has played instrumental roles in both the *rise of and*

---

85. Ibid., 11.
86. Moltmann does not explicitly reference Weber in this text.
87. Ibid., 51, emphasis added.

PROTESTANT GHOSTS AND THE SPIRITS OF CAPITALISM

resistance to global capital. "In short," she asks, "how are we to account for Christianity's culpability for and resistance to global capital?"[88]

It seems Protestants are not alone in seeking a purified prophetic ground on which to stand. Just as the impulse to hold up Luther or Calvin as liberating heroes does not also account for the capitalizing systems their traditions set in motion, Rubenstein outlines broader, more ecumenical, conversations than those highlighted above, where an alternative to global capital is posed from within the Christian tradition. She notes that these conversations consistently leave out a major complicating factor: "the extent to which Christian universalism has been responsible for the emergence of global capital in the first place."[89] While many would avoid such muddy waters, Rubenstein proposes a way through: "And so once again, we are looking for a condition of possibility that might unsettle the very formation it has produced. Once again we are heading for a deconstruction."[90] One need not be well versed in the details of deconstruction to grasp Rubenstein's point: when there is no pure ground on which to stand, when you are up to your neck in a system you helped create but which now constricts, threatening to cut off the breath of life, you look for a place to trouble the system *from within.*

This may be shaky ground—surely not a foundation—and so, will entice our prophetic voices to remain nimble, astute, playful, and even graceful.[91] Calling on the deconstructive work of Jean-Luc Nancy, Rubenstein suggests prophetic space resides with the unrealized potential in Christianity for the dualism-disrupting, auto-deconstructing, inessential essence of "being-with." "It is witness itself to which thinking and practice must return," she urges, describing being-with as "the fundamental mode according to which lives and things

---

88. Rubenstein, "Capital Shares: The Way Back into the With of Christianity," *Political Theology* 11, no. 1 (2010): 105.

89. Ibid., 104.

90. Ibid., 115.

91. See, for example, Catherine Keller, "Talking Dirty: Ground Is Not Foundation," in *Ecospirit: Religions and Philosophies for the Earth,* ed. Laurel Kearns and Catherine Keller (New York: Fordham University Press, 2007), 63–76.

TOWARD A BETTER WORLDLINESS

emerge alongside, by virtue of, up against, and through other lives and things."[92] One might also consider this mode chiefly *ecological*.

As tides rise in Miami and wildfires blaze in Alaska while snow falls in Texas, climate change may confront us with an unbearable yoke. As we turn to look climate change in the face we do well to recall that the Christian tradition maintains resources for transforming yokes for the weary into graciously light burdens. Rubenstein describes this yoked reality—being-with—from a theological perspective. It remains to be seen, though, whether this disruptive potential can also be claimed from within the Protestant tradition. The task may be stickier than it immediately appears since the unique Protestant understanding of grace seems to be tied, as we will see, to separative individualism, commodification, an active/passive binary, and a persistent return to an absolute, nonporous boundary between inside and outside. In particular, it seems grace has been—and continues to be—defined in opposition to exchanges associated with both ecology and economy. Such definitions of grace remain key aspects of the Protestant inheritance; some would say they are the essence of the Protestant message. As we will see in the next chapter, others argue these particularly Protestant characteristics of grace also retain key resonance with the foundational ideals of neoliberal capitalism.

In taking responsibility for what we inherit, we may find ourselves face-to-face with less-than-welcome ghosts of the Reformation tradition. We may also be surprised to welcome less familiar ghosts who graciously empower us to look climate change in the face and exchange this yoke of burden for a life-sustaining, Christomorphic yoke of life-with-others. In the spirit of Luther's eucharistic call to a communal bearing of one another's burdens, we might yet find that just as this yoke materializes as ecological, it simultaneously emerges as sacramental.

---

92. Rubenstein, "Capital Shares," 115.

2

Inheriting the Free Gift: Economic and Ecological Implications

> [I]f capitalism is a religion . . .
> it is definitely a mode of Protestant religion.
> —John Milbank[1]

As[2] Protestant scholars highlight the liberative potential of the reformers' writings on early capitalist practices, the spirit of Max Weber's thesis on the unintended economic consequences of Reformation theology reverberates from within the tradition through Moltmann's *Theology of Play.* Outlining how generations following the reformers lost track of its pivotal and liberating message, Moltmann emphasizes the "paradoxical" nature of the shift from freedom *from* works through justification to a capitalist-driven justification *by* works

---

1. John Milbank, "The Double Glory, or Paradox Versus Dialectics: On Not Quite Agreeing with Slavoj Žižek," in John Milbank and Slavoj Žižek, *The Monstrosity of Christ: Paradox or Dialectic?*, ed. Preston Davis (Cambridge, MA: MIT Press, 2009), 127.
2. Versions of this chapter previously published in "Grace and Climate Change: The Free Gift in Capitalism and Protestantism," *Eco-Reformation: Grace and Hope for a Planet in Peril,* ed. Jim Martin-Schramm and Lisa Dahill (Eugene, OR: Wipf & Stock, 2016) and "Grace in Intra-action," *Entangled Worlds: Science, Religion, Materiality,* ed. Mary-Jane Rubenstein and Catherine Keller (New York: Fordham University Press, 2017).

TOWARD A BETTER WORLDLINESS

through labor, accumulation, and achievement.[3] Yet, what Moltmann identifies as a paradoxical or irrational shift, John Milbank singles out as a rational, indeed inevitable, consequence of a fundamentally flawed theology of grace. As read primarily through the perspectives of Milbank and other theologians identifying with Radical Orthodoxy, gift theory demonstrates that Weber's thesis only identifies the tip of a religio-economic iceberg. Where Weber focuses on what might be considered more secondary aspects of the Protestant tradition (vocation, for example), gift theory takes the discussion of a link between Protestantism and capitalism directly to the heart of the religious tradition: its doctrine of grace.

Milbank, William Cavanaugh, Stephen Long, and others argue that the reformers helped introduce a new concept of gift through their particular articulation of the doctrine of grace that has become pervasive in modern society. Where previous notions of gift encompassed a sense of exchange, the reformers excised reciprocity from the doctrine of grace and thus constructed a gift/exchange dualism. According to this reading, the operative dualism then paved the way for concepts foundational for the rise and global success of a profoundly destructive (and heretical) economic system. Global neoliberal capitalism thus emerges as a tragic—yet logical—consequence of the Protestant doctrine of grace.

Ironically, the two portraits—the heroic liberative reformer (highlighted in chapter one) and the inevitably capitalist reformer (outlined by Milbank and others associated with Radical Orthodoxy) —have emerged nearly simultaneously with extremely limited cross-conversation or acknowledgment. Even among the growing number of Protestant scholars engaging gift theory Milbank's thesis connecting Protestant grace and capitalism is rarely, if ever, highlighted.[4] In some

---

3. "The history of life's reformations and revolutions has up to now revealed an irritating paradoxical nature. The Reformation fought justification by works in the medieval ecclesiastical society with its system of penances, indulgences, and almsgiving on the grounds of a new faith which justified without the works of the law. The Reformation also abolished the holidays, games, and safety valves of that society. This led to the establishment of the Puritan society of penny pinchers and to the industrial workaday world among the very people who had at first insisted on believing that men are justified by faith alone" (Jürgen Moltmann, *Theology of Play*, trans. Reinhard Ulrich [New York: Harper & Row, 1972], 11).

34

INHERITING THE FREE GIFT

cases where gift theory is engaged, Protestant theologians and historians proudly and unambiguously wave the banner of the "free gift." In other cases, Protestant theologians take Milbank's critique of the free gift seriously, but often without acknowledging the economic stakes. The arguments of Milbank and Radical Orthodoxy are philosophically compelling and—unlike those of Weber—theologically sophisticated. They call for serious engagement from any Protestant scholar concerned about ecological and economic justice.

One of Milbank's most persuasive arguments is that the Protestant gift/exchange dualism has saturated modern Western society so that it emerges as authoritative even where the dualism's confessional roots would be rejected. The work of philosopher Jacques Derrida emerges as a key example. With the help of Derrida's logical rigor, Milbank argues the dualism is finally pushed to its logical conclusion: nihilism. By remaining committed to the purity of the gift without exchange, Derrida ends up demonstrating that the gift itself, although highly desirable, is impossible since even simple recognition of a gift by the donee is a return gift to the donor, rendering the gift an exchange rather than a pure gift.[5]

This chapter will outline a widespread and uncritical dependence in the Protestant tradition on the characterization of grace as a free, nonreciprocal gift, followed by an articulation of Milbank's and others' analysis of the ways the free gift is intimately interconnected to three particular ideological foundations of capitalism: separative individualism (through a self/other, inside/outside dualism), commodification, and secularism. The chapter will also examine Milbank's critique of Derrida, outlining the sense in which Derrida's gift seems

---

4. See, for example, Gregory Walter, *Being Promised: Theology, Gift, and Practice* (Grand Rapids, MI: Eerdmans, 2013); Risto Saarinen, *God and the Gift: An Ecumenical Theology of Giving* (Collegeville, MN: Liturgical, 2005); Berndt Hamm, "Martin Luther's Revolutionary Theology of Pure Gift without Reciprocation," trans. Timothy J. Wengert, *Lutheran Quarterly* 29 (2015); and two volumes of collected essays on the topic: *Word - Gift - Being: Justification - Economy - Ontology* (Tübingen: Mohr Siebeck, 2009) and *The Gift of Grace: The Future of Lutheran Theology*, ed. Niels Henrik Gregersen, Bo Holm, Ted Peters, and Peter Widmann (Minneapolis: Augsburg Fortress, 2005). The most recent contribution with chapters dedicated to Gift theory is by Ted Peters, *Sin Boldly!: Justifying Faith for Fragile and Broken Souls* (Minneapolis: Fortress Press, 2015).

5. See Derrida, *Given Time: I. Counterfeit Money*, trans. Peggy Kamuf (Chicago: University of Chicago Press, 1994). More on this below.

to merely interrupt a cycle of exchanges from the outside. Finally, we will examine what Milbank fails to acknowledge: Derrida's counter-capitalist tendencies in what he calls "general economy." In reading Milbank and Derrida critically together, we will find that Milbank's position resonates with a capitalist economy more than he acknowledges and that Derrida's counter-economy may offer important insights of its own for a Protestant rearticulation of an unconditioned gift not absolutely opposed to exchange.

Eco/nomy and Grace

The Lutheran ethical, theological, and historical scholars highlighted in the previous chapter have focused primarily on issues of socioeconomic concern. Awareness is increasing, though, that any economic analysis must also take into account ecological concerns alongside the social since humans are fully interdependent with and embedded in other-than-human creation. However, this shift proves precarious for the Reformation theological tradition. Frequently, the story of the Reformation is told in terms of a protest and prophetic rejection of the overly economized, overly exchangist soteriology of medieval piety. In opposing economies in this way the doctrine of grace claims soteriological space outside exchange. This story easily slides into a general opposition of grace and exchange. Opposing grace to economies and exchange is not nearly as precarious if one only attends to economic concerns. However, embracing ecological concerns complicates the Reformation narrative of grace opposed to exchange since ecological relations prove exchangist at the most basic, sustaining levels of life. Consequently, through an otherwise admirable concern for economic justice, the old antagonism between grace and exchange threatens a resurgence.

Free Gift without Reciprocity or Exchange

Since the publication of *The Gift: The Form and Reason for Exchange in Archaic Societies* in 1924, Mauss's influence has exceeded the bounds of socio-anthropology, sparking important conversations in theology about divine and human giving practices. Church historian Berndt Hamm's recent essay describing the Protestant doctrine of grace in terms of Mauss's gift theory is a prime example. Like Lindberg and Torvend, Hamm describes the unique aspects of Luther's concept of gift by contrasting it with medieval piety and economic practices. Hamm takes the contrast one step further though, arguing that Luther's concept of the gift was innovative, unique, and historically unprecedented. He describes Luther's theology as a "quantum leap" that "developed new criteria for what a gift in its absolute sense really is: a pure giving without the least reciprocal gift, as is only realized in God's gift of grace."[6] For Hamm, this concept of gift was "absolutely never anticipated in the history of religions."[7]

In *The Gift*, Hamm argues, Mauss identifies an ancient and pervasive tendency to assume that every gift deserves and requires a gift in return. Hamm explains that this "primary religious" tendency shaped the history of Christianity from its beginnings but came into heightened focus in the Middle Ages.[8] In this primary religious tendency, both God and creatures are bound to continual relations of debt and obligation to one another. As such, there remains "no such thing as an unconditional gift or grace, no behavior without punishment and no pardon without reparations and atonement."[9] For Hamm then, Luther's concept of gift, which he describes as "free" of exchange and "a pure giving without the least reciprocal gift," emerged in the world as unprecedented.[10]

Hamm does not relent in his insistence that Luther and the reformers held steadfastly to the essential character of grace as nonreciprocal, uncooperative, pure, and free-of-exchange. He ensures that his audience understands that this revolutionary concept of gift was not a matter of peripheral significance or one point of reform

---

6. Berndt Hamm, "Martin Luther's Revolutionary Theology of Pure Gift without Reciprocation," trans. Timothy J. Wengert, *Lutheran Quarterly* 29 (2015): 150.
7. Ibid., 139.
8. Ibid., 128.
9. Ibid.
10. Ibid., 150.

TOWARD A BETTER WORLDLINESS

among others for Luther but remained solidly central in all of his reform work.[11] This was also true for other key Reformation leaders:

> if there was a truth criterion of content for theology and church in the reformation of, say, a Luther, Melanchthon, Zwingli, Bucer, Bugenhagen, Brenz, Bullinger or Calvin . . . then it was the teaching of salvation, under the aegis of a theology of justification, as "pure gift without a gift in return." At stake in this statement was the very center and entirety of the Evangelical *raison d'etre*.[12]

For the reformers, Hamm insists, the gift was nothing if not free and without this unique concept of gift the reformation movement was insignificant.

According to Hamm, the radical nature of Luther's concept of gift can best be appreciated by seeing that Luther's understanding of grace was opposed to the two major forms of medieval piety. The first major form of medieval piety that Luther rejected compared relation to God with commercial exchange and explicitly used economic metaphors of "purchasing" merit and obtaining "eternal profit and interest."[13] This piety Hamm associates with a theological trajectory influenced by Thomas Aquinas. But Hamm suggests Luther went further yet, also rejecting the remnant of exchange in the theological tradition that most closely influenced him. This second type of medieval piety— associated with the Franciscans, Bonaventure, and Duns Scotus— already resisted crass comparisons to economic practices by emphasizing the radical difference between God and creation, and thus the need for humanity to depend on God's mercy and grace.[14] Yet, for Luther this piety retained enough of "the logic of gift and reciprocal gift (*Do ut des*) and the notions of merit and reward" that it was not "able to disturb the mercantilistic logic" of the time.[15] Hamm's point is clear: Luther's theology initiated a previously "unforeseeable and

---

11. Ibid., 126.
12. Ibid., 127.
13. Ibid., 132, citing a 1501 letter from Dr. Sixtus Tucher who was seeking to comfort a grieving nun, Caritas Pirckheimer, "by comparing Christian life and death to a profitable commercial business."
14. Hamm explains, "without this late-medieval forerunner theologically sharpening the idea of gift in the context of grace . . . the radicality of the Reformation's theology of gift is unthinkable" (ibid., 134).
15. Ibid., 130–31. As an example, Hamm points to Luther's disagreements with Gabriel Biel who did

INHERITING THE FREE GIFT

unimaginable" break from economy and exchange.[16] Even Luther's "happy exchange" Hamm characterizes as actually "anti-exchange" in that it "runs counter to every sense of an earthly economic exchange as well as of religious logic of an exchange relationship between God and human beings."[17]

Although Hamm is primarily interested in articulating the theological/spiritual implications of the Protestant concept of gift, a basic contrast to medieval economics—even economics in general —remains key to the way Hamm tells the story of the Reformation. The concept of grace as "free gift" remains pervasive among confessional orientations like Hamm's as well as among Protestant theologians and ethicists concerned with economic justice consequences of the message of the Reformation. For example, as noted in the previous chapter, Carter Lindberg consistently contrasts Luther's theology with an overly economized spiritual system. He characterizes medieval piety as excessively calculated and too economic, insisting Luther's theology was a rejection of such spiritual economization. This contrast was nowhere more clear in Luther's message than in his theology of grace: "Luther turned the medieval logic of salvation upside down. . . . Justification by grace alone sharply undercuts the medieval understanding of testaments as human contributions to divine account books of salvation."[18] Contrasting Luther's theology of grace to a specific economic system and particularly unjust economic practices

---

not conceptualize relations with God as "trade with a heavenly business partner" but as a "loving relation of gift under the auspices of God's immense mercy, generosity and kindness" (ibid., 137).

16. Ibid., 131.

17. Ibid., 148–49. He argues that the happy exchange is actually "anti-exchange" in the following way: "In this passage, Luther attacks the traditional religious motif of gift exchange between God and human beings, in that he reduces it to an absurdity and thus proves the impossibility of any salvifically relevant gift on the part of human beings. For what Christ receives from each human being and takes upon himself that needs atoning is human sin, that is, the anti-gift *per se*. But what he in return grants the sinner is the gift *per se*: his own eternal righteousness, forgiveness and salvation." Other Reformation scholars such as Piotr Malysz and Bo Holm will contest this interpretation by pointing specifically to this happy exchange as evidence that Luther's theology does not contain a gift/exchange dualism (see chapter four).

18. Carter Lindberg, *Beyond Charity: Reformation Initiatives for the Poor* (Minneapolis: Fortress Press, 1993), 97. See also, "Salvation was subjected to measurement. Theology was penetrated by the cumulative logic and calculations of marketing accountancy. Luther's reversal of the medieval theology of achievement by a biblical theology of grace caught the attention of an anxious citizenry" (ibid., 93).

TOWARD A BETTER WORLDLINESS

is one thing. However, Lindberg also tends to apply his critique to economic exchange in general, referring to the rejected system as an "economy of salvation":

> Those who occupied a civic world of producing . . . were fascinated by the idea that earthly treasures could in the end yield heavenly treasures. Contemporaries were engaged in . . . an 'economy of salvation.' . . . In this regard, religion reflected the culture; in religion as in early capitalism, contracted work merited reward. But as Luther himself paradigmatically discovered, spiritual anxiety and insecurity are not 'overcome by calculation and installment plans.'[19]

In describing the rejected piety as an "economy of salvation," Lindberg is no longer just critiquing particular unjust economic practices, but the basic association of God's redeeming work with exchange.[20]

Even for some in the Radicalizing Reformation movement, the concept of grace as free gift emerges in opposition to economics. This movement has recently emerged as one of the most promising interpretive strategies within the tradition, emphasizing justice alongside theological/spiritual concerns.[21] The push to radicalize or reengage the root impulses and values of the Reformation has been intensified in anticipation of the five-hundredth anniversary of the Reformation. The group seeks to employ Reformation themes to move toward "repentance and conversion toward a more just society." Karen Bloomquist, a leader in the movement, argues that "[t]oo often . . . God's justification by grace has been viewed only individualistically and detached from the systemic aspects of social justice."[22] By contrast,

---

19. Lindberg, *Beyond Charity*, 92–93.
20. Unfortunately, Lindberg does not note, as Marion Grau, John Cobb, and others do, the important connection between the "economy of salvation" and the ancient theological term, *oikonomia*, which refers to God's ordering and redemptive work in the "household" of creation. By omitting this connection, Lindberg and others retain the unfortunate tendency in Protestant thought to separate the doctrines of creation and redemption. Ecotheologians Moltmann and Sittler address this consistent tendency as outlined in chapter three (see Marion Grau, *Of Divine Economy: Refinancing Redemption* [New York: T&T Clark International, 2004], 5).
21. On Radicalizing the Reformation movement: "Radicalizing Reformation: A Critical Research and Action Project Towards 2017," http://radicalizing-reformation.com/index.php/en/. Ulrich Duchrow has been a key instigator, with leadership from several of the other theo-ethicists from Chapter One like Chung and Nessan along with Karen Bloomquist who wrote the introduction to *Liberating Lutheran Theology*.
22. Bloomquist, email to the Radicalizing the Reformation group, May 26, 2015.

she insists that "[j]ustification cannot be reduced to being only a subjective, privatized matter, but needs to be closely connected with the more public pursuit of justice."[23] These pursuits must include social, racial, sexual, economic, *and* ecological justice. Bloomquist presses further, urging that insights from Luther's protest of the "dominating powers of his time . . . need to be considered not only appreciatively but also critically and provocatively in relation to the reigning injustices that are especially evident here and now."[24] These are aims intimately connected with those of this project. Yet, Bloomquist also lists the "free gift" as a "distinctive Lutheran tenet" for its prophetic potential to critique "the works-righteousness pervasive in American society."[25] My point is not to discourage this movement, but to demonstrate that the narrative of the prophetic message of the free gift is broadly accepted—articulated not only by those who seek to conserve the tradition, but by those who aim to reform it while simultaneously protesting current injustices in our economic system.

Where the Reformation messages of justification by faith and grace are contrasted to Roman Catholic medieval economization, the danger is broader than just damaging ecumenical relations. In doing so, we risk reinforcing a definition of grace as a rejection of this world's exchanges. Gregory Walter succinctly describes the dangers involved in his analysis of gift theory in terms of Luther's concept of promise:

> The gift that has no relationship to reciprocity or what is already given cannot interact with what comes before the gift, the field into which the gift is given, in any other way than to erase it, trump it, to completely overcome and end that economy. The pure gift does not allow us any interpretive approach to the given except negation, erasure, and interruption. We may signal this problem in theological terms by invoking the tumultuous relationship between grace and nature, or grace and creation.[26]

---

23. Ibid.
24. Ibid.
25. Bloomquist writes, "This is an opportunity to make more public certain distinctively Lutheran tenets, such as how God's grace comes to us as free gift (in contrast to the works-righteousness pervasive in American society)" (ibid.).
26. Walter, *Being Promised*, 40.

TOWARD A BETTER WORLDLINESS

Walter articulates a key insight here. When we contrast God's grace to economy and exchange in general—especially without delineating between the many forms economic exchanges take on—we continue to assert that God only interrupts, annihilates, or overwhelms the exchanges of the world as pure exteriority. This is particularly troublesome when we consider that the exchanges of the world are not only economic but natural. From an ecological perspective it is clear life is lived in and through modes of exchange; the exchanges of O_2 and CO_2 between animals and plants, for example, play a vital role in sustaining life on this planet. Walter, therefore, keenly observes that in the opposition of grace to economy or gift to exchange, oft-repeated antagonisms between nature/grace and creation/redemption re-emerge as a persistent problem for the Reformation tradition.

Dangers of the Free Gift

Ironically, in his most polemical mode, John Milbank would wholeheartedly agree with Hamm's thesis that the Reformation played a significant role in introducing an unprecedented understanding of the gift as free, cut off from any form of reciprocity.[27] However, Milbank emphasizes the shadow side of the free gift. Milbank claims Mauss as an ally in his efforts to reemphasize gift-exchange rather than the free gift. Mauss's study of the gift is a meta-analysis of premodern economies and a fundamental critique of unreciprocal gifting. Mauss argues that instead of the gift idealized as altruistic without expectation of a return in modernity, in premodern societies, gift-exchange was the ideal. In these societies, any idea of a gift as "free" was not only impossible but a contradiction because it undermined the primary role of gifting: social connectivity.

Rather than barter—the utilitarian precursor of capitalism—Mauss

27. This "modern purism about the gift which renders it unilateral," he explains, is "in part the child of one theological strand in thinking about agape which has sought to be over-rigorous in a self-defeating fashion." Milbank refers here to the Protestant theological tradition that, as Anders Nygren explicitly argues in *Eros and Agape*, renders Christian love unilateral with passive receivers as opposed to the reciprocity and exchange of desire (Milbank, "Can a Gift Be Given?: Prolegomena to a Future Trinitarian Metaphysic," *Modern Theology* 11 [1995]: 132).

INHERITING THE FREE GIFT

found that premodern societies and economies are more accurately characterized as gift economies. More than just a guiding economic principle, gift-exchange constituted the society itself.[28] Milbank identifies this as one of Mauss's critical insights: that "gift-giving is a mode (the mode in fact) of social being."[29] For Mauss, more than just objects, gifts include acts, practices, and traditions that transcend economic value and individual meaning.[30] These exchanges remain foundational to society because they are practices binding people together, even over generations.[31] According to Mauss, relationships are not established first and followed by gifts. Rather, gift-exchange creates relationships.[32]

Modern societies "draw a strict distinction . . . [between] things and persons. Such a separation is basic: it constitutes the essential conditions for a part of our system of property, transfer and exchange." This detachment, however, is "foreign" to a system of gift-exchange.[33] Later gift theorists identified this detachment as the "alienable" quality of the free gift.[34] A person could give a gift without expectation of return only where the gift was assumed to be an object, a separable "thing." But in a society of gift-exchange, a gift was seen as inseparable or "inalienable" from its donor because, as Mauss explains, these gifts were imbued in a mysterious or magical way with the

---

28. Marcel Mauss, *The Gift: The Form and Reason for Exchange in Archaic Societies,* trans. W. D. Halls (New York: W. W. Norton, 1990), 46.
29. John Milbank, *Being Reconciled: Ontology and Pardon* (New York: Routledge, 2003), 156.
30. "What they exchange is not solely property and wealth, movable and immovable goods, and things economically useful. In particular such exchanges are acts of politeness: banquets, rituals, military services, women, children, dances, festivals, and fairs, in which economic transaction is only one element, and in which the passing of wealth is only one feature of a much more general and enduring contract" (Mauss, 5).
31. Socio-anthropologist Mary Douglas explains: "Just the rule that every gift has to be returned in some specified way sets up a perpetual cycle of exchanges within and between generations" (Douglas in intro to Mauss's *The Gift,* viii-ix).
32. "The gift is not prior to but coincident with relation such that they are inseparable—interlinked on horizontal and vertical planes, so to speak. As such, 'reciprocity' is inseparable from receiving a gift" (Milbank, "Can a Gift Be Given?: Prolegomena to a Future Trinitarian Metaphysic," *Modern Theology* 11, no. 1 [1995], 136).
33. Mauss, *The Gift,* 47.
34. Mauss does not use the terms "alienable" and "inalienable." These developed out of Mauss's work in a later wave of gift theory aligned with the work of C. A. Gregory and Annette Weiner. See Gregory, *Gifts and Commodities* (London: Academic, 1982) and Weiner, *Inalienable Possessions: The Paradox of Keeping-While-Giving* (Berkeley: University of California Press, 1992).

personhood of the donor.[35] A gift, therefore, was no mere disconnected object, but an extension of the giver so that in giving a gift, one was not merely giving an object, but a part of oneself. In this sense, the gift participated in the personhood of the giver so that exchange resulted in the interweaving of the giver and receiver through their connection to the gift.

Consequently, where reciprocity and exchange are commonly associated today with a crass kind of tit-for-tat or *quid pro quo* (as Hamm does), Mauss demonstrates this understanding of exchange is merely a symptom of the modern understanding of the gift as a separable transaction. By contrast, there were other forms of exchange where the expectation was not merely for the return of the gift itself, but of relationship because the gift embodied the giver. "By giving," Mauss explains, "one is giving oneself, and if one gives oneself, it is because one 'owes' oneself—one's person and one's goods—to others."[36] Once given, the gift did not shuttle between discrete individuals. Rather, such exchanges resulted in lives "mingled together" since this is, as Mauss explains, "precisely what contract and exchange are."[37]

In mingling subject and object, Milbank argues that Mauss "wrote a meditation against Descartes."[38] According to Milbank, the gift/exchange dualism has its roots in significant metaphysical and cosmological shifts associated with nominalism, particularly the philosophical trajectory from Duns Scotus to William of Ockham that "abandoned a metaphysically participatory framework."[39] Before nominalism, the relation between God and world could be seen as mingled or interwoven together by creation's participation in a continuous Trinitarian gift-exchange.[40] Premodern gift-exchange was viewed "not [as] merely social or cultural at all but [as] an aspect

---

35. Mauss, *The Gift*, 24.
36. Ibid., 46.
37. Ibid., 20.
38. Milbank, "Can a Gift Be Given?," 133.
39. Milbank, *Beyond Secular Order: The Representation of Being and the Representation of the People* (Malden, MA: Wiley-Blackwell, 2013), 36.
40. Milbank, *Being Reconciled*, x.

INHERITING THE FREE GIFT

of a cosmic ecology: a vast circulation encompassing natural beings, the gods and the ancestors."[41] But with nominalism, a strong divide emerged between God and creation that Milbank sees functioning in the Reformation emphasis on grace as a unilateral gift from active giver to passive recipient.[42]

Without a participatory sense of exchange, a gift could be given from a god increasingly pushed outside the world, ruling with autonomous and sovereign power over the world that could only passively receive from a divine wholly other. A loss of participation and exchange also allowed forgiveness to be opposed to justice and expressed as a "counterpart of Creation" or even "de-creational" since forgiveness simply erased or uncreated a transgression without simultaneously insisting on reciprocal justice to make right what was put wrong.[43] As modernity progressed, a divine ideal of external—rather than participatory—relations increasingly became a model for human subjectivity in autonomy, self-sufficiency, and the human assertion of *their* will over a passive and inert nature.[44] This development becomes typified in Descartes's modern subject wherein he defined human consciousness over and against an objectified, unconscious material world. By removing human consciousness from the realm of material nature, Descartes's subject/object dualism created the possibility for humans to see nature as object and potential resource, rather than something in which they were inherent participants.

---

41. Milbank, "The Gift and the Given," *Theory, Culture & Society* 23 (2006): 444.
42. Milbank describes this gift as "strictly formalist and unilateral . . . as not expecting a return" (John Milbank, "Can a Gift Be Given?," 123).
43. Milbank, *Being Reconciled*, 45. Milbank draws on an example from Søren Kierkegaard here.
44. See also Michael Northcott, who explains this nominalist division between God's absolute, arbitrary power, and creation set in motion "a new politics, first of the 'divine right' of kings apart from the consent of the governed, and then in the modern era of the social contract according to which the individual is autonomous of the body politic into which she is born until she *contracts* some of her autonomous power by an act of will. This split also gave rise to a new religion in which the individual soul exists as an independent entity within the body, drawn by piety to a life of Puritan self-denial and a related quest for the inner feeling of divine presence. And the split gave rise to a new science in which the body of the earth and the human body become available for investigation and reordering by empirical science, free through nominalist logic from the theologic symbolism of medieval cosmology" (*A Political Theology of Climate Change* [Grand Rapids, MI: Eerdmans, 2013], 43).

Was Luther a Nominalist?

What Milbank does not adequately acknowledge is that the question of Luther's relationship with nominalism is not clear-cut. Historians Heiko Oberman and Steven Ozment demonstrate the complexity of this issue. While at one point Oberman unambiguously concludes that "Martin Luther was a nominalist, there is no doubt about that,"[45] he later complicates this association, focusing on Luther's key break with the nominalist formula that the faithful person need only "do what is within them" to earn God's grace.[46] Therefore, Oberman concludes, "Not merely the 'young Luther,' but the 'youngest Luther,' even before beginning his career as a professor, as a biblical exegete, and eventually as a reformer, has on points which later prove to be cornerstones . . . become independent of the nominalist tradition in which he was reared."[47]

Ozment similarly highlights Luther's rejection of the "do what is within you" formula, yet suggests that despite this difference, Luther's theology retains a key structural influence from Ockham and (as Hamm seems to inadvertently suggest) pushes the nominalist logic even further. Ozment explains that "Following Duns Scotus, Ockham rejected the view that a saving relationship with God depended in any final sense on metaphysical connections between God, grace, and the soul."[48] God's grace, as well as authority of any church institution, could no longer rely on a metaphysical connection or participation in the divine life. Instead, they became contingent on a "divine act," that "from an infinite number of theoretical possibilities God had chosen them to be the instruments of his will in time."[49] Thus salvation and

---

45. Oberman, *Luther: Man Between God and the Devil*, trans. Eileen Walliser-Schwarzbart (New York: Doubleday, 1992), 122.

46. "[T]here is nevertheless reason to believe that Luther at the end of 1509 has become independent of the nominalistic tradition as regards the relation of faith and reason, while retaining till 1515-1516 the doctrine of the *facere quod in se est* in its application to the relation of will and grace" (Oberman, *The Dawn of the Reformation: Essays in Late Medieval and Early Reformation Thought* [Edinburgh: T&T Clark, 1992], 96).

47. Ibid., 103

48. Steven Ozment, *The Age of Reform, 1250-1550: An Intellectual and Religious History of Late Medieval and Reformation Europe* (New Haven: Yale University Press, 1980), 244.

49. Ibid.

INHERITING THE FREE GIFT

authorities of institutions came to rely on God's unilateral declaration. Like Ockham's view of the relation between God and the world, such declaration of worth was not inherent (or participatory), but arbitrary; it depended on the free will of God. As a result, Ozment notes (echoing Weber's argument), "From Luther to the American Puritans the central religious problem of mainstream Protestantism become the certitude of salvation."[50] Thus from Luther to the Puritans who, according to Weber, became model capitalists on account of the radical uncertainty of their preordination, the key question of faith became the "trustworthiness of God's word and promise." From this, Ozment concludes: "It is not farfetched to see here the legacy of Ockham."[51]

Whether or not Luther was a nominalist—or even more nominalist in his theology of grace than Scotus, Ockham, and Biel—the more pressing (but interconnected) question is whether Luther's theology of grace can abide by a more participatory cosmology and soteriology. We might grant that Luther was, in important ways, influenced by the nominalist tradition. However, to say that this tradition categorically outweighed other key influences of Luther's thought—namely, patristic Christian theologians and Scripture—seems unlikely. So, another important question arises: How much have we read Luther's theology of grace through the lens of nominalism-become-modernity that turned the Western world so decisively away from an indwelling divine presence in the world and humanity? To suppose we have read Luther apart from this lens seems nearly impossible—and yet, increasingly imperative.

Modern Ubiquity of the Free Gift

Given the ambiguity around the question of Luther's nominalist influences and in spite of Milbank's polemics, I find the critique of

50. Ibid.
51. Ibid. Graham Ward and John Montag also argue that Luther was both influenced by and resisted nominalism. Montag adds that "Luther recognized the inadequacy of this nominalist restriction, and . . . tried to reinvent—or at least reinvoke—the lush kind of *communicatio/participatio* between God and creation allowed by the pre-Scotist hierarchy of being" ("Revelation: The False Legacy of Suárez," in *Radical Orthodoxy: A New Theology*, ed. John Milbank, Catherine Pickstock, and Graham Ward [New York: Routledge, 1999]).

47

TOWARD A BETTER WORLDLINESS

Protestant grace as a popularization of a gift/exchange dualism unavoidable for addressing an eco-Reformation in our current climate.[52] Milbank's claim that the free gift has become pervasive in modern society is especially difficult to deny. Even after all traces of religious thought have been erased or forgotten, the gift/exchange binary has taken on a life of its own.

Milbank finds that the free gift has been particularly influential in modern ethics. By idealizing selfless, altruistic, and sacrificial giving, modern and postmodern ethics have assumed that a gift in the form of an ethical gesture is best given without any anticipation of a return gesture. Milbank focuses on Jacques Derrida's and Emmanuel Levinas's "other-oriented ethics," directing particular attention to Derrida's often-cited analysis of Mauss's gift theory in *Given Time*. Here, Milbank argues, the purism of the modern free gift is taken to its extreme—but logical—conclusion, whereby the possibility of the gift and giving itself is annihilated.

In *Given Time* Derrida laments that in spite of the title of Mauss's book, he never actually arrives at the gift; everything Mauss wrote concerned economy and exchange. Reciprocity, return, exchange, and debt all turn a gift into poison—the fitting translation of the German *Gift*. Mauss's gift-exchange, Derrida argues, "puts the other in debt [appearing] to poison the relationship, so that 'giving amounts to hurting, to doing harm.'"[53] Even a verbal expression of gratitude turns a gift into exchange since the recognition of a gift acknowledges a good deed, and thus reciprocates the gift. Mauss insists on a definition of gift that can only be given with the expectation of a return. To Derrida, a gift that returns to its origin erases the gift, transforming it into exchange. Consequently, according to Derrida, "[f]or there to be a gift, there must be no reciprocity, return, exchange, countergift, or debt."[54] As such, the gift emerges as impossible.[55]

---

52. See important responses to Milbank in Rosemary Radford Ruether and Marion Grau, eds., *Interpreting the Postmodern: Responses to 'Radical Orthodoxy'* (New York: T&T Clark, 2006).
53. Jacques Derrida, *Given Time: I. Counterfeit Money*, trans. Peggy Kamuf (Chicago: University of Chicago Press, 1994), 12.
54. Ibid.
55. Derrida does not use the term impossible in the common way—something Milbank does not

INHERITING THE FREE GIFT

Milbank argues that in spite of the fact that Derrida, a Jewish-born "rightly passing as an atheist"[56] philosopher, would have no conscious intention of upholding Protestant doctrine, he assumes the modern gift/exchange dualism and demonstrates its logical conclusion in impossibility and nihilism. Milbank's claim also gains support from a far less sophisticated source that seems bent on inserting itself into this chapter. The grammar checker on my word processor indefatigably objects to the phrase *free gift*, underscoring the phrase in red with the explanation that this is a "redundant expression." Apparently, the gift *by definition* is free: free of debt, reciprocity, and exchange.

The pervasive social influence of the Protestant theology of grace in the form of the free gift might be rather heartwarming for confessional Protestants if it was not also bound to condemning economic and ecological consequences. In particular, Milbank and Mauss emphasize the implications of the gift/exchange dualism evident in commodification and individualism. Max Weber demonstrated the ways in which the Protestant tradition contributed to the loss of mystery, magic, and the sacred in a world of commodified goods. Many current ecologically or economically concerned theologians lament the loss of the sacred in relations of commodification.[57] However, many also fail to recognize that commodification depends on a particular pattern of relationship and a certain view of the self in an individualist ontology and that these have been shaped by the idealization of the free gift. This is a significant insight Mauss adds to Weber's thesis connecting the Protestant tradition and capitalism. Where Weber regretted a

---

acknowledge. On "the impossible," see Jacques Derrida, "A Certain Impossible Possibility of Saying the Event," trans. Gila Walker in W. J. T. Mitchell, ed. Arnold I. Davidson, *The Late Derrida* (Chicago: University of Chicago Press, 2007) as well as John Caputo, *The Prayers and Tears of Jacques Derrida* (Bloomington: Indiana University Press, 1997).

56. Derrida, and Geoffrey Bennington, *Circumfession*, trans. Geoffrey Bennington (Chicago: University of Chicago Press, 1993), 155.

57. "But what we have lost," as Larry Rasmussen reminds us in *Earth-Honoring Faith*, "is the sense of the sacred." Max Weber called it disenchantment. Rasmussen further describes it as the loss of the numinous from the common where the "holy is leached from the ordinary, and the mystical is cut away from the everyday. Use, utility, and possession measure all value, just as all are relative to human appropriation and significance. The (human) subject determines the worth of all else, as object" (*Earth-Honoring Faith: Religious Ethics in a New Key* [New York: Oxford University Press, 2013], 264).

49

TOWARD A BETTER WORLDLINESS

certain disenchantment of the world, Mauss similarly indicates that inalienable gifts were, in a way, enchanted by the giver so that the receiver not only receives an object, but relational participation in the giver.

Milbank also takes up the question of the Christian trajectory toward disenchantment, arguing that this "crucial theological issue today" involves the theological constructs that underwrite commodification.[58] "In ancient times," he explains, "objects were not yet commodities, and so were seen as specific things with specific characteristics liable to achieve specific but not quite predictable effects."[59] Gift-exchange was possible "in part because of a certain belief in the animation of objects."[60] When presents lost their inalienable qualities, gifts that were once extensions of the giver became mere objects, commodities. Where gifts once wove the fabric of an interconnected society, commodification designates passive objects awaiting human inscription of meaning. Commodities shuttle between separative parties with no enduring relational ties over time.

An alienable or free gift, for example, makes it possible for me to go to a grocery store to purchase milk without any prior, or continued, relationship to the grocer, the farmers, the cows, or the land on which they were raised. I can enter the building, purchase my commodified cow product and leave without any debts, established relationship, further obligations, or responsibilities to any of these providers. The shadow side of such purchasing practices becomes evident when we consider our relationship to something less wholesome than milk. Waste, for example, functions by this same logic since it involves rendering something separable from a continuous cycle of rights and responsibilities. I can throw something out as "waste" or excess only

---

58. He argues that this tendency to "disenchant" cosmologies is not "entirely loyal to its own nature," but that in actuality Christianity "at its liturgical and sacramental heart, propose[s] a heightened enchantment" (Milbank, *Beyond Secular Order*, 17).

59. Milbank, "The Gift and the Given," 446. See also C. A. Gregory, *Gifts and Commodities* on the connection between alienable gifts and commodification.

60. Ibid., referencing Jacques T. Godabout and Alain Caillé, *The World of the Gift*, trans. Donald Winkler (Montreal: McGill-Queen's University Press, 1998).

INHERITING THE FREE GIFT

by unconsciously assuming that something is an object, alienable from my person.

For Milbank, the kind of gift prioritized marks more than theological or ecclesial difference. The ideal gift also marks the difference between individualist ontologies (on which capitalism depends) and relational, or gift-exchange ontologies.[61] For Milbank, creation participates in and is upheld by its participation in the continual gift-exchange between the members of the Trinity. For Mauss too, while the gift/exchange dualism lies at the root of the alienation of property, the alienable gift of commodification implies isolated individualism since the exchange of property involves cutting the ties between giver and receiver that create community. As William Cavanaugh explains in his Milbank-influenced critique of Luther's eucharistic theology, the alienable gift marks a "radical differentiation between what is mine and what is thine"[62] because exchange becomes a "spatial transfer of goods between individuals."[63] Rather than a gift tying together members of a community, the alienable gift shuttles between isolated individuals, leaving no necessary obligation to other members of a body. Milbank argues that when Western society shifted from a cosmology of continual gift-exchange where creation participated in divine reality to a gift/exchange dualism, the groundwork was laid for commodification, isolated individualism, and ultimately, neoliberal capitalism. Thus he polemically identifies capitalism as "a mode of Protestant religion" that, since it relies on the free gift that Mauss declared antisocial, offers a "theological legitimation of a new sort of 'amoral' economic practice."[64]

---

61. "Just as Christianity transforms but does not suppress our 'given' social nature which is exchangist, so also Christian theology transforms, utterly appropriates to itself the ontological task, but does not abandon it in suspension, by elevating itself above it . . . in the name of a purely unilateral (and univocal) gift prior to that circular reciprocity which is, indeed, consequent upon *esse*" (Milbank, "Can a Gift Be Given?: Prolegomena to a Future Trinitarian Metaphysic," 131–32). Milbank's gift theory does not engage ecology, but remains firmly in the social and economic spheres.

62. William T. Cavanaugh, "Eucharistic Sacrifice and the Social Imagination in Early Modern Europe," *Journal of Medieval and Early Modern Studies* 31 (Fall 2001): 592.

63. Ibid.

64. Milbank in Slavoj Žižek and John Milbank, *The Monstrosity of Christ: Paradox or Dialectic?* (Cambridge, MA: MIT Press, 2009), 127 and 129. Cited in Jeffrey Robbins, "The Monstrosity of Protestantism," *Expositions* 4, no. 1 & 2 (2010): 93.

TOWARD A BETTER WORLDLINESS

It is important also to understand Milbank's theological motivations in upholding the value of gift-exchange rather than the free gift. Just as for Luther and Calvin, the Augustinian tradition remains decisive for Milbank. However, in Milbank's gift ontology, he chooses to emphasize what the reformers seem to deemphasize: the continuous relational exchange of the Trinity. This relational gift-exchange, Milbank argues, is a necessary precursor to the divine unilateral gift that Luther and Calvin made primary. Consequently, the ideal gift is not prior to, but concomitant with relation in a primary Trinitarian gift-exchange. Milbank explains, "For Augustine the *donum* that is the Holy Spirit is not only a free one-way gift (though it is also that), but in addition the realization of a perpetual exchange between the Father and the Son."[65] Milbank argues such continuous relational and reciprocal Trinitarian gift-exchange is necessarily foundational to any kind of nonreciprocal gift.

Therefore, while Milbank leaves room for the possibility of an "offering without return," similar to the gift idealized by the reformers, he insists that such a gift always remains secondary to a primary and continual gift-exchange.[66] Christianity, he argues, is a successful integration of the unilateral (free) gift with reciprocal gifts. The problem with the Protestant Reformation, according to Milbank, was that it fundamentally altered the integration of free and reciprocal gifts by idealizing the unilateral gift while dualistically opposing it to reciprocal giving. Milbank aims to redefine the exemplary or idealized divine gift. Rather than the pure, free, or unilateral gift idealized by the reformers, Milbank argues that the ideal Christian gift is never good "outside the hope for a redemptive return to the self."[67] Sometimes, in a fallen world, we do give sacrificially or without a return, but in light of the resurrection a truly Christian theology must insist that "we are always receiving back as ever different a true, abundant life (this is the Gospel)."[68]

---

65. Ibid., x.
66. Ibid., xi.
67. Ibid., 155.
68. Ibid.

INHERITING THE FREE GIFT

Since capitalism works against an ontology that is participatory —and thereby Trinitarian—this particular economic system can only be regarded as "heresy." Fellow Radical Orthodoxy theologian Stephen Long describes Milbank's position:

> Capitalism is a Christian heresy because of the loss of the orthodox doctrine of the Trinity according to which the world is created through, in, and for participation with God, who is not some bare divine unity defined in terms primarily of will, but who is a gift who can be given and yet never alienated in his givenness. Once the doctrine of the Trinity is reduced to bare divine simplicity, a new "secular" politics emerges from within Christianity that makes capitalism possible.[69]

This new secular politics also takes on a form of gift/exchange dualism in the opposition of the idealized gift, free of compulsion, characterizing private life and the compelled contract employed in public life.

Milbank's main concerns seem to be economic, social, and ecclesial, so he does not focus on ecological implications. However, Christian environmental ethicist Michael Northcott agrees with Milbank's assessment of the destructive influence of the nominalist shift away from a participatory ontology in Western modernity and adds that the nominalist turn marked a decisive shift in the church's previous prohibition of mining. When nominalism removed a perceptible correlation between God's will and the earth, the church no longer felt mining was a sacred violation of the earth: "If, as Ockham argued, there is only an arbitrary relationship between physical created order and divine moral will, there are no theological grounds for restraining the reordering of the earth by miners and in the forges and metal works that coal fed."[70] In response to nominalist shifts, religious leaders lifted their long-held ban on coal mining. This newly admissible form of income created the "material base of the emergent capitalism of Germany."[71] At a time when we are realizing, as Northcott explains,

---

69. Stephen Long, *Divine Economy: Theology and the Market* (New York: Routledge, 2000), 259. See "Capitalism as Heresy" (258–60) on Long's interpretation of Milbank on why capitalism is heresy.
70. Northcott, *A Political Theology of Climate Change*, 55.
71. Ibid.

53

TOWARD A BETTER WORLDLINESS

that "the fossil fuel economy was not possible without capitalism," and furthermore, that it seems impossible to conceive of a capitalism that is not wholly dependent on fossil fuels,[72] an ecotheology that aims to be eco-Reformational is pressed to address some key questions about its doctrine of grace, relation to nominalism, and corresponding concept of the ideal gift. Therefore, one of the most pressing questions appears to be whether a Lutheran theology of grace can faithfully, accurately, and exclusively be described, as Berndt Hamm insists, as a free gift exclusive of participation and exchange.

Capitalizing Tendencies of Milbank's Gift-Exchange

Milbank persuasively demonstrates the detrimental effects of the free gift. However, as he rails against the heresy of capitalism and the nihilism of Derrida's other-oriented ethic, Milbank fails to take seriously the counter-capitalist character of Derrida's gift within the context of Derrida's wider project. Rather than leading toward nihilistic individualism, Derrida's insights may be an important corrective to tendencies that push Milbank's own Trinitarian gift-exchange toward a growth-centered economy, an idealization of the separative substantial subject, and colonizing tendencies.

Mauss's work piqued Derrida's deconstructive interest by means of its overlapping themes, foundational also for Western metaphysics: time, being, and gift. These three themes, Derrida notes, share a particular economy of symbolic exchanges. In Western metaphysics, time, being, meaning, and economy (or gift-exchange) are symbolized as a circle; their end goal predictably emerges as a return to their origin. Derrida describes this as an Odyssean economy beginning at home, journeying away from home, and struggling to return to one's origin.[73] In Derrida's early work he refers to this philosophical system

---

72. Ibid.
73. See Derrida, *Given Time*, 7–8. One need not be engaged in philosophical discourses to be affected by this symbolic logic. In the *Politics of Deconstruction*, Susanne Lüdemann explains, "In this sense, Derrida observes, our everyday language is 'neither harmless nor neutral. It *is* the language of Western metaphysics and carries with it an array of assumptions'; these assumptions are also operative even if one knows nothing about them—even if one is not a philosopher or an academic and has never read a word of Plato, Hegel, Heidegger or Derrida himself" (Susanne Lüdemann,

as "logocentrism" and describes how its permeating influence in Western thought has trained our concepts so that we desire presence, a center, a foundation, identity, sameness, sovereignty, and dominion.

Derrida's project, beginning with *Of Grammatology* and continuing in his late work on the animal, consists in deconstructing hierarchical oppositions (man/woman, human/animal, self/other, etc.) that result from a logic dependent on a single, certain center or foundation. Not only does Derrida seek to reverse these hierarchical oppositions, he also demonstrates that the favored term (human, for example) depends on the excluded term (animal) for its very definition.[74] Here, the favored term is interrupted, infected, or as Catherine Belsey writes, "invaded" by the "other"—the secondary term. For Derrida, the binary between self and other or subject and object that Milbank aligns with Derrida's gift is undermined by Derrida's demonstration that the self (that which is thought to be self-sufficient) "is produced outside itself."[75] Consequently, Belsey succinctly describes Derrida's much-maligned and misunderstood project or "method" of "deconstruction" as an "analysis of the inevitable invasions of the other into the selfsame."[76]

So here we have come full circle, so to speak, since, for Derrida, the selfsame is another term for the circle of the same or a system of exchanges tightly bound so that there is no loss, no gift given without a return to complete the circle. This is the perspective from which Derrida approaches Mauss's gift. He associates the gift-exchange cycle with the circle of the same where every gift is met with a return. Describing Derrida's gift, John Caputo explains, "The gift is an event, *é-venir*, something that really happens, something we deeply desire, just because it escapes the closed circle of checks and balances, the calculus which accounts for everything, in which every equation is

---

Politics of Deconstruction: A New Introduction to Jacques Derrida [Stanford: Stanford University Press, 2014], 56–57).

74. See Derrida, *The Animal That Therefore I Am*, ed. Marie-Louise Mallet, trans. David Wood (New York: Fordham University Press, 2008).

75. Catherine Belsey, *Poststructuralism: A Very Short Introduction* (New York: Oxford University Press, 2002), 73.

76. Ibid.

TOWARD A BETTER WORLDLINESS

balanced."[77] For Derrida, the "impossibility" of the gift is what makes it so deeply desirable, and thus such an important motivation for finding possibility where there is none to be found.[78]

As we have seen, in spite of vastly divergent ethical, theoretical, and religious concerns, Derrida's unilateral gift disconcertingly aligns with traditional Protestant assumptions of gift.[79] Indeed, some of Derrida's language does seem perplexingly close to theological proponents of absolute transcendence. In *Given Time*, for example, he writes, "But is not the gift, if there is any, also that which interrupts economy? That which, in suspending economic calculation, no longer gives rise to exchange? That which opens the circle so as to defy reciprocity or symmetry, the common measure, and so as to turn aside the return in view of the non-return?"[80] If *economy* here implies not just the exchange of finances or goods, but every exchange—even those necessary for the founding of relationships and our ecosystems—then what kind of interruption does Derrida desire? A welcome intrusion? If it is an intervention by something wholly other, does the gift, as wholly other, transcend the world and all exchanges that make life possible in the world? "Not that it remains foreign to the circle," Derrida writes, "but it must *keep* a relation of foreignness to the circle."[81] The gift, it seems, is not alien to the circle and all those economies that make up our human and other-than-human worlds.

Where Derrida gives comfort with one phrase, however, he seems to undermine it with the next: the gift "must *keep* a relation of foreignness to the circle, a *relation without relation* of familiar foreignness. It is perhaps in this sense that the gift is the impossible."[82] But what kind

---

77. John Caputo, *The Prayers and Tears of Jacques Derrida* (Bloomington: Indiana University Press, 1997), 160.

78. See Derrida on the impossible in "A Certain Impossible Possibility of Saying the Event," in *The Late Derrida*, ed. W. J. T. Mitchell and Arnold I. Davidson, trans. Gila Walker (Chicago: University of Chicago Press, 2007): 223–43, and as described by Caputo in *The Prayers and Tears of Jacques Derrida*, 169 and on.

79. See Catherine Keller's argument in Catherine Keller and Stephen D. Moore, "Derridapocalypse," in *Derrida and Religion: Other Testaments*, ed. Yvonne Sherwood and Kevin Hart (New York: Routledge, 2005): "might Derrida's own 'gift' not harmonize, hauntingly, with the triumphant chorale of God's absolutely free and transcendent gift, *charis*, grace, *sola gratia*—a unilateral, pure omnipotence, whether coming from above or from the future?" (203).

80. Derrida, *Given Time*, 7.

81. Ibid.

INHERITING THE FREE GIFT

of bond is a relation without relation? If the gift is related without being related, must it enter the circle by force? For theologians, in particular, Derrida's phrasing, while entirely coincidental, may carry extra baggage. Theologian Karl Barth's absolutely transcendent God of wholly otherness also retained some necessary relation to the world of economy and exchange: "In the resurrection the new world of the Holy Spirit touches the old world of the flesh. But it *touches* it as a tangent to a circle, which is, *without touching it.*"[83] Analogously, does Derrida's gift touch the circle of worldly exchanges only as a tangent touches a circle: that is, without *really* touching it? How does a touch without touch or relation without relation *materialize?* Given such seeming congruence between Derrida's gift of "relation without relation" and Barth's divine gift of "touch without touch," the ecofeminist issues at stake here are worth stating explicitly: for the sake of a desire for something wholly other, does Derrida himself succumb to a *phallogocentrism* wherein the gift inseminates the world of economic and ecological exchange from the outside? Protestant theologies such as Barth's have had a problem with nature either interrupted or annihilated by grace. Is it also the case with Derrida's gift?

The association between Derrida's gift and anti-economic theologies of radical exteriority is tempting indeed. It is, nonetheless, misplaced when we look at Derrida's wider project, particularly his early distinction between general and restricted economy. In his 1978 essay, "From Restricted to General Economy," Derrida builds upon Georges Bataille's insistence on the need for a general economy. Bataille introduces this distinction with questions potentially more relevant today than when first written. Urging a broader application and engagement within economics, Bataille asks, "Shouldn't productive activity as a whole be considered in terms of the modifications it receives from its surroundings or brings about in its surroundings? In other words, isn't there a need to study the system of human production and consumption within a much larger framework?"[84] One

---

82. Ibid., 7. Emphasis added.
83. Karl Barth, *Der Römerbrief, Zweite Fassung 1922* (Zürich: Theologischer Verlag, 1989), 6 in Gregory Walter, *Being Promised*, 39. Emphasis added.

57

TOWARD A BETTER WORLDLINESS

is reminded of Wendell Berry's "Great Economy" here.[85] Bataille goes on to contrast this larger understanding of economics with a "restricted economy." This economy is restricted not merely because economic considerations are artificially cut off from environmental exchanges, but also because it is a symbolic economy where space for the difference of loss is excluded and the (circular) return remains inescapable. Such a system cannot abide difference, uncertainty, or anything like "the impossible" that resists calculation. The restricted economy is a swirling vortex, sucking everything into its singular aim; no room remains for loss or the unredeemed. Ideally, everything finds its meaning, the symbol always hits its mark, and every investment finds a return. As Arkady Plotnitsky explains, "Any restricted political economy, however, be it Adam Smith's, Hegel's, or Marx's, would still be predicated on the value of meaning, and particularly conscious meaning—meaningful investment, meaningful expenditure of labor and capital, meaningful production and conservation."[86] In a restricted economy, everything must be utilized, every investment returned, and every profit reinvested to maximize growth.

To resist this restricted circle of exchanges, Derrida does not introduce an anti-economy, but suggests, as Bataille does, a counter-economy that they call the "general economy." In Derrida's 1978 essay, he addresses Smith's economics through Hegel's closed system/circle of absolute knowledge.[87] Here, general economy emerges as a strategy to create some space for the play of difference, uncertainty, and multiplicity by preserving space for loss within the restricted economy. For Hegel, Smith's economic system emerged as the ultimate Christian economy because it depends on a system of resurrection: ideally, every loss is returned and every expenditure capitalized.[88] Therefore, according to Derrida and Bataille, difference or loss is

---

84. Georges Bataille, "The Meaning of General Economy," *The Accursed Share: An Essay on General Economy, Vol. 1: Consumption,* trans. Robert Hurley (New York: Zone Books, 1991), 20.
85. See introduction.
86. Arkady Plotnitsky, "Re-: Re-Flecting, Re-Membering, Re-Collecting, Re-Selecting, Re-Warding, Re-Wording, Re-Iterating, Re-et-Cetra-ing . . . (in) Hegel," *Postmodern Culture* 5, no. 2 (1995): 20–21.
87. Derrida, *Writing and Difference,* trans., Alan Bass (Chicago: University of Chicago Press, 1978).
88. Mark C. Taylor explains, "Derrida, following Bataille, sees in Hegelianism a transparent translation of the foundational principles of a capitalistic market economy" ("Capitalizing (on)

precisely what Hegel's system could not accept. Derrida describes the "force of this imperative: that there must be meaning, that nothing must be definitely lost in death."[89] Arkady Plotnitsky reflects on the influence of capitalist economics on Hegel, explaining, "Adam Smith's political economy was a major influence on Hegel during his work on *The Phenomenology of the Spirit*. . . . From *The Phenomenology* on, economic thematics never left the horizon of Hegel's thought, the emergence of which also coincides with the rise of economics as a science, which conjunction is, of course, hardly a coincidence."[90] For Hegel, material and religious economies both work "by securing a return on every investment."[91] While Hegel claims to preserve the negative through double negation, Derrida contests that this is just what is lost, since no space remains outside of sublation/capitalization/resurrection.

When no space remains for loss, there cannot be room for a more Abrahamic economy of traveling to new lands with no hope for a return home.[92] Derrida, the Jew who "passes" for an atheist, has no space in Hegel's capitalizing/resurrection economy. So, he (with Bataille) makes room for some things to exceed or fall outside this restricted economy. In "From Restricted to General Economy," Derrida resists this particular kind of economy with a different (general) economy, not the aneconomic gift.[93] Here, general economy emerges as the space for difference at the margins of a restricted economy.

So, early on Derrida counters one economy with another rather than an exterior annihilation. But is this the case with Derrida's gift

---

Gifting," in *The Enigma of Gift and Sacrifice*, ed. Edith Wyschogrod, Jean-Joseph Goux, and Eric Boynton [New York: Fordham University Press, 2002], 53).

89. Derrida, "From Restricted to General Economy: A Hegelianism without Reserve," *Writing and Difference*, 256–57.

90. Arkady Plotnitsky, "Re-: Re-Flecting, Re-Membering, Re-Collecting, Re-Selecting, Re-Warding, Re-Wording, Re-Iterating, Re-et-Cetra-ing . . . (in) Hegel," 1, cited in Grau, *Of Divine Economy*, 8.

91. Taylor, "Capitalizing (on) Gifting," 55.

92. This language of an "Abrahamic" economy is inspired by Emmanuel Levinas who opposed the Odyssean economy to the Abrahamic in "The Trace of the Other": "To the myth of Odysseus returning to Ithaca, we wish to oppose the story of Abraham leaving his fatherland forever for a land yet unknown, and forbidding his servant to bring even his son to the point of departure" (349, quoted in Grace Jantzen, *Becoming Divine: Towards a Feminist Philosophy of Religion* [Bloomington: Indiana University Press, 1999], 249).

93. See Grau's comparison of early and later Derrida on the gift in "Erasing 'Economy': Derrida and the Construction of Divine Economies," *Cross Currents* 52, no. 3 (2002).

TOWARD A BETTER WORLDLINESS

in *Given Time*? Further into this text, Derrida clarifies: the gift is not a transcendent exteriority. The gift (*if* there is any, he often adds) "does not lead to a simple, ineffable exteriority that would be transcendent and without relation."[94] How is it that the gift, if there is any, might interrupt economy while not remaining exterior to it? Derrida continually returns to Baudelaire's short story, "Counterfeit Money," as he engages the question of the gift and economy. In Baudelaire's story, the narrator's friend makes a gift of a counterfeit coin to a beggar. Derrida notes the true ambiguity of this gift of alms. On the one hand, it may have the effect of simply circulating as a "true" coin, allowing the beggar relief from his poverty. In this case, since the counterfeit coin would have the same effect as a true coin, the difference between them would effectually be none. This result, however, is not guaranteed for, on the other hand, its use could result in the unsuspecting beggar's arrest. In effect, the narrator's friend has interrupted or tainted a closed and trustworthy economy (where every symbol hits its mark) with a measure of indeterminacy which is the mark of the gift itself. Alongside authentic money, inside this economy, the counterfeit coin circulates, all the while creating the possibility for something new, unknown, and disruptive from within the circle of the same.

Where counterfeit money masquerades as honest currency it participates in economy while also disrupting it. Recall the quotation highlighted above, now read in a different light: "it must *keep* a relation of foreignness to the circle, a relation without relation of *familiar foreignness.*" Retaining a relation of familiar foreignness, the counterfeit coin interrupts, though not from a purely exterior location. The gift of a counterfeit coin introduces some wiggle room, play, or room for difference into the economy of the same. This play leaves the circle just loose enough to allow for the possibility of something new and different to disrupt the circle of the same. *If* the counterfeit coin does protest the circulation by means of interruption, it will not be from outside the economy. The effects of the counterfeit coin come

94. Derrida, *Given Time*, 30.

INHERITING THE FREE GIFT

forth from *within* the depths of that otherwise circumscribed circulation.[95] As in a segregated 1960s soda shop counter sit-in strategy, protestors—like the counterfeit coin—inserted themselves into an oppressive system closed off from difference and with an active passivity waited for the system to collapse from its own vulnerabilities. Such a counterfeit (*contre / faire*: against / doing) resists the drilling, pumping drive of *laissez-faire* (let, leave to do) capitalization and production—not over and against, but from within.[96]

By proposing a different kind of economy with Bataille—one that abides difference, loss, the unexpected, and the surprise of the impossible—Derrida is clearly not opposing the gift to all forms of exchange, just those modes of exchange that have no room for difference or investments of uncertain returns. Where Derrida claims to desire the gift as if it were "outside" economy, it is primarily the symbolic, Hegelian, restricted economy he seems to have in mind.

Refusing to recognize the counter-capitalist potential of Derrida's gift proves unfortunate for Milbank's project. In ignoring the connection Derrida draws between capitalism and resurrection, Milbank creates his own economy of exclusion and capitalized gains. As Derrida strives to make room for uncertainty and difference, we might also add that he makes space for grace as a noncircular gift that might just disseminate rather than turn into a good investment for the giver. When applied to Milbank's ethic, Derrida's critique of restricted economy and the necessary capitalization of every loss hits its mark. "So long as there is loss," Milbank insists, "there cannot be any ethical, not even in any degree. . . . *To be ethical therefore is to*

---

95. In "Erasing 'Economy': Derrida and the Construction of Divine Economies," Marion Grau suggests that the differential economy of the early Derrida is an "'economy that is ambiguous enough to seem to integrate noneconomy'" (365–66, citing Derrida, *The Gift of Death*), whereas the later Derrida (especially in *Given Time*) desires the gift that is outside of economy altogether. As I have shown above, there are indeed phrases in *Given Time* that seem to suggest he desires something that transcends economy. I have intended to demonstrate, though, that this is not where he ends up with his main trope of the counterfeit coin.

96. While the prefix *contre* can take the form of a binary opposition—"against"—Catherine Keller's counter-apocalypse and Marion Grau's counter-economy reveal a Derridean-influenced strategy: "To criticize without merely opposing; to appreciate in irony, not deprecate in purity," "it knowingly performs an analog to that which it challenges" (Keller, *Apocalypse Now and Then: A Feminist Guide to the End of the World* [Minneapolis: Augsburg Fortress, 2006], 19 and Grau, *Of Divine Economy*, 19–20, respectively).

61

TOWARD A BETTER WORLDLINESS

believe in the Resurrection, and somehow to participate in it. *And outside this belief and participation there is, quite simply, no 'ethical' whatsoever."*[97] Milbank's ethic *requires* the confession of Christian orthodoxy. Outside this confession no hope remains for an ethical gesture. Such exclusivism goes to the root of his concept of gift since, here, the gift is never good "outside the hope for a redemptive return to the self."[98] For Milbank, this is the definition of the Gospel—that we *always* receive back, for to receive back is to participate in the resurrection and the unreturned gift denies the resurrection. Milbank draws his circle of gift-exchange tight: his ethical act must be a good, capitalized investment, continually returning to shore up the security of an orthodox self. Where Derrida desires some wiggle room within economy, Milbank is not willing to grant him that hospitality.

In addition to Milbank's failure to recognize the capitalizing tendencies of a gift-exchange that must return to its origin as well as the counter-capitalist potential of Derrida's gift, Catherine Keller also argues that Milbank does not recognize his own vulnerabilities to separative individualism. Keller affirms the move toward ontological reciprocity in her essay, "Is That All?: Gift and Reciprocity in Milbank's *Being Reconciled,*" yet offers a caveat regarding Milbank's particular gift-exchange: "Whether Milbank himself breaks out of the trap of the substantial subject remains to be seen."[99] Keller suggests that for all of Milbank's emphasis on participation and reciprocity, in the end, his doctrine of God cannot abide by the flux and uncertainties of life in and with the world. For him, the relational, reciprocal flow between God and creation only goes so far because of his commitment to a traditional doctrine of God as absolute. Keller notes that this would account for Milbank's careful avoidance of any language of "interdependence," suggesting he is not prepared to think seriously about reciprocity between God and the world. Consequently, Milbank's

---

97. Milbank, *Being Reconciled,* 148. Emphasis added.
98. Ibid., 155.
99. Keller, "Is That All?: Gift and Reciprocity in Milbank's *Being Reconciled,*" in *Interpreting the Postmodern: Responses to 'Radical Orthodoxy,'* ed. Rosemary Radford Ruether and Marion Grau (New York: Bloomsbury T&T Clark, 2006), 21.

INHERITING THE FREE GIFT

ontology of participation only reaches into the world "as a supernatural donation, from the transcendent outside, beyond, after all."[100] With an anthropology and ontology of participation in God from the transcendent outside, material relations must follow suit. Keller's analysis demonstrates that Milbank's gift-exchange lacks a truly mutual exchange between God and creation, and thus reveals he is not yet willing to move beyond the ideal of external relations characteristic of the modern separative subject.

Theologian Marion Grau's postcolonial rendering of the gift strikes a similar tone of skepticism regarding the extent to which Milbank is actually willing to affirm exchange between God and creation. To Keller's assertion of Milbank's inability to avoid the sovereign separate subject, Grau adds suspicion regarding Milbank's "call to resistance against capitalism and globalization."[101] She notes that while Milbank "assumes that ethical exchanges among human agents are reciprocal," he yet reserves the "true gift" as divine redemption and forgiveness where "God remains only a giver, yet is never a recipient in a gift exchange."[102] The historical/material implications of such a lack of reciprocity become clear when Grau also notes that Milbank remains wholly invested "in a hegemonic sense of 'Western' orthodoxy that is unthinkable without the forces of the British Empire, past and present."[103] By holding to a pure core of Christianity without acknowledging the ways that such orthodoxy supported and was enforced by colonial forces on "native" people who were characterized as passive receivers of the unilateral gift of colonial rule, Milbank's own gift ideals are undermined.

In various ways Milbank's gift-exchange does not live up to its promise of a more reciprocal, counter-capitalist, ecological gift structure. Rather than an alternative, it would merely repeat some of the most deleterious aspects of modernity: growth-dependent

---

100. Ibid., 31.
101. Grau, "'We Must Give Ourselves to Voyaging': Regifting the Theological Present," in *Interpreting the Postmodern*, 146.
102. Ibid., 147.
103. Ibid.

economics, the sovereign modern subject, and Western colonialism. While the critique of the free gift and its connection to foundational aspects of capitalism remains an important insight, an alternative to Milbank's gift-exchange must be explored.

Toward an Ecologically Exchangist, Unconditioned Gift

We live in an interdependent world of continual eco/nomic gift-exchange. Theologians and religious people are now pressed to reflect seriously on the way we envision divine action in relation to this exchangist world. Is divine grace merely an interruption of the systems of creation that sustain life in the world? How then do we reconcile this with a God who is both creator and redeemer?

In order to resist unjust and consuming economic systems, we might say grace is opposed to economy and its exchanges and that in this opposition grace disrupts or protests an unjust system. This seems to generally characterize the approach of many economically engaged Protestant theologians today, but the ecological implications, as we have noted, are dangerous. Environmental advocate Bill McKibben has persuasively argued in his reflections on the book of Job that in this age of global climate crisis, we humans have become de-creators.[104] In this context, do we really want to profess that the work of redemption is de-creational?[105] Can we live with the consequences? Can we survive them?

Is it possible to articulate an understanding of grace that is characteristically Protestant and not a rejection of economy/exchange but of undemocratic, colonizing, unjust, and unsustainable economies? Rather than opposing grace to economy and exchange, we might seek an articulation of grace that works by an alternate relational economy and thus makes space for incarnations of grace-filled relationships in the world.[106] In contrast to Milbank's particular articulation of divine

---

104. Bill McKibben, *The Comforting Whirlwind: God, Job, and the Scale of Creation* (Cambridge, MA: Cowley, 2005).

105. See Milbank's characterization of Protestant forgiveness (in Kierkegaard among others) as de-creation above.

106. Drawing on biblical and patristic trickster figures, Marion Grau's *Of Divine Economy: Refinancing*

INHERITING THE FREE GIFT

gift-exchange, Keller notes that while grace would be meaningless apart from its unconditionality, we may yet affirm a graceful reciprocity that emerges as asymmetrical but interdependent.[107] A key task for us thus emerges: to distinguish between the unconditioned and merely free gift.

Before we can address this task, however, it will be important to address grace and its ecological stakes more directly. In doing so, we will arrive at one further confounding fact regarding the Protestant tradition and ecological concerns: in spite of a history of opposing the nonreciprocal character of grace to the reciprocities of nature, prioritizing redemption over and against creation, and emphasizing faith as primarily a personal, individual matter, many ecotheologians of various theological traditions indicate that the twentieth-century ecotheological movement first began to find its voice in the prophetic, poetic prose of Protestant pastor, Joseph Sittler. We have not quite come to any satisfying conclusion with regard to grace and ecology. There is more, yet, to the story.

Redemption is an excellent example of finding ways to disrupt oppressive economic systems through counter-economies—that is, through disruptions from within an economic system rather than seeking an overthrow from a transcendent exterior as she argues Milbank suggests (in "We Must Give Ourselves to Voyaging").

107. Keller, "Is That All?," 32.

3

Ecology of the Gift: The Ecotheologies of Joseph Sittler and Jürgen Moltmann

What do you have that you did not receive?
—1 Corinthians 4:7

We have no ontological status prior to and apart from communion.
Communion is our being; the being we participate in is communion,
and we derive our concrete selves from our communion.
—Joseph Haroutunian in Joseph Sittler, *Essays on Nature and Grace*[1]

It may be surprising, given the contested and ambiguous eco/nomic track record of the Protestant tradition, to note that many scholars unambiguously acknowledge that the ecotheological movement first began to find its voice in the mid-twentieth century with Lutheran pastor Joseph Sittler.[2] Indeed, even for Sittler, the tradition—and its doctrine of grace, in particular—does not escape criticism. Sittler

---

1. Joseph Haroutunian, *God With Us* (Philadelphia: Westminster, 1965), 148, quoted in Joseph Sittler, "Essays on Nature and Grace," *Evocations of Grace: The Writings of Joseph Sittler on Ecology, Theology, and Ethics*, ed. Steven Bouma-Prediger and Peter Bakken (Grand Rapids, MI: Eerdmans, 2000), 174.
2. See Dieter T. Hessel and Rosemary Radford Ruether, "Introduction," *Christianity and Ecology* (Cambridge, MA: Harvard University Press, 2000).

TOWARD A BETTER WORLDLINESS

especially notes the devastating effects of overly personalized models of redemption, including what he calls a "truncated doctrine of grace."[3] Even more than the early date of his ecotheology and his critical analysis of the Protestant tradition, what makes Sittler's work noteworthy is his willingness and ability to rethink the doctrine of grace in terms of ecological reality. In addition, Sittler saw from an early point the interconnectedness of concepts of grace and selfhood. As a result, he also constructs a profoundly graced ecological self.

While Sittler did not engage gift theory, remarkably, his ecological grace can be seen to anticipate current ecotheologian Anne Primavesi's concept of ecological gift-exchange. As we will see, this easy confluence seems to be due to the fact that Sittler, unlike most Protestant theologians, considers grace as concomitant *with* relation, rather than a precursor to it. While gift discourse has maintained a nearly exclusive focus on the social realms of gift-exchange, Anne Primavesi's work emerges as a significant exception to this anthropocentric focus. In her essay, "The Preoriginal Gift—and Our Response to It," Primavesi applies gift theory to the ecological exchanges of the world, thereby challenging her readers to pay attention to gifting structures and idealized gifts within the realm of other-than-human creation.[4] From this perspective, life itself—not just human society, as in the case of Mauss—emerges through a continual (and constitutive) flow of gift-exchanges. Applying gift theory to ecological exchanges, Primavesi describes the "essential contributions to present gift events made by 'more than' those participating in them now. They include antecedent generations of living beings: all those who, by their lives, their labor, their deaths, their vision, and their patient endeavors have made such events presently possible."[5] Importantly, here gift-exchange begins to emerge as a network or a

---

3. Sittler, "Called to Unity," *Ecumenical Review* 14, no. 2 (1962): 177–87.

4. Anne Primavesi, "The Preoriginal Gift—and Our Response to It," in *Ecospirit: Religions and Philosophies for the Earth*, ed. Laurel Kerns and Catherine Keller (New York: Fordham University Press, 2007). See also Primavesi, *Gaia's Gift: Earth, Ourselves and God after Copernicus* (New York: Routledge, 2004).

5. Ibid., 218.

ECOLOGY OF THE GIFT

web rather than in lines of linear causality from giver, through gift, to receiver.

Primavesi and Sittler articulate a compelling vision of the grace-infused and gifting nature of reality. However, where Sittler excels at articulating grace and the self in terms of ecological reality, he does not adequately address the key and corresponding issue of God's relation to this ecological and exchangist reality. Where Sittler lacks key shifts in a doctrine of God, theologian Jürgen Moltmann adds compelling and important insights.

Rather than focusing explicitly on grace, Moltmann's key contributions to ecotheological concerns lie in his articulation of the ecological and social consequences of a Western Christian doctrine of God that has idealized separation and self-sufficiency. He also addresses the persistent Protestant divide between creation and redemption by reframing redemption as God's creative moment on the cross and creation as a beginning in and through redemption. Where Sittler highlights the deleterious effects of a Protestant divorce of the doctrine of creation from redemption, he does not yet offer a constructive and systematic alternative. Moltmann, on the contrary, successfully reintegrates them and, in the process, shifts from a doctrine of God idealizing the supreme individualist to a Trinitarian, *perichoretic*, and relationally ecological doctrine of God and creation. In doing so, Moltmann demonstrates the ways that individualism and a God/world dualism are critically interconnected. When God is kept apart from creation God becomes the absolute subject and the world God's object. In this case, God emerges as the ultimate separative individualist.

In the work of Joseph Sittler and Jürgen Moltmann themes of grace and self, redemption and creation, and the relation between God and world emerge as key loci for a Reformation tradition concerned with addressing intertwined issues of ecological and economic justice. When analyzed from the perspective of Primavesi's ecological gift, however, this chapter will also demonstrate that at key points, both theologians

69

revert to a unilateral gesture that puts their remarkable ecological-exchangist theologies and ontologies at risk.

Sittler's Ecological Self, Radically Dependent on Grace

Sittler began writing about ecology in a theological context dominated by a neo-orthodox presumption of anthropocentrism. The emphasis on human redemption and God's revelation from pure exteriority was so strong it verged on anti-creationism—what Sittler called an "almost proud repudiation of the earth."[6] Even those who may not have been radically opposed to naturalism were fundamentally unfamiliar with basic ecological concepts. Sittler's early students recall audiences wholly unfamiliar with the term "ecology."

In spite of a neo-orthodox insistence on God's redemptive action in terms that ended up devaluing creation or opposing it to the reciprocating ways of the natural world, Sittler consistently grounded his ecotheology in grace. He explains he chose grace rather than more obvious choices—like a doctrine of creation and its corollary ethic, stewardship—because he needed a theological perspective central enough for the task he had in mind.[7] Grace, he argues, is the only doctrine broad and crucial enough to encompass the necessary scope of environmental ethics.[8] Sittler recognized that an environmental ethic had to move hearts and minds toward transformation and he questioned whether any doctrine other than grace could do that within the Protestant tradition.

However, Sittler also emphasized the Protestant doctrine of grace because in it he identified a root of the ecological problem. In his

---

6. Sittler, "A Theology for Earth" in *Evocations of Grace*, 24. He also writes that he "felt a deepening uneasiness about that tendency in biblical theology, generally known as neo-orthdoxy, whereby the promises, imperatives, and dynamics of the Gospel are declared in sharp and calculated disengagement form the stuff of earthly life" (ibid.).

7. Sittler, *Gravity and Grace: Reflections and Provocation*, ed. Thomas S. Hanson (Minneapolis: Augsburg Fortress, 2005), 2.

8. Bakken explains the strategy of Sittler's theological approach, arguing that "Sittler deliberately cast environmental ethics in terms of highly charged religious doctrine central to Christian, particularly Lutheran, piety—namely grace and christology—rather than in terms of teachings that are less central (but more commonly connected to environmental concerns), such as creation and stewardship" (Sittler, *Evocations of Grace*, 5).

ECOLOGY OF THE GIFT

famous 1961 New Delhi address to the World Council of Churches, Sittler argued that the general lack of interest in the environment and ecology was the consequence of an overly personalized Christology and a correlating truncated doctrine of grace. The reformers restricted the scope of grace to a personal remedy for a sinful condition, a break in the individual's relationship with God. With grace focused exclusively on the person, the material consequences were disastrous: "Enlightenment man could move in on the realm of nature and virtually take it over because grace had either ignored or repudiated it."[9] Where Christ's saving work is relegated to human spheres alone, the doctrine of grace fails to account for God's redeeming work in all creation.

Ironically, the very tradition that defined sin as being turned in on the self[10] tragically justified an anthropocentric turn, placing the human at the center of the cosmos, God's interest, and God's redemptive work. Thus he argues that the very doctrines meant to give life and open up our inward turn closed us off from significant relations and ethical responses to other-than-human creation. As a remedy, Sittler reinterprets Luther's Augustinian definition of sin, *incurvatus in se*. Rather than emphasizing this as a description solely of the individual human soul in relation to God, Sittler describes sin as the incurved focus of anthropocentrism and individualism.[11] With Luther and Augustine, Sittler maintains that the only fitting cure for the inward curve is the outward turn of grace.

Along with anthropology and a definition of sin, Sittler recognizes that the understanding of grace will also need to be transformed. In the introduction to a collection of Sittler's works, Peter Bakken explains that, for Sittler, "the reality of grace is not simply that divine acceptance whereby an individual's sins are forgiven, but a disturbing, even violent energy that is a living and active presence in the whole of creation. It is grace not against or above or identical with nature, but grace *transforming* nature."[12] For Sittler, grace takes on a communing

---

9. Sittler, "Called to Unity," in *Evocations of Grace*, 43.
10. *Incurvatus in se*: Augustine, as emphasized by the reformers.
11. See Sittler, *The Care of the Earth* (Minneapolis: Fortress Press, 2004), 11 and 22.

character of "the whole giftedness of life."[13] Rather than a mere model of God's concession to human materiality in the bread and wine, Sittler argues that the Eucharist should be interpreted as the ultimate model of the unity of nature and grace, the spiritual and the material.

At his most provocative, Sittler offers inspiring ecological views of the human, grace, salvation, and Christ. The human is not a static being, grace is not a state, salvation is not individual or merely personal, and Christ's work does not exclude the other-than-human. By his later writings especially, Sittler's view of reality has been fundamentally reshaped so that he understands it to be fluid, interconnected, and constantly becoming.

The Ecological Self

The depths of Sittler's understanding of grace may yet be hard for many Protestants—so well trained by both theology and modernity to assume an original separative self—to swallow. As much-loved as Sittler is, in Lutheran theological circles it is not clear that the radical nature of Sittler's self and grace are fully appreciated. Note how Peter Bakken, for example, introduces Sittler's work in the collection, *Evocations of Grace*. Describing Sittler's concept of self and grace, Bakken writes, "human interiority is affected by interactions with the world of nature—our 'sense for the world.'"[14] Bakken sees Sittler's understanding of the self as an interior affected by exterior experiences and relations. I would argue, however, that Sittler is doing something much more radical than reflecting on the effect of the external "environment" on interior selves. Where Bakken seems to yet assume the existence of a self before this interaction, Sittler acknowledges an affect deeper than the emotional, psychological, experiential, or even existential aspects of natural life. In other words,

12. Peter Bakken, "Introduction: Nature as a Theater of Grace: The Ecological Theology of Joseph Sittler," in *Evocations of Grace: The Writings of Joseph Sittler on Ecology, Theology, and Ethics*, ed. Steven Bouma-Prediger and Peter Bakken (Grand Rapids, MI: Eerdmans, 2000), 5.

13. Sittler, *Gravity and Grace*, ed. Thomas S. Hanson (Minneapolis: Augsburg Fortress, 2005), 3.

14. Bakken, "Introduction: Nature as a Theater of Grace: The Ecological Theology of Joseph Sittler," in *Evocations of Grace*, 14.

ECOLOGY OF THE GIFT

he is intuiting the ways that the "exterior" constitutes the "interior." In using language such as "constituting" and "transaction," Sittler reflects on the truth that we fundamentally would not be ourselves—and not just our psychic, emotional selves, but material and spiritual selves as well—without these others.

This profoundly ecological reality marks a shift from separative, externally relating human agents to relational ontologies based on co-constitutive interactions. Where many relational ontologies only account for human sociality, there may yet be an original self that secondarily enters into social dynamics and is psychologically shaped in relationship with others. However, an ecological, biological, relational ontology such as Sittler's radically shifts the location of relational exchange in relation to the self. Here, there is no original self, no original starting place of pure "me." The relational exchanges do not start with human interaction once we are born or once we become self-conscious or rational. From this perspective, we might say that the self is never and has never existed outside gift-exchange with humans, other-than-humans, and the divine.

Rather than the substantial individualist, Sittler envisions the self as a collective meeting point of multiple influences and life forms. He writes, "human beings 'occur' rather than are amidst their ecological context or web of relations."[15] Nothing can be seen to exist on its own or as its own because "things are what they are, and do what they do, and have the force they have because they are where they are in a vast and intricate ecosystem."[16] Here, Sittler has been inspired, in part, by early twentieth-century mathematician and philosopher Alfred North Whitehead's compelling alternative to substance metaphysics based on decisive shifts made necessary by the discoveries of quantum physics. Citing Whitehead, Sittler explains that we can no longer assume anything like "simple location" remains possible.[17] Inspired both by recent revelations in quantum physics and nature poets, Whitehead insisted that the idea that some "thing" resides in one place at one

---

15. Sittler, "Essays on Nature and Grace," *Evocations of Grace*, 153.
16. Ibid.
17. Ibid., 152.

73

TOWARD A BETTER WORLDLINESS

time on its own is an erroneous philosophical assumption of modern science. Whitehead calls this fallacy "simple location." Rather than isolated substances, reality emerges as profoundly interconnected and relational. "In a certain sense everything is everywhere at all times," Whitehead explains. "For every location involves an aspect of itself in every other location."[18] We cannot assume that reality is composed of things like substances that can be said to be firmly fixed in time and space and inherently separable from a field of relational influences. Rather than substances, states, or essential qualities, Sittler begins talking about the self as an intersection of multiple gifts—and grace in terms of "occasions."[19]

Humans exist, he insists, only in and through communion since no self exists outside a web of relations.[20] Rather than a static substance with delineated interior and exterior, the self is a fluctuating "intersection" of multiple organisms and influences. "We are constituted by our transactions with nature," he insists. "Selfhood is not simply finding out and clarifying all the potentialities of the self as individual. There is no selfhood that is not at the same time a self existing in the grid of all selves. *I have no self by myself or for myself. I really have no identity that I can specify except the intersection point of a multitude of things that are not mine. They have been given to me.*"[21] This self is profoundly, radically, and decisively graced—given from multiple divine and creaturely others.

Sittler recognized these unseen relationships and interdependencies with the human, divine, and other-than-human world as grace. He saw nature as a field of grace, a web in which humans find themselves. In his thought, grace emerges as a mode of connectedness that unites us in communion with God, the earth, and each other so that nature is held up by grace, rather than interrupted by it. As a transcendent "energy of love" that works through and with the mundane web of our

---

18. Sittler, *Gravity and Grace*, 44.
19. "Occasions" of reality is a term Sittler gets from Whitehead. *Evocations of Grace*, 155. On Whitehead and occasions of reality, see *Process and Reality*, ed. David Ray Griffin and Donald W. Sherburne (New York: Free Press, 1978).
20. Sittler, "Essays on Nature and Grace," *Evocations of Grace*, 174.
21. Sittler, *Gravity and Grace*, 44–45, emphasis added.

74

ECOLOGY OF THE GIFT

interdependent connections, grace could no longer be seen as a "state." Where simple location is now suspect, Sittler added, grace can also no longer be merely personal. He insists the "location of grace" must now be articulated in terms of "reality-in-relations," meaning that "things are what they are, and do what they do, and have the force they have because they are where they are in a vast and intricate ecosystem." Where grace is no longer a state, he sees it instead in occasions as the "energy of love." Consequently, the place of grace is the "webbed connectedness of man's creaturely life."[22]

Sittler's concept of self and grace address consistent concerns with Protestant theologies: that they assume and encourage a God/world dualism and a personal and individualist understanding of redemption and anthropology. As his understanding of grace develops with an ecological ontology, it becomes clear that, for Sittler, creation is not interrupted by grace, but held up by it. Where sin is interpreted as the turning in of the self toward separative individualism and away from an interdependent and relational reality, the opening of grace emerges as not merely the result of restored relation with a transcendent divine but in and through the gifts of multiple others—both divine and creaturely. Consequently, we might conclude that Sittler (presumably inadvertently) echoes Mauss's key insight that the ideal gift is concomitant with relation rather than its precursor. Just as Mauss insists that the gift coincides with societal relationship rather than preceding them, Sittler similarly shifts grace to cohere with and through ecological relations that can be understood as a web of continual gift-exchange. Indeed, he remarkably affirms Joseph Haroutunian's insistence that in the ecological self we find relationality from the beginning: "We have no ontological status prior to and apart from communion. Communion is our being; the being we participate in is communion, and we derive our concrete selves from our communion."[23] No self exists that is not the result of a multitude

22. Sittler, Evocations of Grace, 161.
23. Joseph Haroutunian, God With Us, 148, quoted in Joseph Sittler, "Essays on Nature and Grace," Evocations of Grace: The Writings of Joseph Sittler on Ecology, Theology, and Ethics, 174.

75

of gifts.[24] Consequently, we have no self outside of grace, nor before relationship.

Compelling as Sittler's ecological and occasional style remains, one also finds unresolved questions along with inconsistencies and tensions where one would hope for clarity. Where his understanding of reality becomes remarkably ecological, it remains unclear how this ecological reality can best be expressed in familiar Christian terms and doctrine. In particular, it also remains unclear how this ecological reality relates to the divine life—specifically, a doctrine of God.

Without addressing this key question, we are left with a radically altered view of reality, yet suggestions of a traditionally transcendent God. For example, Sittler commonly repeats Calvin's metaphor of creation as a theater for God's grace, which implies some safe distance yet between God and creation. Similarly, he also insists, at times, that this web of connections is a vehicle or stage for God's saving work, but is not itself a giver of grace. Finally, Sittler also suggests the metaphor of God as placenta for the world. While a beautifully unconventional and feminine metaphor, it still (though less-so than "theater") maintains God's traditional place as exterior sustainer.

While Sittler insists on a union of the spiritual and material, the holy and mundane, it remains unclear how or where God is present in, with, and under the world. He consistently regards grace as "inherent in and given in, with, and under the creation,"[25] but fails to expound on the ways God is put at risk or becomes vulnerable to the world as a result of this profound relationality. Granted, we can assume such conclusions would have put his appeal to an audience in a theologically and religiously anthropocentric landscape at risk. Yet, without such a doctrine of God, it seems that articulating a theology of grace in the world may, in the end, be a rather clever way to think ecologically without yet tainting a traditionally transcendent God, thus reserving significant space for the idealization of the unilateral gift.

24. Ibid., 172.
25. Sittler, "Essays on Nature and Grace," 75.

Moltmann's Indwelling Divine

Some thirty years after Sittler, Jürgen Moltmann's work can be seen as a resolution of many of Sittler's unresolved tensions. In resisting systematic theological methodologies, Sittler also sacrifices doctrinal coherence.[26] This is particularly evident in his doctrine of God. In not focusing on a doctrine of God, this early ecotheologian did not critically examine the God/world relation, and thus was not able to extend his ecological reality in a consistent way from the world to the relation of God and world. Moltmann, on the contrary, addresses these concerns by emphasizing an interdependent, indwelling, and communitarian divinity. He demonstrates influential connections between a dominating human sovereign subject and the modern Western doctrine of God which he describes as "monotheistic monarchianism," suggesting instead a perichoretic, Trinitarian God in relation. Moltmann also reconciles the doctrines of creation and redemption—a crucial shift for a tradition that, at times, verges on anti-creationism in order to emphasize the transcendent, redemptive power of God.

Like Sittler, Moltmann's work is a response to an antagonism between nature and grace in the tradition of the reformers. Moltmann explains that this nature/grace dichotomy, already present in Reformation thought, became only further reinforced during the WWII-era German theological debates. Here, the theological justification of or resistance to Hitler's rise to power and ideologies were at stake. In debates between Protestants of the Barmen Declaration and supporters of German National Socialism, the options for Protestant thought on nature were merely two: either a person supports "natural theology," interpreted as a way of reading God's will in Hitler's rise to power and God's orders of nature in nation and race, or a person assents to a theology of God's Word, revealed over and against the world—especially including National Socialism.

---

26. He explains in the introduction to his later work, *Essays on Nature and Grace*, that he has found the systematic methodology inadequate for constructing an ecological theology. He suggests, instead, that our form should be consistent with our content. Therefore, an ecological theological method is needed.

Moltmann reflects with regret that even some forty years later this singular divide remains. His work, *God in Creation*, is an attempt to chart a new path that avoids this unfortunate binary. To address this concern, he decides to continue the work he began in *Trinity and the Kingdom*, developing a doctrine of the Trinity that is not only social, but ecological in its indwelling character. Moltmann has developed a reputation as a theologian who has helped revitalize the doctrine of the Trinity by demonstrating its relevance for social and ecological concerns.[27] As Joy McDougall explains, "Moltmann traced the ills of modern Christian theology specifically to the eclipse of its trinitarian understanding of God."[28] Some of these deleterious effects include an apathetic, dispassionate doctrine of God that keeps God detached from the joys and pain of life in the world and a corresponding anthropology that idealizes self-sufficiency and separative relations. In *Trinity and the Kingdom*, Moltmann describes the traditional Western Christian doctrine of the Trinity as "monotheistic monarchianism." In Western trinitarian thought, the perichoretic, or mutually indwelling, communion of the three persons has been deemphasized in favor of an emphasis on the united power of one God. Where an emphasis on oneness subordinates the threeness, God emerges as a divine monarchical figure with "disastrous consequences for the Christian life of faith" because it has "provided a theological justification for structures of domination and subordination in the familial, political, and ecclesial realms of human existence."[29]

Rather than a single, all-powerful monarchical God idealizing the absolute sovereign subject and the separative individualist, Moltmann suggests the doctrine of the Trinity reveals that God's being is in community. Taking up the Cappadocian idea of Trinitarian *perichoresis*, Moltmann suggests that in the *koinonia* of the Trinity, each person does not stand on their own separate from the others, but interpenetrates

---

27. Joy McDougall notes, "During the last thirty years no theologian has played a more pivotal role in revitalizing trinitarian doctrine and its implications for Christian praxis than German Reformed theologian Jürgen Moltmann" (*Pilgrimage of Love: Moltmann on the Trinity and Christian Life* [New York: Oxford University Press, 2005], 6).

28. Ibid.

29. Ibid.

ECOLOGY OF THE GIFT

and dwells within each other. This is, of course, a claim with powerful social implications. As McDougall explains, "The practical significance of Moltmann's social trinitarian program rests on his bold claim that trinitarian fellowship not only describes divine community but also prescribes the nature of true human community."[30]

In *God in Creation*, Moltmann demonstrates the ways that monotheistic monarchianism has justified domination over other-than-human creation as well by linking the transcendent, monotheistic God to the modern sovereign subject. The traditional doctrine of God maintains God as the absolute transcendent subject. Where God is absolute subject, the world becomes "His" object of creation and redeeming work. If this is the divine ideal—the image in which humans have been made—then they too are bound to re-create this subject/object divide, granting themselves the role of subject and actor and creation as passive object.

Moltmann contrasts monotheistic monarchianism with an "ecological doctrine of creation" that "implies a new kind of thinking about God."[31] Rather than building from an assumption of absolute distinction between God and world, Moltmann shifts to a "recognition of the presence of God in the world and the presence of the world in God."[32] Where other ecologically oriented approaches have emphasized the role of the Son in creation, Moltmann explains, "we shall proceed differently, and shall present the trinitarian understanding of creation by developing the third aspect, creation in the Spirit."[33]

Where Sittler fails to address how God relates to an interdependent reality, Moltmann's perichoretic God becomes the origin and archetype of an interrelational creation. Thus, created ecological, mutually interdependent, and nondualist relations reflect their Trinitarian and communal creator. Moltmann explains:

30. Ibid., 7.
31. Moltmann, *God in Creation* (Minneapolis: Fortress Press, 1991), 13.
32. Ibid.
33. Ibid., 9.

79

TOWARD A BETTER WORLDLINESS

> Our starting point here is that all relationships which are analogous to God reflect the primal, reciprocal indwelling and mutual interpenetration of the trinitarian perichoresis: God in the world and the world in God; heaven and earth in the kingdom of God, pervaded by his glory; soul and body united in the kingdom of unconditional and unconditioned love, freed to be true and complete human beings. There is no such thing as solitary life.[34]

Moltmann's alternative to the absolute divine subject emerges as a social, communitarian, interpenetrating, Trinitarian doctrine of God—an inspired model of ecological, interrelational, reality: "God in the world and the world in God. . . . All living things—each in its own specific way—live in one another and with one another, from one another and for one another."[35] This changes the emphasis of ideal, divine relationships from detached power-over to dwelling with. The result is a "non-hierarchical, decentralized, confederate theology" that resists any concept of subjectivity as one-sided and dominating.[36]

Such shifts in a doctrine of God and God/world relations reverberate also in Moltmann's reinterpreted and reintegrated doctrines of creation and redemption. Rather than a detached sense of God creating the world and relating to it as pure exteriority, Moltmann insists that "God creates the world, and at the same time enters into it. He calls it into existence, and at the same time manifests himself through its being. It lives from his creative power, and yet he lives in it."[37] In *God in Creation*, Moltmann is continuing the work of reinterpreting soteriology begun in *Theology of Hope*. Here, already the theologian resists the personalism and privatism of Protestant soteriologies, arguing the human is not saved from sin outside of history, but in and through it. In his ecotheological work, though, he expands this soteriology beyond the exclusivity of human history to all creation.[38]

---

34. Ibid., 17.
35. Ibid.
36. Ibid., 2.
37. Ibid., 15.
38. Although there are common themes, commentators also note a drastic shift between these texts. William French, in particular, argues that Moltmann's work in *God in Creation* "calls into question the adequacy of Moltmann's own earlier radical eschatological agenda" in *Theology of Hope*. French continues, emphasizing the anti-naturalism implicit—and at times, explicit—in his eschatological focus in *Theology of Hope*: "Where once he challenged us *not* to live in 'the world' as our 'home,'

ECOLOGY OF THE GIFT

Like Sittler, Moltmann points to the problem of the personalization of faith during the Reformation that can be seen as a consequence of limiting the scope of God's redemptive work to the human personal plane. By compartmentalizing faith and science and limiting scriptural interpretation to personal salvation, this tradition limited the potential scope of theological reflection on the ways the human interacts with the natural world.[39] To counter this limited scope, Moltmann emphasizes the expansive nature of Christ's work beyond the human sphere. He explains, "the first Christians saw Christ in all natural things and all natural things in Christ."[40] But in a void of soteriological interpretations of creation, nature is left vulnerable to use and resource allocation for human aims.

Resisting this personalized—and thus anthropocentric—focus, Moltmann reintegrates creation and redemption, remarkably finding inspiration in Jewish mysticism with Kabbalah rabbi Isaac Luria and his teaching of *zimzum*. In developing this teaching, Luria was addressing the logical problem of maintaining God's omnipotence and omnipresence, while also insisting that the world is not God. Rather than a divine event of absolute will over creation,[41] Luria explains that creation is the result of the omnipotent and omnipresent God's self-concentration or contraction. The infinite creator pulls back Godself in order to make room for something outside of God. This contraction creates the *nihil* or void of God that becomes space for the creation of

---

Moltmann now in *God in Creation* shifts direction to hold that the 'messianic promise' is that 'the world should be 'home'" (5). Where once he charged us 'no longer to live amid surrounding nature,' now he holds that nature is our 'home country,' and that 'society must be adapted to the natural environment' (p. 46). Once he held that 'the recognition that man does not have nature but history means an overcoming of all the naturalistic or quasi-naturalistic ways of thinking.' Now he holds that 'theology must free belief in creation from this over-valuation of history' (p. 32)" (80) (William C. French, "Review: Returning to Creation: Moltmann's Eschatology Naturalized," *The Journal of Religion* 68, no. 1 [1988]: 78–86).

39. Moltmann, *God in Creation*, 35.

40. Moltmann, "The Resurrection of Christ and the New Earth," in *Resurrection and Responsibility: Essays on Theology, Scripture, and Ethics in Honor of Thorwald Lorenzen*, ed. Keith D. Dyer and David J. Neville (Eugene, OR: Pickwick, 2009), 54.

41. Moltmann associates this view with Barth and his doctrine of decrees. Here, Moltmann is working to find a mediating position between Barth's doctrine of decrees and Tillich's doctrine of emanation.

TOWARD A BETTER WORLDLINESS

the world. So, in creating the world, God moves outside of God with the ultimate aim of returning all things to Godself.

Moltmann reinterprets Luria's *zimzum,* applying it to the cross and resurrection. He associates the *nihil* of creation with the *nihil* Christ faced on the cross. Consequently, creation becomes a first act of salvation that is then repeated on the cross. Moltmann explains, "the nihil in which God creates his creation is God-forsakenness, hell, absolute death; and it is against the threat of this that he maintains his creation in life."[42] Here, creation emerges as a first redemption, while redemption on the cross materializes as a new creation. Each is a repetition of the other so that implicit tension between Protestant articulations of creation and redemption dissolve.

For such a remarkable emphasis on the perichoretic nature of God in relationship, Moltmann's insistence on a "fundamental" or "sustaining foundation" for the flux and flow of relationality is jarring. "For only the Spirit of God exists *ex se*"—out of Godself alone—Moltmann asserts. "It is therefore the Spirit," he insists, "who has to be seen as the sustaining foundation of everything else, which does not exist *ex se* but *ab alio et in aliis,*" that is, the other from another.[43] Indeed, the world functions in another, from another, and God too exists in this manner. However, Moltmann's insistence on the *ex se* of the Spirit throws any exchangist, perichoretic relation *between* God and creation into question.

Sallie McFague's skepticism regarding the truly communal nature of relational trinities such as Moltmann's is relevant here. She expresses concern that in social-communal trinities, the "point of the trinity [can still be] protecting God from any dependence on the world."[44] Rather than true God/world relationality, God in community within Godself may serve as a way to ensure that God can be community without the world. Moltmann, she explains, does better at ensuring that we do not end with God's relationship to Godself. However, the danger

---

42. Moltmann, *God in Creation,* 87.
43. Ibid., 11.
44. McFague, *Models of God: Theology for an Ecological, Nuclear Age* (Minneapolis: Fortress Press, 1987), footnotes, 223. McFague is referring to *The Trinity and the Kingdom of God* here.

ECOLOGY OF THE GIFT

still remains "since he is afraid to allow God any dependency on the world."[45] Despite Moltmann's efforts to disrupt the monarchy of the one God, the danger of "a picture of the divine nature as self-absorbed and narcissistic" still remains.[46]

McFague makes a key point here. In order for exchange to appear as such—and not mere narcissism—there must be interchange across difference. In Moltmann's case, if God only exists out of Godself, does the divine only receive in exchange with Godself? For Moltmann, it seems, the gift within God is exchangist, and our world too is exchangist, but there is no receptivity in God from the world. Suddenly, the gift is unilateral again. There is communication within God, but only God is communicating with creation—God does not receive communion back from creation. One is left to wonder: Is this communion after all?

The Free Gift, Soil, and Climate Change

Both Sittler and Moltmann insist on ecological reality and want to affirm a relational and exchangist God. With Sittler's emphasis on the ecological self and grace within (rather than interrupting) creation and Moltmann's interpretation of the cross of redemption as a repetition of the redemption in creation, these early ecotheologians take significant strides to address consistent Protestant ecological issues. However, Anne Primavesi calls for attention to gifting structures within the exchanges of creation. Unfortunately, doing so reveals that at key places these theologians revert to the presumption of a unilateral gift. Mauss and Milbank note the deleterious effects of the free, unilateral gift on social and economic relations. But what effect does the unilateral gift have on ecological systems of exchange? Where we have seen that the free gift also implies an alienable gift structure implying relations of commodification between human agents and their gift "objects," a model of ecological gift-exchange demonstrates that the implications for our relation to the other-than-human world are

45. Ibid.
46. Ibid.

TOWARD A BETTER WORLDLINESS

broader yet. To illustrate, take, for example, the mundane case of soil in relation to the unilateral gift.

The liturgical hymn, "Lord Let My Heart," commonly sung before the reading of the Gospel in American Lutheran churches today, explicitly links the human heart to soil: "Lord let my heart be good soil, open to the seed of your word."[47] Drawing on the Genesis account of humanity formed from humus, the gathered worshiping assembly is weekly reminded of this link that is also annually enacted in the solemn exhortation on Ash Wednesday to "Remember you are dust and to dust you shall return." These rituals and hymns remind us that a shared Jewish-Christian anthropology has long maintained a link between human bodies and the soil.

Grounded in an ancient Judeo-Christian humus/human connection, this hymn also depends on a more recent logic. It relies on the logic that the human heart and soil are linked primarily by a common characteristic: receptivity, passivity, and inertness. The hymn's central metaphor only works if the chanting assembly holds a basic—likely unconscious—assumption that just as the human heart passively awaits God's saving activity, so also the soil remains empty, inert, awaiting human activity to make it redemptively productive.

Global environmental advocate Vandana Shiva demonstrates the material implications of these modern conceptualizations of the human heart, soil, and fossil fuel dependence. In researching the social, economic, ecological, and long-term agricultural impact of India's shift to industrial agriculture in the 1960s, Shiva was surprised to find soil explicitly described by European agriculturalists as "an empty container."[48] She soon found this metaphor functioning as a basic assumption of the Western modern industrial agricultural paradigm, where soil was seen as "an empty container for holding synthetic fertilisers."[49] The connection between widespread synthetic fertilizer

---

47. Handt Hanson, "Lord Let My Heart Be Good Soil," *Evangelical Lutheran Worship: Pew Edition* (Minneapolis: Fortress Press, 2006), Hymn 512.
48. Shiva, "Soil Papered Over," speech given at the Seizing the Alternative Conference, Claremont, CA, June 2015.
49. Ibid.

ECOLOGY OF THE GIFT

use and climate change is still relatively unknown, but agricultural innovator and environmental activist Wes Jackson explains: "What wasn't recognized until more recently was the full extent to which agriculture contributed to [climate change]. We now know that land use, which includes agriculture, is second only to power generation as a greenhouse gas emitter, ahead of transportation."[50] In addition to massive amounts of fossil fuels needed to create synthetic fertilizer, we now also know that when the nitrogen from synthetic fertilizers evaporates, it can combine with oxygen to make nitrous oxide, a greenhouse gas *three hundred* times more potent than carbon dioxide.[51] Paralleling the human heart in common articulations of grace, Shiva notes how in modern Western agricultural practices soil is envisioned as passive and inert, awaiting redemptive and life-giving action from a purely exterior source. Consequently, it seems that where a unilateral or free gift is functioning, an intimate link between the human heart and soil can have widespread and devastating effects on the earth's ecosystems.

Rather than a hollow vessel awaiting a redemptive gift from pure exteriority, Shiva notes that ancient Indian farming practices trained farmers to preserve the productive potential of the soil by encouraging the biodiversity of its vast communities of microorganisms. Shiva explains that these ancient agricultural practices flowed from an understanding of a relationship of reciprocity and mutuality—a kind of gift-exchange—between humans, the land, and its diverse communities of microorganisms.

From an agricultural perspective, Shiva explains, "biodiversity is the alternative to fossil carbon."[52] Where soils are rich in diverse microorganisms, there is no need for synthetic fertilizers. Such biodiversity results from attention to and care for the billions of microorganisms inhabiting healthy, lively, fruitful soil. Shiva reminds

50. Wes Jackson, "The Land Institute," "Issues" accessed July 5, 2015, http://www.landinstitute.org/our-work/issues/#.
51. EPA, "Overview of Greenhouse Gases," http://www3.epa.gov/climatechange/ghgemissions/gases/n2o.html.
52. Shiva, *Soil Not Oil: Environmental Justice in an Age of Climate Crisis* (Brooklyn, NY: South End Press, 2008), 130.

TOWARD A BETTER WORLDLINESS

us that many ancient agricultural practices saw soil not as an empty container awaiting the saving action of a pure exteriority, but as a living community calling for care and communication.[53] It seems, in other words, that the worldview Shiva articulates remained cognizant of the multiple human and other-than-human gifts humans utterly rely on. Rather than affecting merely human spirituality, this illustration of the connection of conceptualizations of the human heart, soil, and fossil fuels demonstrates the ways that our concepts of gift (corresponding with models of grace) affect not just our relations with other humans, but the ways we seek to work with the other-than-human world to sustain human existence.

In preserving the unilateralism of the gift, do not Moltmann and Sittler inevitably end up reinscribing the sovereign self and its externalities that they set out to disrupt? Is this the necessary result of any Protestant ecotheology? One wonders if in Sittler and Moltmann the Protestant tradition finds its limit—the point at which it can go no further toward exchangist, reciprocal relations between God and creation. Given the rising stakes of climate change, however, it seems necessary now to press beyond economies that originate in a unilateral gesture, and so, idealize the gift free of exchange.

McFague's insight that exchange must transgress lines of difference will also continue to reverberate through this study of gifting patterns in our theologies of grace and redemption. We will find we need exchange, but more specifically, we need exchange that does not stay within the circle of relative familiarity and sameness, but engages—and thereby, honors—difference. Without exchange with and through difference, we will find, as McFague does with Moltmann's Trinitarian exchange, that God can remain community within Godself, and thus still has no need for creation. Here again, creation emerges as ultimately expendable.

However, in a sense, this *ex se* might yet be redeemed, as we will see in the final chapter. It might be that in giving God is, in a sense, giving

---

53. Shiva emphasizes that these practices were characteristic of ancient Indian farming techniques in particular.

ECOLOGY OF THE GIFT

out of Godself, and so, continually beside Godself, only ever Godself out of Godself, with the other in communing communication. But as McFague points out, the specter of the sovereign self remains unless this self can be shown to be interrupted, in a sense, by an other. For this to be the case, the divine must truly be able to receive from, be affected by, and be-with the world. This kind of exchange certainly cannot maintain any kind of "foundation"—it is much too shifty, much too "non-hierarchical [and] decentralized."[54] Nor can we oppose it to anything like the reciprocity of returned relation. Certainly, we would want to avoid the binding reciprocal relations that look more like tit-for-tat or *quid pro quo*, but as we will find, our options are certainly not limited to either unilateral gifting or bondage to debt.

54. Moltmann, *God in Creation*, 2; see above.

4

The Gift Revisited:
Unconditioned and Multilateral

Rings and other jewels are not gifts, but apologies for gifts.
The only gift is a portion of thyself.
Thou must bleed for me.
—Ralph Waldo Emerson, "Gifts"[1]

The reach of our daily mundane decisions and actions has never before been so nonlocal. In earlier moments of the ecotheological movement, the interconnectedness of the world could be seen romantically as a redemptive goal toward which God was drawing the world. But today, we find that such interconnections, rendering our daily decisions so nonlocal and disproportionately influential, are harder to romanticize. When mundane and seemingly insignificant decisions about what to eat and how to get to work result in disastrous, even global effects, we are forced to acknowledge the risk involved in interconnection. It seems clear our yoke of interdependence may unfold as our undoing as easily as our redemption. In a world of dynamic systems where effects are disproportionate to causes, Newtonian, linear space-time causality

---

1. Emerson, "Gifts," *Essays and Lectures* (New York: Penguin Putnam, 1983).

TOWARD A BETTER WORLDLINESS

becomes increasingly suspect. Linear causality fundamentally depends on an atomistic view of the universe where separable individual parts can be broken down into smaller and smaller parts, all relating externally and inertly as in a machine. However, today, it is evident that we would not be facing a climate crisis if the world actually functioned as isolated atoms in a void or as isolated individuals, each autonomously directing their own futures.

Those of us in Western and Euro-American contexts might also observe a kind of connection fatigue as the more oppressive expressions of a capitalist society compel us to remain continually plugged into our work, a twenty-four-hour news cycle, and constant availability through social media.[2] Rather than liberation, such interconnection may leave us with an intensified sense of the light cloak-turned-iron yoke of material possessions.

Where connections increasingly emerge as not merely romanticized connectedness but a basic condition of reality—as a given, so to speak—the task of theology turns toward emphasizing the need for what Catherine Keller has called "connection that counts."[3] In her early work, Keller describes the perils and possibilities of gender relations. For women struggling to recall their own sense of self and resisting identifying only with the needs and desires of others, Keller urges her readers to not settle for a dualistic choice between a shored-up self and relation. Indeed, she suggests, "relation can either foster dependency, or test and nurture freedom."[4] Keller intuits that what women striving for a more defined and empowering sense of self desire is not really less connection but more meaningful, liberating, and transforming connection—not the yoke of patriarchal roles, but of solidarity, symbiosis, and mutual empowerment.

In today's climate crisis, where the interconnections of the world seem to hold possibilities for both devastation and redemption, the

---

2. My thoughts on the risks and underside of connections are indebted to Jenna Supp-Montgomerie's response to Jane Bennett's paper at the 2014 Drew Transdisciplinary Theological Colloquium.

3. Keller, *From a Broken Web: Separation, Sexism and Self* (Boston: Beacon, 1988), 3.

4. Ibid.

THE GIFT REVISITED: UNCONDITIONED AND MULTILATERAL

response of women weighed down in self-depleting dependencies holds true across gender differences: what we desire is "not less but more (and different) relation; not disconnection, but connection that counts."[5] When we find we are unable to extricate ourselves from interdependent relations without denying the continuously unfolding mode of reality, what we need is not freedom from interdependencies, but connections that liberate, that open possibilities for meaningful relation and empowering responsibility. The need for *grace-filled connection* runs deep.

We have outlined the perils of continuing with the Protestant majority tradition to emphasize that grace reveals itself in antagonistic or annihilating relation to the exchanges and interconnections of the world. What then will grace look like if it is not to merely interrupt or annihilate the eco/nomies of the world? Can grace become something like a mode of connection that counts, celebrating interdependence and knitting bodies within bodies into symbiotic communities, rather than acting as a key mode of the modern separative individual? Through the work of Sittler and Moltmann, we have seen characteristics of this understanding of grace begin to emerge. Yet, we also noted a persistent tendency to prioritize or revert to the unilateral gift. As we will see, this is the case more broadly as well.

Although connections between Milbank's critique of Reformation understandings of grace and economics remain widely under-recognized, Protestant theologians have responded extensively to theological aspects of Radical Orthodoxy's critiques. Such replies vary widely. Among them, Kathryn Tanner is the only theologian to deal extensively and explicitly with the economic issues at stake. With Tanner, we find we will be able to make a key distinction between the free or unilateral gift and the unconditioned gift. As such, Tanner begins to help us see the outlines of a gift that remains distinctively Protestant, while resisting the impulse to define itself in opposition to exchange.

Another key insight emerges in the work of theologians Risto

---

5. Ibid.

TOWARD A BETTER WORLDLINESS

Saarinen and Niels Henrick Gregersen. They introduce a new category of gift-giving that helps disrupt a presumed impasse between Derrida's nonreciprocal and Milbank's necessarily reciprocal gifts—each of which, as we have seen, display capitalizing vulnerabilities. By delineating between the unilateral, bilateral, and multilateral gift, Saarinen and Gregersen help us see that while Milbank and Derrida seem to be on opposite ends of the gift spectrum, they are actually joined by a common assumption of bilateral gift practices. The multilateral gift thus emerges not only as a potent metaphor of ecological gifting, but a further illustration of how an unconditioned gift may resist circulating back to the giver (thus resisting capitalizing tendencies), and yet, does not emerge as alienated (thus avoiding a separative, commodifying ontology).

Where Derrida and Protestant theologians are joined in a similar desire for the gift that resists a return to its origin, the multilateral gift emerges as a way to do just that while refusing an opposition to the exchanges of the world. In examining the implications of a multilateral gift, it becomes clear that the concerns Protestant theologians respond to in rejecting exchange would be better addressed by protesting linear, bilateral causality than a flat-footed, "here I stand, I can do no other" rejection of exchange. Just as Milbank argued with the reciprocal and nonreciprocal gifts, there are ontological implications. The multilateral gift structure requires an alternate description of reality that can account for internal relations. So, in concluding, we will explore physicist Karen Barad's quantum ontology where material reality itself, and not just biological reality, emerges in what we might identify as a kind of multilateral gift-exchange.

The Unconditioned Gift, Distinguished from Pure, Unilateral, or Free Giving

The possibility of articulating the noncircular gift that disseminates rather than returning to its origin while refusing to reject exchange begins to emerge in Kathryn Tanner's important work on the Protestant tradition and economic ethics. In *Economy of Grace,* she

THE GIFT REVISITED: UNCONDITIONED AND MULTILATERAL

acknowledges increasing concerns with antisocial and unjust aspects of capitalism. Similar to theo-ethicists and historians such as Duchrow and Lindberg, Tanner organizes her economic critique around the assertion that a Protestant theology of grace offers a liberating alternative to current economic practices. However, Tanner's methodology demonstrates a key difference from other reformation economics where grace offers a "radical alternative to the present system."[6]

Like many others, Tanner suggests a methodology of comparing grace and economics in the same symbolic system.[7] Yet, Tanner's approach emerges as unique since most others compare religion and economics within a theological symbolic system and thus end up shifting away from the impurities of exchange. The result is a predictable contrast between the idolatrous god of economy/exchange and the true God of grace. Tanner has taken the reverse strategy, placing religion and economics in conversation within an *economic* symbolic system. In terms of a gift/exchange dualism, this methodological shift is significant as it allows her to avoid repeating this common Protestant binary. As we saw in chapter two, by taking on the language of idolatry, these critiques often end up pitting God against money and economics, thereby implicitly reinforcing the idea that grace only interacts with these worldly exchanges as a rejection, interruption, or annihilation. Tanner's unique methodology allows her to avoid the trap of posing the Christian story of grace against all economy and exchange by suggesting that "the whole Christian story is a vision of economy, a vision of a kind of system for the production and circulation of goods."[8] Where the majority of Christian thought has treated economics as a "second tier of theological concern, an optional addition or supplement to those strictly God-oriented questions that form theology's central domain,"[9] Tanner's methodology demon-

---

6. Kathryn Tanner, *Economy of Grace* (Minneapolis: Fortress Press, 2005), x.
7. Ibid.
8. Tanner, *Economy of Grace*, xi.
9. Ibid., 3.

93

strates that "Christianity is every bit as much about economic issues as an account of the way prices are determined by marginal utilities."[10]

A successful avoidance of the gift/exchange, grace/economy binary should not be taken as an indication that Tanner subscribes to Milbank's shift toward gift-exchange, however. While Milbank and others affirm gift economy as a viable alternative to capitalism, Tanner remains skeptical. She notes that where inalienable gifts maintain ties in the form of debt between giver and receiver, oppressive relationships, like those the Reformers opposed, remain. If the gift is never cleanly cut from the giver, it not only creates relational ties, but a tangle of indebted and obligated relationships. Where objects of exchange are inalienable from the donor, "this simply means that gift exchanges turn into explicit loans." She remains particularly concerned that this kind of gift "suggests that gifts are a kind of common property or loan never fully possessed by the recipient."[11]

From Tanner's perspective, all gift-exchange runs on "debt and credit, in which primary obligations derive from the delegation, or holding in trust, of inalienable property."[12] Since oppressive debt is a key aspect of capitalist economy, Tanner concludes that gift economy is not an acceptable alternative to capitalism. In fact, Tanner rejects all forms of debt as counter to God's redemptive work. Even in our theologies, she argues, "notions of debt, contractual obligation, loan, even stewardship, should be written out of the Christian story about God's relations to the world and our relations with God and one another, in light of an understanding of grace that is fundamentally incompatible with them."[13] In this way, while avoiding a structural contrast between grace and any exchange, Tanner does insist that grace be fundamentally different from—a kind of protest against—the kinds of exchanges that "presuppose private property and conditional loans or grants associated with inalienable forms of possession."[14]

10. Ibid., xi.
11. Ibid., 54.
12. Ibid.
13. Ibid., 56–57.
14. Ibid., 56.

THE GIFT REVISITED: UNCONDITIONED AND MULTILATERAL

Consequently, Tanner rewrites redemption stories, erasing debt-laden atonement theories and replacing them with a soteriological narrative of God's way of grace fighting to oppose and cancel the tangles of debt that oppress us.

For the purposes of this project, Tanner's key insight arrives in the form of an insistence that grace as the "unconditioned" gift may be distinguished from "pure," "unilateral," or "free" gifts. The unconditioned gift is not unilateral or pure of exchange since God does not desire debt, but does call for a "proper return."[15] In this case, a proper return means giving a gift forward. Rather than returning the gift vertically to God, God's gift creates givers on the horizontal plane. The gift is unconditioned because God does not give where there is merit, but where there is need, and the proper return is not given back to God, but to our neighbors, rendering receivers not passive but empowered givers.[16]

The unconditioned gift disrupts oppressive and antisocial economic systems because it is fundamentally noncompetitive. Tanner's protest grace works in congruence with the principle of noncompetitiveness she develops in *God and Creation in Christian Theology* and *Jesus, Humanity, and the Trinity*. There, Tanner articulates a God/world relation where the two are not in competition such that in order for one to increase, the other must decrease.[17] This has been a consistent problem for Protestant thought where God's freedom and power is purchased at the expense of human dependence and passive receptivity.

Unfortunately, Tanner's notion of a noncompetitive relationship between God and world depends on a reiteration of the Protestant

---

15. Ibid., 69.

16. "God's giving does not then humiliate us or work to keep us in an inferior's position of debt. God in giving to us does not bring about our debilitating dependency upon God; God does not in that sense seek to give unilaterally, to be the only real giver. God is, instead, eager for us to become givers in turn and is doing everything possible to make that happen" (ibid., 72).

17. "This non-competitive relation between creatures and God is possible, it seems, only if God is the fecund provider of *all* that the creature is in itself; the creature in its giftedness, in its goodness, does not compete with God's gift-fullness and goodness because God is the giver of all that the creature is for the good" (Tanner, *Jesus Humanity and Trinity*, 3). Tanner furthermore adds, "Unlike this co-operation among creatures, relations with God are utterly non-competitive because God, from beyond this plane of created reality, brings about the *whole* plane of creaturely being and activity in its goodness" (ibid., 4).

theme of an absolute ontological separation between God and creation: "This relationship of total giver to total gift is possible, in turn, only if God and creatures are, so to speak, on different levels of being, and different planes of causality."[18] In other words, God and world are not in competition because they do not share the same space—they are on different planes of reality.[19] Here, Tanner fails to conceptualize a model of difference that does not rely on separation. God may affect the world in soteriological gestures, but fundamentally, God and world do not compete with one another because they do not ontologically intersect.[20]

Familiar suspicions regarding the relation between gift and economy or God's presence with the world rise again. While Tanner avoids reiterating the gift/exchange binary on one level, on another level, she reintroduces a strict divide between giver and receiver in an effort to assert noncompetitive relations.

The Multilateral Gift

Tanner has chosen to address the relation of grace and exchange through explicit engagement with economics. Others engage gift theory with more confessional concerns in mind. Although Piotr Malysz, Bo Kristian Holm, Niels Henrik Gregersen, and Risto Saarinen generally avoid the economic implications Milbank articulates and leave ecological concerns unaddressed, their specific focus on Luther's theology proves insightful in-as-much as it reveals a new distinction in gift discourse between bilateral and multilateral gifting.

In spite of Berndt Hamm's decisive stand for the reformer's alliance with the free gift, among other Lutheran theologians who deal with gift theory, no clear consensus has emerged regarding the compatibility of Milbank's gift-exchange and Luther's theology of grace. For example,

18. Ibid.
19. Ibid.
20. Miroslav Volf echoes a similar thesis pairing noncompetition with separate realms of reality: "It's different with God. True, God is infinitely richer and more powerful than humans. But God and human beings do not occupy the same space. We are not competitors for the same goods. . . . God is incomparably greater—on a completely different plane than we are" (Volf, *Free of Charge: Giving and Forgiving in a Culture Stripped of Grace* [Grand Rapids, MI: Zondervan, 2005], 45–46).

THE GIFT REVISITED: UNCONDITIONED AND MULTILATERAL

while Finnish scholar Risto Saarinen remains skeptical about the applicability of gift-exchange for Lutheran theology, he does suggest that the active/passive binary functioning in interpretations of Luther's justification is misguided.[21]

Polish-American Piotr Malysz and Danish Bo Kristian Holm argue, contra Saarinen, that Luther's theology of justification is more similar to Milbank's gift-exchange than not.[22] Malysz responds to William Cavanaugh's Milbank-influenced essay comparing medieval and reformation eucharistic theologies.[23] Countering Cavanaugh's critique of Luther's eucharistic theology, Malysz argues that, for Luther, the gift is "inalienable" from the giver so that "there are no individualistic

---

21. A Lutheran theologian from Finland, Saarinen has been engaging in ecumenical dialog with the Russian Orthodox Church. He notes that the Eastern Christian tradition takes a different perspective on gift-giving that does not result in the need to insist on the passivity of the receiver. The Eastern Orthodox "giver-oriented" perspective avoids these problems and allows for a certain understanding of cooperation between God and humanity in salvation while yet avoiding Pelagianism. From this perspective, "giving in general only makes sense when the receiver is in some way active" (Risto Saarinen, *God and the Gift: An Ecumenical Theology of Giving* [Collegeville, MN: Liturgical, 2005], 9). He argues, for example, that no one would give to an inanimate object. Yet, in the Western tradition with the strong emphasis on the passivity of the receiver, there is danger of misunderstanding that God's gifts are for persons and not inanimate objects. The receiver-oriented perspective, "has prohibited us from seeing the other side of the coin, namely, the giving that occurs in the process of receiving" (ibid., 6).

Saarinen argues that the answer to this issue is a reversal in perspective. Rather than viewing the exchange from the receiver's point of view, he argues we should see this act of giving from the giver's perspective. Where the focus is on God as the "eminent giver," the receiver's activity can be seen as "mirroring the abundant giving" (Intro to Holm and Widmann, eds., *Word - Gift - Being: Justification - Economy - Ontology* [Tübingen: Mohr Siebeck, 2009], 11). Consequently, reception is not necessarily passive, but includes "a process of giving and transmitting the gift received" (Saarinen, *God and the Gift*, 3). Saarinen argues a Lutheran theology of justification can embrace this kind of active reception from a giver-orientation. Therefore, he concludes, Luther is "not completely unilateral in his theology of love, since he admits the moments of reception and circulation" (ibid., 57–58).

22. This happy exchange theme also leads Malysz to revisit the question of reciprocal relations between God and humanity. Malysz suggests that Luther allows for an element—admittedly limited and markedly asymmetrical—of interdependence between God and creation. Malysz rejects the common Reformation view of the doctrine of justification that demands humanity's absolute passivity before God and lack of reciprocity. God's own Godliness, he argues, awaits the return of trust and faith from creation. "What is returned to God is precisely his Godhood ['"not in substance but God in us"'], which is thus shown to be not an abstraction but a reality with a creation-wide impact. As Luther explains, 'God has none of His majesty or divinity where faith is absent'" (Piotr Malysz, "Exchange and Ecstasy: Luther's Eucharistic Theology in Light of Radical Orthodoxy's Critique of Gift and Sacrifice," *Scottish Journal of Theology* 6, no. 3 [2007]: 299). In effect, God cannot be God—cannot exercise the essence of Godhood—without creation. While God justifies the creature, the creature then justifies "God as God indeed" with their faith and newly given ability to be gifts to one another.

23. Malysz responding to William Cavanaugh, "Eucharistic Sacrifice and the Social Imagination in Early Modern Europe," *Journal of Medieval and Early Modern Studies* 31, no. 3 (2001): 585–605.

TOWARD A BETTER WORLDLINESS

'boundaries between what is mine and what is thine' here."[24] Malysz argues that Luther's "happy exchange" is a key example of inalienable giving since in this exchange at the heart of Luther's doctrine of justification, the result is not just a transfer of goods but a relational union between Christ and the sinner.

Similarly, Holm argues that Milbank's "purified gift exchange" is actually a better description of Luther's doctrines of grace and justification than the "pure gift." He even argues that, from a certain perspective, Luther is more exchangist than Milbank himself.[25] For Holm, the heart of Luther's doctrine of justification is the happy exchange that creates a union between Christ and the human. Luther describes this union-creating exchange in terms of a marital relationship. In Luther's "Freedom of a Christian," he uses the metaphor of bride and bridegroom, writing, "It follows that everything they have they hold in common, the good as well as the evil. . . . Christ is full of grace, life, and salvation. The soul is full of sins, death, and damnation. Now let faith come between them and sins, death, and damnation will be Christ's while grace, life, and salvation will be the soul's."[26] In terms of the Protestant tradition and gift theory, this focus on union between Christ and the human is significant. In "love, giver and gift are identical," Holm writes. "[B]oth partners give identical gifts, themselves, and give them simultaneously."[27] Here, Christ both *gives* and *is* the gift within a relational exchange rendering the gift

---

24. Malysz, "Eucharistic Sacrifice," 301, citing Cavanaugh, 597.
25. See Holm, "Justification and Reciprocity, 'Purified gift-exchange' in Luther and Milbank," in *Word—Gift—Being*, 89. Holm accuses Milbank of effectively obscuring reciprocity in the process of purifying gift exchange. Milbank explains that Mauss's archaic gift exchange must be purified of its agonistic characteristics which would lead to dominating relations of indebtedness or competitive giving. In order to purify gift exchange he applies Pierre Bourdieu's standards: the return gift must be delayed (after a certain amount of time) and for it to be a gift it must be a "non-identical repetition." In other words, giving back the same ugly scarf, even ten years later, will still be received as an insult rather than a gift. Holm argues that employing these two conditions on the gift actually obscures the reciprocity of the gift rather than celebrating it since, for Bourdieu, these two conditions served not only to "distinguish gift from contract but also . . . to blunt our awareness of the gift economy." While Milbank has to resort to conditions that were intended by Bourdieu to obscure reciprocity, Holm argues that a "celebration of reciprocity and exchange can be found at the heart of Luther's doctrine of justification" (ibid., 100).
26. Luther, "The Freedom of a Christian, 1520," *Luther's Works* 31:351.
27. Bo Holm and Peter Widmann, "Word—Gift—Being, Introduction," in *Word—Gift—Being*, 12.

THE GIFT REVISITED: UNCONDITIONED AND MULTILATERAL

inalienable because it does not shuttle between two separative parties, but creates community between Christ and the human.[28]

Emphasizing the community created between Christ and the human through gift-exchange, Holm takes the metaphor a step further, arguing that this is not only an exchange but a *mutual* exchange —effectively between equals. However, here is where Holm's argument seems to falter. The argument for a relation of mutuality relies on a significant shift Holm notes in the conception of marriage relationships in the thirteenth century. During this time, love-poets such as Gottfried of Strasbourg shifted marriage metaphors away from hierarchical relationship toward "the ancient idea of 'one soul in bodies twain.'"[29] This metaphor of unity and mutuality, previously used to describe the ideal male friendship, was now used to describe heterosexual marriage. Because of these conceptual shifts in the understanding of heterosexual marriage, Holm argues Luther's sixteenth-century happy exchange should be seen as an expression of mutuality rather than hierarchy. However, Holm does not give persuasive evidence that Luther was familiar with these sources or that they directly influenced his writing. Historical issues aside, we might remain skeptical about the gendered power dynamics at work here. It is, after all, still the case that Christ is aligned with the saving male while all the feminized soul brings to the exchange is of negative worth: "sin, death, and damnation."[30]

Holm deals with this explicit inequality between Christ and the

---

28. This insight, as we will see in the next chapter, will remain a key insight and important defining characteristic of the Finnish Interpretation of Luther.
29. Holm, "Justification and Reciprocity, 'Purified gift-exchange' in Luther and Milbank," in *Word—Gift—Being*, 103.
30. Lutheran feminist theologian Kathryn Kleinhans notes these oft-repeated feminist concerns about Luther's gendered marital metaphors even as she argues that constructive readings of Luther's happy exchange can prove remarkably resonant with feminist concerns in "Christ as Bride/Groom: A Lutheran Feminist Relational Christology," in *Transformative Lutheran Theologies: Feminist, Womanist, and Mujerista Perspectives*, ed. Mary J. Streufert (Minneapolis: Fortress Press, 2010), 127. For other feminist readings of Luther's happy exchange that acknowledge the dangers while insisting on constructive potential see also Elisabeth Gerle, "Commercial Transaction or Loving Embrace?," *Passionate Embrace: Luther on Love, Body and the Sensual* (Eugene, OR: Cascade, 2017) and Else Marie Wiberg Pedersen, "This Is Not About Sex?: A Discussion of the Understanding of Love and Grace in Bernard of Clairvaux's and Martin Luther's Theologies," *Dialog* 50, no. 1 (2011): 15–25.

Christian by identifying the exchange as "realized reciprocity": "what is not equivalent in an absolute sense—God and man; righteousness and sin; life and death—and not symmetrical—God can give, humans cannot—and therefore not part of reciprocal communication is elevated to equivalence due to participation, elevated to symmetry due to love, and elevated to reciprocity due to God's self-giving. And so the divine gift *is* exchange."[31] For Holm, God's gift to humanity is the gift of participatory exchange in the divine life. God gives the gift of mutual relationship, choosing to identify as equal what is not equal. Therefore, according to Holm, "Luther's use of the marriage metaphor 'creates' equality between God and man."[32]

One wonders at this point if we have arrived at a structure of gift/exchange different from the unilateral gift at all. Isn't the creation of mutual relations a primary gift—and a unilateral one at that? Holm seems to confirm this suspicion: "Human beings are receivers, indeed even 'pure receivers' in a certain sense, but the object received by man and given by God, in Luther's theology, is actually the exchange itself, which according to Luther is beneficial for man and pleasing for God."[33] Despite Holm's efforts to affirm exchange, the basic structure of Protestant unilateral gifting remains. Here, the gift (the creation of mutual relationship—deeming equal what is not equal) remains primary and only secondarily gives way to or opens the way for exchange. Holm's blind spot lies in failing to identifying the "creation" of mutuality as a gift in itself.

The Protestant tendency to revert to a primary unilateral gift that secondarily gives way to exchange repeats itself again in Niels Henrick Gregersen's otherwise promising and insightful essay, "Radical Generosity and the Flow of Grace."[34] Through most of his essay, Gregersen remains impressively cognizant of dangerous power dynamics that might turn generosity and grace to domination and

---

31. Holm and Peter Widmann, "Word—Gift—Being, Introduction," in *Word—Gift—Being*, 12.
32. Holm, "Justification and Reciprocity, 'Purified gift-exchange' in Luther and Milbank," in *Word—Gift—Being*, 103.
33. Ibid., 116.
34. Gregersen, "Radical Generosity and the Flow of Grace," in *Word—Gift—Being*.

THE GIFT REVISITED: UNCONDITIONED AND MULTILATERAL

control.[35] Indeed, one of his main objectives is "to articulate a doctrine of grace that is generous in a graceful manner, that is, without turning violent."[36] Such sensitivity, a demonstrated willingness to articulate grace beyond the personal forgiveness of sins, and the articulation of multilateral giving are promising indications for a worldly theology.[37] This potential, however, makes Gregersen's ultimate conclusions all the more disappointing.

Gregersen opens by outlining the dangers of dichotomous giving, synonymous with the alienable gift. While Gregersen does not explore economic connections, he does emphasize the interpersonal danger of the dichotomous gift: that our generosity gives without consent, and thus slips into domination.[38] Meaningfully, if inadvertently, for this project, in order to elucidate the importance of giving that does not turn to domination and control, Gregersen turns to a historic eco-friendly source: Ralph Waldo Emerson. Gregersen suggests Emerson was the first to point to the problem of giving in his 1844 essay, "Gifts." His alternative to dichotomous giving anticipates Mauss's work almost eighty years later. Emerson argues that to be truly generous, the giver's gift must not be something separable, but must be a gift of a part of the giver's self: "Rings and other jewels are not gifts, but apologies for gifts. The only gift is a portion of thyself. Thou must bleed for me."[39]

Where Mauss emphasizes the power of the gift to dissolve separation (or illusions of separation) between giver, gift, and receiver, Emerson

---

35. He cites Ralph Waldo Emerson's observation that "Behind generosity lurks a violent and wolfish urge to encompass the world" (ibid.,127). Gregersen begins by clearly identifying the potential dangers of grace by focusing on the theme of generosity. He cites postcolonial philosopher Romand Coles who writes, "Indeed, it is difficult to write of generosity today without conjuring up images of the terror wrought by a religion that at once placed the movement of *caritas* and *agape*, giving and love, at the foundation of being and swept across the Americas during the Conquest with a holocaust of 'generosity'" (ibid., citing Romand Coles, *Rethinking Generosity: Critical Theory and the Politics of Caritas* [Ithaca, NY: Cornell University Press, 1997], 1).

36. Gregersen, "Radical Generosity," 140.

37. Continuing the above quote, he writes that another important task for a doctrine of grace today is to maintain "the principal theological motif that grace is not merely a divine reaction to the sinfulness of man, but essentially emanates from the excess of divine nature itself, rooted in God's eternal love" (ibid.).

38. Gregersen also makes a connection between separation and dichotomous relations, explaining, "only if a logic of separation takes the lead at the expense of the phenomenon of the gift is a division of giver and receiver tactically assumed, whereby the gift is reified as an encumbering object" (ibid., 132).

39. Emerson in ibid., 125.

TOWARD A BETTER WORLDLINESS

emphasizes the importance of giving in love. According to Emerson, "We can receive anything from love, for that is a way of receiving from ourselves."[40] Love breaks down divisions between "what is mine and what is thine" to the point that a gift truly given in love cannot slip into domination because it is also a gift given from ourselves to ourselves. Gregersen's elucidation is worth quoting at length:

> [T]he redeeming power of love consists in the fact that in expressions of love the donor hands over to the receiver a mutual relationship that makes it possible (even attractive) to receive the gift unreservedly. Giving out of love involves a sharing of the giver ("a portion of thyself") with the other, and receiving love means receiving from within the mutual relationship itself ("receiving from oneself"). In this manner the gap between the giver and the receiver is overcome, at least momentarily.[41]

Gregersen suggests that such an emphasis on the redeeming power of love, creating union in gifting relationships, is just what has been underemphasized in Reformation soteriologies. Grace is not just for the forgiveness of sins since grace is limited to a gift with unilateral dimensions when only seen as a declaration of forgiveness. In a relationship of love, a humbling view of the self in interdependent relation to others emerges, resisting generosity's "wolfish urge to encompass the world."[42]

The most unique—and for the purposes of this project, significant—contribution Gregersen offers is in suggesting an alternative to both a "logic of separation" between giver or receiver and Milbank's gift-exchange in suggesting that "in the midst of a *network of relations* and interchanges we might find generous actions that exceed the mere condition of an exchange object."[43] The shift to a "network of relations" depends on work Saarinen offers on Augustine and the gift. Saarinen uniquely differentiates between the unilateral, bilateral, and multilateral gifts, noting that the common modern conception of gift-giving—even for Mauss—involves a threefold

---

40. Ibid.
41. Gregersen, "Radical Generosity," 126.
42. Ibid., 127.
43. Ibid., 132. Emphasis mine.

102

THE GIFT REVISITED: UNCONDITIONED AND MULTILATERAL

structure: giver, gift, and receiver. Where Mauss emphasizes nonbinary relations between these three in shifting away from the unilateral gift, Saarinen notes he still remains within a threefold bilateral structure. By contrast, he argues the Christian tradition "has extended this structure by adding a fourth element, the beneficiary, at least since Augustine's *De Trinitate* argued its validity based on the structure of sacrifice."[44]

Gregersen notes that cases of bilateral gifting can seldom be identified in social contexts, and therefore remain "artificial." He expands on Saarinen's insight, arguing that the human-divine relation should not be seen as bilateral with immediate or postponed counter-gifts since "the grace of God initiates and facilitates a wider circulation of gifts."[45] As in the case of the beneficiary which is neither giver, gift, nor direct receiver, in some cases, "beneficial actions are carried out in complex networks of interchange between, say, agent A, B, C and an unknown number of D's."[46] Models of divine/human gifting should allow for more than bilateral gifts since a multilateral gift can account for an excessive flow and disseminating distribution of gifts.

We should note that the effect of multilateralism is similar to Tanner's unconditioned gift that, as distinguished from unilateral or pure gifts, encourages the gift to continue exchanging. However, where Tanner rejects gift exchange on account of her concern that it maintains structures of indebtedness, the multilateral gift allows for a continual exchange of gifts that are not intended to return to their origin (as in restrictive debt relations) but disperse. Gregersen explains, "The grace of God initiates and facilitates a wider circulation of gifts. With the gift of grace, human beings receive an impulse to pass on the gifts of grace to other creatures within a multidimensional network of giving and receiving."[47] Overflow is never a precondition for receiving divine generosity in a multilateral gift structure because the beneficiary merely receives a gift as a result of a gift exchange

---

44. Holm and Widmann, on Saarinen in "Word—Gift—Being, Introduction," in *Word—Gift—Being,* 10.
45. Ibid., 13.
46. Gregersen, "Radical Generosity," 132.
47. Holm and Widmann, on Gregersen in "Word—Gift—Being, Introduction," in *Word—Gift—Being,* 13.

TOWARD A BETTER WORLDLINESS

between a giver and receiver. Furthermore, since relational gift exchange remains primary, such exchanges constitute us, creating the possibility of being giving and receiving selves in the first place. Preconditioned giving would only be possible in a bilateral gifting scenario, for as the recipient is empowered to pass on a gift given in love and in a multilateral context, gifts become part of us in such a way that there no longer remains a pre-existing self.

Unfortunately, in the end, Gregersen's articulation of the multilateral gift relies on the omnipotence of God. When he opens with such sensitivity to concerns about wolfish desires to dominate, the return to omnipotence and a reprioritization of unilateral power is confounding. Gregersen explains the need for omnipotence as a need for God to give without loss. "It is solely almightiness that can truly set free," he argues, "because omnipotence does not lose itself when giving, but precisely actualizes itself as almighty by making its creatures independent as partakers in divine power."[48] By returning to omnipotence—God as unlimited power for and source of giving—Gregersen also ends up reiterating the same old Protestant gift structure: "Through God's unilateral giving, reciprocity is engendered. The pure gift sets otherness free, free to pass on (to the neighbor) and free to give praise (to God)."[49] Once again, the unilateral gift is primary, and only secondarily gives way to relational interchange: "If the beginning of all things is God's radical generosity, and if salvation of all things comes through the flow of grace, then the end of all things is the mutual inherence of God and the world."[50]

In light of this persistent pattern of reverting to a primary unilateral gift that gives way to gift-exchange—even when a theologian expresses the goal of asserting a key element of exchange at the heart of Lutheran theologies of grace—it seems important to recall that Milbank's argument was not that the Protestant gift denies exchange altogether. Rather, he is concerned that the Protestant gift reversed

---

48. Ibid., 142. Gregersen cites Kierkegaard here: "'only omnipotence can retain itself all along as it gives itself away'" ("Radical Generosity," 142).
49. Ibid., 143.
50. Ibid., 144.

104

THE GIFT REVISITED: UNCONDITIONED AND MULTILATERAL

the *priority* of gift models by making the unilateral gift primary, and thus the divinely inspired ideal. Consequently, efforts to reveal simply a reliance on or appreciation of exchange within Protestant theologies of grace fail to get at the heart of the matter if, in the end, they confirm the priority of the pure gift.

The Noncircular Gift and Multilateral Gifting

Gregersen's only reference to Milbank's work is in critique of Derrida. Consequently, he fails to note Milbank's key point on the prioritization of unilateral gifting over exchange. Gregersen also uncritically accepts Milbank's reading of Derrida as a nihilist. In doing so, Gregersen misses a key connection between his work and Derrida's. In fact, Saarinen, Holm, and Gregersen all assume Milbank's reading of Derrida's gift as nihilistic, and thus collectively miss what would likely be clarifying points of connection.

For example, along with drawing upon Emerson, Gregersen also relies on Nietzsche's critique of controlling gift patterns. Inspired by Nietzsche's concerns, Gregersen notes that a world-consuming compulsion must be kept in check by reserving space for difference within a community of love. In order to avoid a kind of generosity that might slip into a one-sided demonstration of force or a desire to swallow the world, Gregersen points to Nietzsche's insistence that space be reserved for the other. Generosity entails sharing widely, but in order to remain truly graceful, "some *slack* is needed, to provide some elbow room for the recipient."[51] For Derrida, as for Nietzsche, the space reserved for difference is the space of loss that makes room for the "bad investment" that does not return to its origin. Instead, the noncircular gift playfully and indiscriminately disseminates to many others.

Rather than pursuing these connections, Gregersen and others conclude that Derrida is a nihilist, which suggests he flatfootedly

---

51. Gregersen, 128. Gregersen only says that these two—self-sharing, communing, generosity, and space to respect difference—must be balanced. Gregersen's dismissal of Derrida as a nihilist and "slanderer" of the gift is particularly unfortunate here since Derrida offers a more nuanced model for maintaining unity and difference.

declares there is nothing in the space where God, meaning, truth, and so on once stood. This would, however, be too determined, too certain for Derrida. Rather than absolute nothingness, the place of loss for Derrida is, as Gregersen himself notes (invoking Nietzsche), the place for wiggle room, play, the space for difference, the other, and a multiplicity of exchanges. This space does not remain stable, but undecidable, as Derrida would say. What will be is not determined by a pure-gift essence, but by relational interactions that take place at the boundaries between "you" and "I."

Take, for example, Derrida's invocation of the "Holy of Holies" in his middle-period work, *Glas.* In the Jewish temple, the Holy of Holies is traditionally in the center of the temple and interpreted as the place of God's pure, unmediated presence. Biblical scholar Stephen Moore comments on Derrida's reference to this site of what was understood as God's pure presence in the center of the temple. As Moore explains, according to "Josephus, the first-century Jewish historian, whose description of the Herodian temple is the most detailed we possess, the Holy of Holies contained 'nothing at all [*ouden holōs en autō*].'"[52] In response, Derrida reflects on the surprise of the "non-Jew when he opens . . . or violates the tabernacle . . . and after so many ritual detours to gain access to the secret center, he discovers nothing—only nothingness. . . . The tent of the tabernacle, the stone of the temple, the robe that clothes the text of the covenant—is finally discovered as an empty room, is not uncovered, never ends being uncovered, as it has nothing to show."[53] Nothing, *nihil*: based on a flat reading of this text alone, one could sympathize with those who label Derrida a nihilist, and thereby dismiss his work and its applicability for theology. Note, however, that Derrida writes in the last sentence that the emptiness "never ends being uncovered." Such phrasing intimates that his conclusion about the Holy of Holies is not so much a closure of meaning as a different kind of opening of possibilities.

---

52. Stephen Moore, *Mark and Luke in Poststructuralist Perspectives: Jesus Begins to Write* (New Haven: Yale University Press, 1992), 38.
53. Moore, 38, citing Derrida, *Glas*, 49a–50a.

THE GIFT REVISITED: UNCONDITIONED AND MULTILATERAL

Look, too, at Yvonne Sherwood's reading of *Glas*. The biblical scholar notes that here the philosopher

> refers to the Torah and synagogue of his past, but he also evokes a sense of the Babylonian Talmud by assembling different and contradictory voices on the same page. Implicitly, in the subtext of his writing, he evokes midrashic ideas and strategies and a style of biblical criticism which has been marginalized by logocentric ideals of empiricism and rationality. When he advocates reading *d'une certaine manière* ("in a certain way") he seems to place himself among the rabbis who urged '*al tiqre*: that is, "do not read it" (i.e., in its conventional form).[54]

Given Sherwood's emphasis on Derrida's playful evocation of midrashic strategies, I would argue that Derrida is not interested in finally determining whether there is or is not a presence. This would only return us to a binary logic (logocentrism or the logic of presence) again. What inspires Derrida is the indeterminate, unresolvable tension—the play—between absence and presence. He says this is where desire begins, in the teasing play between absence and presence, in other words, in the unresolvable question: Is there something or is it nothing?[55] Significantly, Derrida contrasts his view with a centered, substantial, atomistic physics: "For what is discovered here is that there is no nucleus of meaning, no conceptual atom, but that the concept is produced within the tissue of differences."[56] Here, Derrida refers to a structure of meaning where a concept, much like a multilateral gift, emerges within the exchanges between "the tissue of difference." Does this not suggest something like a shift from centered, substantial, isolated gift to a gift that emerges *in exchange*?

In Derrida's early work—a paper presented at Johns Hopkins, which was his first introduction to an English audience—he addresses the idea of the center, certainty, meaning, and truth more explicitly. In "Structure, Sign, and Play in the Discourse of the Human Sciences,"

---

54. Yvonne Sherwood, *The Prostitute and the Prophet: Reading Hosea in the Late Twentieth Century* (New York: T&T Clark, 2004), 197.

55. See, for example: "The supplement is maddening because it is neither presence nor absence and because from the start it breaches both our pleasure and our virginity" (*Of Grammatology*, trans. Gayatri Chakravorty Spivak [Baltimore: Johns Hopkins University Press, 1997], 168).

56. Derrida, "From Restricted to General Economy," *Writing and Difference*, trans. Alan Bass (Chicago: University of Chicago Press, 1978), 267.

107

TOWARD A BETTER WORLDLINESS

Derrida opens by explaining that the logic characterizing Western metaphysics is the logic of centrism. This logic seeks foundations, certainty, and original truths to resist anxiety before the unknown. Derrida then outlines the event in recent history of the loss of this center when interpretations of truth and reality became subject to interpretation themselves. This loss of center, he attributes to "the Nietzschean critique of metaphysics," "the Freudian critique of self-presence, that is, the critique of consciousness, of the subject, of self-identity and of self-proximity or self-possession," and to "the Heideggerean destruction of metaphysics, of onto-theology, of the determination of Being as presence."[57]

Derrida concludes that there are "two interpretations of interpretation, of structure, of sign, of play."[58] In other words, there are two basic responses to the loss of centered certainty in, for example, an absolute presence—a determinate meaning—in the Holy of Holies. The first kind of response he aligns with Levi-Strauss's reading of Rousseau, where the loss of the center is mourned as the absence of an absolute origin. This response, I would suggest, also characterizes Milbank's and Gregersen's interpretation of Derrida since they seem to align de-centering with a loss of center and meaning. The second response Derrida aligns with Nietzsche, who affirms the loss of a solid center of meaning because it provides an opportunity for meaning to be continually produced within the play of differences. Nietzsche's response is a "joyous affirmation of the play of the world and of the innocence of becoming, the affirmation of a world of signs without fault, without truth, and without origin which is offered to an active interpretation. This affirmation then *determines the noncenter otherwise than as loss of the center*."[59] These concluding remarks cast suspicion on

---

57. Derrida, "Structure, Sign, and Play," *Writing and Difference*, 280.
58. Ibid., 292.
59. Ibid. Suggestions of Derrida's later occupation with the animal and modern Western humanism follow: "There are thus two interpretations of interpretation, of structure, of sign, of play. The one seeks to decipher, dreams of deciphering a truth or an origin which escapes play and the order of the sign, and which lives the necessity of interpretation as an exile. The other which is no longer turned toward the origin, affirms play and tries to pass beyond man and humanism, the name of man being the name of that being who, throughout the history of metaphysics or of ontotheology—in other words, throughout his entire history—has dreamed of full presence, the

THE GIFT REVISITED: UNCONDITIONED AND MULTILATERAL

a dismissive conclusion that Derrida is a nihilist. They suggest that, for Derrida, the noncenter is not something he mourns because, rather than an absolute loss of a center/meaning, it is an affirmation of the infinite extension of the center where meaning is continually produced. In other words, "The absence of the transcendental signified extends the domain and the play of signification infinitely."[60] These are not flat-footed concluding words suggesting a closure, but conclusions affirming an opening of possibilities.

This is a key connection between Derrida and Nietzsche's work that Gregersen misses. On the one hand, he affirms Nietzsche's call for space for the other, for difference, as a key aspect of a gift that will not turn to overpowering violence. On the other hand, he labels Derrida a "slanderer" of the gift—seemingly for affirming Nietzsche's same insights. In associating Derrida's work and gift with nihilism, Gregersen and others seem to assume the role of Levi-Strauss, who mourns the center purely as a loss. In this sense, we might agree that Gregersen seems to miss an opportunity by dismissing Derrida's gift as nihilist. Given his stated aims to articulate an understanding of grace outside the realm of forgiveness of sins, it seems he would have benefited from a de-centered gift extended through multiple exchanges in fields of difference.

In the spirit of reciprocal giving, let me also suggest that Derrida's gift, particularly as articulated in *Given Time*, would have benefited from Saarinen's and Gregersen's delineation of unilateral, bilateral, and multilateral gifts. It seems that despite the opposing views of Derrida and Milbank on the gift, they are joined by a linear understanding of gift practices. While Derrida's gift emerges as unilateral, Milbank's Maussian concept of gift remains bilateral in that it does not account for the gift within a vast network of multilateral exchanges. Both unilateral and bilateral gifting structures imply an

---

reassuring foundation, the origin and the end of play. The second interpretation of interpretation, to which Nietzsche pointed the way, does not seek in ethnography, as Levi-Strauss does, the 'inspiration of a new humanism' (again citing the 'Introduction to the Work of Marcel Mauss')" (ibid.).

60. Ibid., 280.

assumption of linear causality while the multilateral gift accounts for a kind of gift that does not abide by linear or direct causality. As Saarinen points out, the multilateral dimension emerges by accounting for the beneficiary who does not directly receive a gift, but who benefits from an indirect gift-exchange through both time and space.

A multilateral gifting model would have helped Derrida avoid the trap of a gift/exchange dualism while maintaining the benefits of the noncircular gift. I suggest that both Derrida and Protestant theologians of grace fall into the trap of gift/exchange not because the noncircular gift is necessarily anti-exchangist, but because it is anti-exchange within a bilateral gifting model. In a bilateral gifting structure, a gift can only go out from the donor and either return to the donor or refuse to return. If the gift returns, the circle is completed and the donor's investment is capitalized. If the gift refuses to return, it stays with the donee as an alienated gift. By contrast, where there is a network of relations rather than a single giver and receiver accounted for, a multilateral gifting structure allows the gift to be given from the donor where it may continue to be laterally exchanged, that is, without returning to the donor. I would suggest that a multilateral gift truly accounts for what it seems Derrida was most concerned about in gifting structures: Affirming a gift economy that resisted a logocentric, Western metaphysical, Odyssean return to the origin and a gift that disseminates or spreads widely and indiscriminately, that is, without precondition. The multilateral gift would have allowed Derrida the possibility of avoiding a gift/exchange dualism while preserving the noncircular aspect of the gift.

Rather than opposing gift to exchange as Derrida does, I am arguing that the unconditioned gift emerges as the multilateral gift which may or may not return the gift to the origin, but also continually engages in exchange. Like the noncircular gift, it might not be redeemed to the giver. It may not be capitalized, nor is it necessarily nullified or alienated if it does not return. Like Tanner's and Gregersen's gift, it may disseminate or spread freely by empowering and inspiring further giving.

THE GIFT REVISITED: UNCONDITIONED AND MULTILATERAL

Here, gifts are given "in the midst of a network of relations and interchanges"[61] so that resonance with both Sittler's and Primavesi's ecological gifts may also be discerned. A shift away from both unilateral and bilateral models toward a multilateral mode of gift giving where "things are what they are, and do what they do, and have the force they have because they are where they are in a vast and intricate ecosystem"[62] complements Sittler's ecological self, further illustrating the ways this self emerges as constituted by multiple gifts within a web of relations. We also might recall that Primavesi's ecological gift-exchange accounts for the "essential contributions to present gift events made by 'more than' those participating in them now. They include antecedent generations of living beings: all those who, by their lives, their labor, their deaths, their vision, and their patient endeavors have made such events presently possible."[63] This is an excellent example of a gift received laterally by a beneficiary rather than a giver or receiver. The nonlinear causality or lateral nature of this gift applies to both time and space. As Primavesi demonstrates, gifts may be received by beneficiaries wholly outside an immediate exchange of gifts but who have profited from a prior exchange. Consequently, it would seem that Primavesi's ecological gift-exchange requires a model that makes room for something other than the direct or linear cause-and-effect characteristic of both unilateral and bilateral gifts.

In addition to Primavesi and Sittler, this gift structure seems more in line with Derrida's general economy which maintains its own interconnection with post-Newtonian nonlocality. In *Complementarity: Anti-Epistemology After Bohr and Derrida*, literature and cultural theory scholar Arkady Plotnitsky offers an original reading of Derrida alongside Niels Bohr's quantum physics. Plotnitsky describes the influence of quantum theory on Bataille's general economy which, as

---

61. Gregersen, "Radical Generosity," see above.
62. Sittler, "Essays on Nature and Grace," *Evocations of Grace: The Writings of Joseph Sittler on Ecology, Theology, and Ethics*, ed. Steven Bouma-Prediger and Peter Bakken (Grand Rapids, MI: Eerdmans, 2000), 153.
63. Primavesi, "The Preoriginal Gift—and Our Response to It," *Ecospirit: Religions and Philosophies for the Earth*, ed. Laurel Kerns and Catherine Keller (New York: Fordham University Press, 2007), 218.

TOWARD A BETTER WORLDLINESS

we noted in chapter two, was taken up by Derrida as an alternative to the capitalizing restricted economy where every sign hits its mark and every investment returned. Through extensive research and analysis of both Bohr's physics and Derrida's deconstruction Plotnitsky concludes, "one can ascertain not only the general economic character of quantum mechanics, particularly Bohr's complementarity, but also a kind of 'quantum mechanical' and complementary character of general economy. Genealogies of both ideas overlap."[64] Indeed, Derrida's symbols of meaning production suggest a shift from classical atomistic physics when he writes, as we have seen, that he wants to account for the ways the "concept is produced within the tissue of differences," rather than in a "nucleus of meaning" or "conceptual atom."[65]

We are observing a different logic emerging—one resisting linear cause and effect from solid, sovereign, and atomistic agents. According to Descartes and Newton, material reality is composed of distinct and mostly inert parts that relate to one another only externally. That is, they act only when acted upon so that an effect has a clear cause within a linear timeline. One can see how either unilateral or bilateral gifting structures neatly fit within such a model of reality.

Since these were descriptions of physical reality, it is not immediately clear that these descriptions would or should apply to divine giving. Clearly, theological discourse is not physical science and Newton's physics is not a theology. However, Coole and Frost argue, regarding the Cartesian-Newtonian influence on philosophy, that "while scientific theories cannot simply be imported into philosophy, the tropes and rhythms they suggest can transform theoretical discourses."[66] I would suggest that, particularly in this case, the same is true of theology as well.

Rather than exchange in general, it seems that the issue really at stake for Protestant theologians is a sense of needing to resist a sense of

---

64. Plotnitsky, *Complementarity: Anti-Epistemology After Bohr and Derrida* (Durham, NC: Duke University Press, 1994), 18.

65. Derrida, "From Restricted to General Economy," *Writing and Difference*, 267.

66. Coole and Frost, eds., *New Materialisms: Ontology, Agency, and Politics* (Durham, NC: Duke University Press, 2010), 13.

THE GIFT REVISITED: UNCONDITIONED AND MULTILATERAL

linear causality between God and humanity and in creaturely relations mirroring this relation. For example, when theologians reject economics or exchange in general, they often associate these with a calculated kind of exchange: tit-for-tat, *quid pro quo*, or *do et des*.[67] Therefore, I am suggesting that they are primarily concerned with disrupting a sense that I do something to get God's reward or that I would act a certain way in order to get God to do something for me—a directly causal gift-exchange. But if this is the case, instead of rejecting exchange as an opposition to the divine gift, might such concerns be better addressed by an alternate ontology that could account for multilateral gifts and a self located in and constructed through multidimensional relationships—a self "existing in the grid of all selves . . . [where] I have no self by myself or for myself [and] really have no identity that I can specify expect the intersection point of a multitude of things that are not mine."[68] In such an ontology, reality itself emerges through exchange and internal relations where linear causality loses its descriptive power.

Intra-Active Gifting

This disruption of direct causality intuited in Primavesi's eco-gift, Sittler's ecological grace, and Derrida's general economy requires an alternate ontology where material relations affect one another internally. As an alternative to Newtonian linear causality and Cartesian dualism between (human) subject and (nonhuman) object, Karen Barad constructs a relational ontology she calls "agential realism."[69] Trained as a physicist in quantum field theory, Barad and her work embody a refusal to divide knowledge by disciplinary boundaries—particularly between the sciences and humanities—by

---

67. See, for example, in Hamm, "Martin Luther's Revolutionary Theology of Pure Gift without Reciprocation," trans. Timothy J. Wengert, *Lutheran Quarterly* 29 (2015) and Gregersen,"Radical Generosity and the Flow of Grace," in *Word—Gift—Being*.
68. Sittler, *Gravity and Grace*, ed. Thomas S. Hanson (Minneapolis: Augsburg Fortress, 2005), 44–45.
69. Karen Barad, *Meeting the Universe Halfway: Quantum Physics and the Entanglement of Matter and Meaning* (Durham, NC: Duke University Press, 2007).

TOWARD A BETTER WORLDLINESS

identifying herself as quantum field theorist, feminist, post-structuralist, and queer theorist.

At least since the discoveries of quantum physics, a separative view of reality cannot be supported. As Plotnitsky drew our attention to enlightening connections between Derrida's work and that of Niels Bohr, so also Barad engages Bohr's work in significant and constructive ways. Building from Bohr's philosophy-physics, Barad explains that the basic structure of reality should not be seen as atoms that bounce off of each other through external relations. Something much more fluid, porous, and relational characterizes the "foundations" of reality. Barad argues that where *inter*action still implies that an original, pure substance or self exists that then subsequently engages in relational exchanges, we would better describe our relations with the human and other-than-human world in terms of *intra*-actions. Moving from interaction to intra-action marks a shift from assumptions of human alienability from the world—a relation enacted in modern scientific methodologies. Rethinking the modern scientific goal of objectivity by assuming separation from the world as an object of observation, Barad insists, "'We' are not outside observers of the world. Nor are we simply located at particular places *in* the world; rather, we are part *of* the world in its ongoing intra-activity."[70] Intra-action thus describes the way that all matter—not just human being since it does not depend on anything such as self-consciousness or some other exclusive human designation—comes to be. Barad's intra-action takes relational ontology past the boundaries of social or even biological life to the level of subatomic materialization.

Barad is rethinking the ontological assumptions that consciously and unconsciously order our worlds, economies, politics, gender relations, sciences, relations with the other-than-human, and more. In particular, Barad moves to rethink linear causality and its implicit separative individualism as key organizing metaphors of modern thought. In other words, she seeks to provide an alternative to

---

70. Karen Barad, "Posthumanist Performativity: Toward an Understanding of How Matter Comes to Matter," *Signs: Journal of Women in Culture and Society* 28, no. 3 (2003): 828.

THE GIFT REVISITED: UNCONDITIONED AND MULTILATERAL

a worldview that posits the existence of discrete entities that interact with one another in a locally determinate causal fashion, wherein change is the result of one event (the cause) causing another event (the effect) and causes effect the motion of entities moving through space in accord with the linear flow of time. The assumptions that support this view include the following: the world is composed of individual objects with determinate properties and boundaries, space is a given volume in which events occur, time is a parameter that advances in linear fashion on its own accord, and effects follow their causes.[71]

Linear causality becomes suspect because it assumes partners remain essentially and ontologically the same before and after the meeting and that time moves in a linear fashion. Such external relations do not jive with accounts of reality where "partners do not precede the meeting."[72] In other words, the need for a shift in models comes not just from a newfound complexity of factors affecting a situation or phenomenon, but because parties constitute one another in their relations. As Barad explains,

> future moments don't follow present ones like beads on a string. Effect does not follow cause hand over fist, transferring the momentum of our actions from one individual to the next like the balls on a billiards table. . . . Our (intra)actions matter—each one reconfigures the world in its becoming—and yet they never leave us; they are sedimented into our becoming, they become us. And yet even in our becoming there is no "I" separate from the intra-active becoming of the world.[73]

Intra-actions do not remain external but cause ontological shifts in the parties involved, affecting the very nature of causality in time and space.

Along with assumptions such as linear time and linear cause and effect that support a view of separative substances, we might also include the gift/exchange dualism along with assumptions that constrain grace to separative, personal, individual relations. The fact that matter does not just interact externally or at a distance might be interpreted as a kind of multilateral gift-exchange. Employing the

---

71. Barad, "Nature's Queer Performativity," *Kvinder, Køn, & Forskning* 12 (2012): 45.
72. Donna Haraway, *When Species Meet* (Minneapolis: University of Minnesota Press, 2008), 4.
73. Barad, *Meeting the Universe Halfway*, 394.

TOWARD A BETTER WORLDLINESS

terminology without citing the (gift) theory, Barad writes, "'Individuals' are infinitely indebted to all others, where indebtedness is about not a debt that follows or results from a transaction but, rather, a debt that is the condition of possibility of giving/receiving."[74] It seems most Protestant theologians define and are concerned with debt that results from a transaction. But where there is no original essential selfhood that secondarily enters into social exchange relations there remains no original starting place of pure human selfhood or materiality that remains outside of, or prior to, intra-active exchanges. Where interconnections of exchange remain primary, they open the possibility in the first place of giving and receiving by constituting the subject within this network of gifts.

The question of the primacy of either a pure gift or exchange is, in short, a question of whether we start as original, essential, substantial selves that subsequently enter into social exchange relations or if we have always already been relational, and therefore, in relationships of exchange. Where Moltmann, Sittler, and many others seek to strengthen a sense of human connection with other humans and all creation, Barad takes a different approach.[75] Rather than striving to articulate how we *make* connections, how we feel less alienated or divorced from our social and ecological communities, for Barad, connection is a given, part of the fabric of reality. The question then is not how to connect (or reconnect) with the world around us. Where connection is the opening act, we cannot simply stop at the acknowledgment that our fates are tied to each other's, but are led on to the next question: *Given* this kind of primary relationality, what kind of responsibility is called for? What kind of connections will "test and nurture freedom"—particularly, as the Reformers called for, freedom for responsibility and service to the neighbor? For Barad the interconnectedness of reality is the opening for the ability to respond

---

74. Barad, "On Touching—The Inhuman That Therefore I Am," *differences: A Journal of Feminist Cultural Studies* 23, no. 3 (2012): 7. See also Barad, "Quantum Entanglements and Hauntological Relations of Inheritance: Dis/continuities, SpaceTime Enfoldings, and Justice-to-Come," *Derrida Today* 3, no. 2 (2010): 240–68.

75. Barad, "Deep Calls unto Deep: Queer Inhumanism and Matters of Justice-to-Come" (paper presented at the Drew University Transdisciplinary Theological Colloquium, Madison, NJ, 2014).

THE GIFT REVISITED: UNCONDITIONED AND MULTILATERAL

since our selves, our consciousness, and our ethical agency only emerge in intra-action. For modern thinkers anything other than autonomy, sovereignty, and full consciousness or self-awareness put the ethical subject and an ability for responsibility in question. But for Barad, rather than diminishing ethical agency and responsibility, these multiple meeting points between what is mine and what is thine—entanglements with others—become the knots of relationality through which response/ability—the ability to respond to the other—becomes possible. In other words, Barad writes, "What if we were to recognize that differentiating is a material act that is not about radical separation, but on the contrary, about making connections and commitments?"[76] Indeed, what if differentiating is not about separation but "connection that counts"?[77]

Gifting within the Tissues of Exchange

In defending the free or pure gift, do we end up actually preserving something key to the Reformation message, or do we inadvertently sustain Western modern assumptions of the world and reality that are no longer scientifically or biblically tenable, let alone ecologically sustainable? By insisting on the gift-exchange at the heart of Luther's theology of grace, Holm and Malysz suggest an intriguing way forward. Unfortunately, any potentially fruitful alternatives are cut off by gendered power dynamics that reabsorb Luther's happy exchange metaphor into active/passive and gift/exchange dualisms. With the articulation of a multilateral gift as a mode of nonlocal, nonlinear ecological gifting, we have been constructing an alternative to both unilateral and bilateral gifting with their corresponding economies, cosmologies, and ontologies. While the gendered power dynamics of the happy exchange keep it from signaling a potentially fruitful alternate eco/nomic ontology, as we will see, a closely related metaphor may do just that. Rather than hierarchical or separative relations, we may find that Luther's interpretation of the *communicatio*

76. Barad, "Nature's Queer Performativity," 47.
77. Keller in *From a Broken Web*, see introduction above.

TOWARD A BETTER WORLDLINESS

idiomatum holds a key for eco/nomic transformative potential from within the tradition.

We have begun to see just how limiting the solid separative self is in accounting for grace. Rather than deemphasizing the reformers' insights into God's graciousness, the multilateral noncircular gift extends the profound implications of grace beyond an anthropocentric worldview to our most mundane realities and relations. In the process, a necessary interconnection between the doctrines of grace and creation is reaffirmed. From a relational and ecological perspective where grace emerges "within the tissue of differences," the space of grace would no longer be found in a nucleus—whether human, atomic, or a Holy of Holies—but flowing through the material relational spaces between and within a multitude of creatures who see grace not solely as something that rights their relationship with the divine, but that sustains, inspires, and enlivens by providing alternate life-giving modes of relation.

In some of the most mundane cases, then, it may be undecidable whether certain gifts are divine or creaturely—is our daily bread a gift purely from God if others, both human and non, have contributed, even giving their lives (yeast!) for it? And yet, isn't there something divinely graceful in the fact that all these contributions have assembled into a concrete and particular gift that, this day, sustains our life's work and service? Isn't there something sacred in the tie between what we might call mine and another's, in what I might call "you" and "me," or between what we might traditionally call spiritual and material, the Godly and the worldly?

5

Communicating Grace

I in them and you in me, that they may become completely one,
so that the world may know that you have sent me
and have loved them even as you have loved me.
—John 17:23

This *communicatio* of divine and human *idiomatum* is a fundamental law
and the master-key of all our knowledge and of the whole visible
economy.
—Johann G. Hamann[1]

One[2] of the most pressing tasks facing humanity today is to formulate
alternative models of economy and exchange among humans and
between humans and the other-than-human world. In so doing, we
construct new ways of being in the world and new understandings of
ourselves in relation to a multitude of others. Many ecotheologians and
ethicists suggest that this is a task suited precisely for religions with
their vast imaginative resources for constructing alternate economies,
cosmologies, and modes of relation.[3] Building from the insight that

---

1. Johann Georg Hamann, *Hamann: Writings on Philosophy and Language*, ed. Kenneth Haynes (Cambridge: Cambridge University Press, 2007), 99.
2. Portions of this chapter published in "Communicating Grace," *Currents in Theology and Mission* 43, no. 4 (2016): 22–26.

modes of being in the world and models of selfhood are intimately related to the models of gifting we assume, the previous chapter explored the alternate mode of unconditioned and multilateral gifts. Refusing a reliance on capitalizing gains, this gift also resists the tendency of the free gift toward alienated giving. More than a mere way beyond Milbank's and Derrida's reciprocal/nonreciprocal impasse, this mode of giving provides a profoundly ecological and promising economic model built on cooperative rather than growth-dependent and competitive relations. But what does this model of gifting look like in terms and tropes more familiar to Protestant theology? The way to think about grace and justification beyond the individual—*pro me*—remains unclear. Recall that even with promising moments in Sittler, Moltmann, Holm, and Gregersen's work, these theologies continue to revert to a unilateral gift. Given the consistency of this tendency, we have wondered whether we have reached the point where a Protestant concept of grace can go no further.

I suggest that the Protestant tradition can and has gone further. Protestant ecotheology need not resign itself to ultimately asserting a unilateral divine gesture behind layers of earthly exchange because resources for envisioning alternate economies and modes of relation can be found in marginalized aspects of Luther's Christology and theology of grace that emphasize profound union between God and creatures. Specifically, I suggest that the multilateral and unconditioned gift finds profound expression in Luther's unique and particularly scandalous interpretation of the ancient christological understanding of the relation between the human and divine in Christ: the *communicatio idiomatum.*

Bo Holm and Piotr Malysz sought to disrupt a gift/exchange dualism in Luther's work by emphasizing Luther's "happy exchange" as an exchangist gift at the heart of Luther's doctrine of justification. We concluded, however, that this particular expression of exchange is marked by power dynamics that bring us back to where we began—that

---

3. For example, see Larry Rasmussen in *Earth-Honoring Faith: Religious Ethics in a New Key* (New York: Oxford University Press, 2013) and John Grim and Mary Evelyn Tucker, *Religion and Ecology* (Washington, DC: Island Press, 2014).

is, with an active/passive binary explicitly tied to gender roles and an assumption of divine impassibility. What remains to be seen is whether an interaction between God and creation can be articulated from a Protestant perspective as truly relational in the sense that there is not only exchange from God to creation, but also from creation to God. Intimately related to the happy exchange, Luther's interpretation of the *communicatio idiomatum* suggests a remarkable reciprocity between creator and creature.

An interesting and particularly relevant debate is emerging about the interpretation of Luther's articulation of this doctrine and the extent to which he allows for a mutual exchange between God and creation. Where many before and after Luther have been willing to affirm a gift from creator to creature, most stopped short of affirming the reverse—that the creator also receives from creation, resulting in properties improper to traditionally conceived divinity: vulnerability, suffering, weakness, and even death. In the twentieth century some theologians have argued that Luther, by contrast, insisted this effect/affect must be felt within divinity itself. The formative effect of this doctrine on Luther's soteriology, sacramentology, doctrine of justification, and more has been convincingly demonstrated.[4] Others have argued that the extent to which Luther is ready to challenge divine impassibility has been exaggerated.

The economic implications of the debate about the proper interpretation of Luther's *communicatio idiomatum* are not widely unacknowledged. In addition to influence on Luther's soteriology, sacramentology and doctrine of justification, I will demonstrate that this christological teaching also drives Luther's social and economic ethics, especially the community chests he encouraged and helped envision. I will also suggest that if Protestant theologies are going to be able to offer an alternative to growth-dependent and alienating economies, then our theologies of grace must be shown to incorporate union. For this, we will turn to the relatively recent Finnish

---

4. Johann Anselm Steiger, "The *communicatio idiomatum* as the Axle and Motor of Luther's Theology," *Lutheran Quarterly* 14 (2000).

interpretation of Luther, paying special attention to their engagement with gift theory in relation to Luther's theology of grace. In the Finnish interpretation of Luther's theology of grace, we see a significant shift from the alienable to the inalienable gift. I will add, though, that it is important also to acknowledge a certain level of difference-preserving mutual exchange between God and creation in this union. Instead of the purely unilateral gesture commonly associated with Luther's articulation of grace, Luther's rendition of the communication of Christ's divine and human properties affirms the communication (or mutual—even if unequal—sharing) of *property* as profoundly Christomorphic and graced.

With grace, communication refers to more than just dialog or a transference of information as would again suggest separative relations where a gift of information is sent from one party across empty space to another. Building from its etymological connections with communion and community, communicating grace emerges as a mode of indwelling interconnection that empowers relations of care and response. As such, it seems this particularly scandalous interpretation of the *communicatio idiomatum* also prompted Dietrich Bonhoeffer, who we will engage in the final chapter. Here, we will explore Bonhoeffer's Christomorphic ontology of being-with, a radical departure from the modern Protestant orientation around the self as isolated individual, as well as his prophetic proposal for a "better worldliness," profoundly animated by Luther's interpretation of the communication of properties.

Early Christian Intimations of the *communicatio idiomatum*

Jaroslav Pelikan explains that the relation between the divine and human as well as between the first and second persons of the Trinity give "creedal status" to the "bond between creation and redemption."[5] As Moltmann, Sittler, and other ecotheologians emphasize, however, this bond has not been emphasized enough in the Protestant tradition.

---

5. Jaroslav Pelikan, *The Christian Tradition: A History of the Development of Doctrine, Vol. 1: The Emergence of the Catholic Tradition: (100-600)* (Chicago: University of Chicago Press, 1971), 172.

COMMUNICATING GRACE

Sittler, for example, wrote of a near "repudiation" of creation for the sake of human salvation. Protestant soteriologies have placed strong emphasis on the absolute passivity of creation to receive the gracious acts of God. This active/passive dualism has consequently meant a strong emphasis on dualistic relations between God and world. As we will see, however, in some strands of Protestant thought, this strict dualism was held in tension with a soteriology that depended on union and even exchange between God and creation. Luther especially emphasized this soteriology and remained remarkably consistent with it. In contrast with Hamm's insistence that Luther's concept of grace was unprecedented among the world's religions, let alone the Christian religion, it will become clear that Luther maintained strong ties with early Christian soteriologies, especially those following from Athanasius and the Alexandrian school, as antecedents that influenced his theology of grace. We will see that Luther's dependence on this school of Christian thought becomes most evident in his particular articulation of the *communicatio idiomatum*.

First intimations of what emerged as the *communicatio idiomatum* can be found in the writings of Ignatius of Antioch (c. 50–between 98 and 117), who emphasized both the "oneness of Christ and the reality of his twofold mode of existence."[6] However, Tertullian (c. 155–c. 240) first addressed the question of the relation between the two natures of Christ, emphasizing that the human and divine characteristics remain distinct in Christ.[7] The traits were, in Tertullian's words, "not confused but conjoined."[8] Any mutable characteristic of Christ, such as suffering or learning, was due to his humanity and did not alter his divine attributes of immutability.[9] However, as early church historian J. N. D. Kelly points out, "these careful distinctions did not prevent Tertullian from using expressions like 'God allows Himself to be born,' 'the

---

6. J. N. D. Kelly, *Early Christian Doctrines*, revised edition (New York: HarperCollins, 1978), 143.
7. Ibid., 151.
8. Tertullian, in ibid., 152.
9. In this regard, Tertullian anticipates the Antiochene position. For church leaders shaped by the Antiochene school of Christian thought, their soteriologies depended on the preservation of God's omnipotence and impassibility. While maintaining Christ's dual nature, then, they emphasized the preservation of difference and distinction between the human and divine natures of Christ.

123

sufferings of God,' 'God as truly crucified, truly died.'"[10] Such language clearly anticipates the *communicatio idiomatum*.

Augustine (354–430) regards the relation of the two natures as a kind of "mixture" that is not a combination of two natures into a new nature. He also insists, like most others through Chalcedon, that this union of natures is particular to the person of Jesus Christ and not a generalizable divine nature united to a generalizable human nature. Around the same time, Apollinarius (d. 390) wrote of a "composite nature" in Christ, which patristic scholar Richard Norris suggests is a less-developed form of the *communicatio idiomatum*.[11] Apollinarius was expanding on the thought of Athanasius (c. 296–373) who arose as an important figure in the Nicene debates with Arius and his followers. Athanasius's soteriology depended on a strong union between divinity and humanity. His famous conclusion to *On the Incarnation* is characteristic: "For the Son of God became man so that we might become God."[12] While Athanasius has become famously identified with this divinizing conclusion, he too was relying on the thought of those who came before him. Irenaeus of Lyons (c. 130–202), for example, similarly wrote that God "became what we are in order to make us what he is himself" and that "[i]f the Word became man, it was so men may become gods."[13]

Athanasius's soteriology became associated with what became known as the Alexandrian school. By the time the Council of Chalcedon (451) became necessary, the Alexandrian school had developed a soteriology and corresponding Christology distinct from what was known as the Antiochene school. Antiochene Christology relied on an understanding of the Logos coming to dwell in the human Jesus. Where Alexandrians emphasized a soteriology dependent on a union between God and humanity, the Antiochene school emphasized the preservation of God's divine characteristics and humanity's human

---

10. Kelly, *Early Christian Doctrines*, 152.

11. Richard A. Norris Jr., ed. and trans., *The Christological Controversy* (Minneapolis: Fortress Press, 1980).

12. Athanasius's famous conclusion of *On the Incarnation* was that the Logos became human so humans may become god—not in the same sense as the Logos, but "by appointment and grace."

13. Irenaeus, *Against Heresies*, Book V, Preface.

COMMUNICATING GRACE

characteristics. Each side held to some level of both union and distinction, so the difference was a matter of emphasis that resulted in different soteriologies and Christologies.

Arguing against the Antiochene position, Cyril of Alexandria insisted that the Logos coming to dwell in a human did not account for the kind of soteriological shift that was needed. Cyril's Christology was a mature articulation of Athanasian soteriology. For Athanasius, the "heart of Christianity" is "the presence of God amid human kind, made human."[14] God's saving work was in the incarnation and it was essential for Athanasius that the Logos suffer and die the death owed by all humanity. In this death, the debt to God's honor was paid and death itself was overcome. Therefore, Christ must be the incarnation of the fullness of God because only the properties of the fullness of God would save humanity and make them divine. If God merely came to dwell in human flesh through Jesus, incarnation was inadequate to save more than just humanity. Cyril argues, "how then can he be said to have become the Savior of the cosmos, and not rather [only] of man, as a pilgrim and traveler through whom we have also been saved?"[15] For the Alexandrians, the relation between God and creation could not be adequately expressed as an indwelling. Emphasizing the unity of divine and human, Cyril insisted that the union in Christ is such that both his divinity and his humanity subsist in one hypostasis.

Such a union concerned Antiochenes, who felt that the humanity of Christ became swallowed by the Logos. Nestorius, archbishop of Constantinople, opposed Cyril's hypostatic union, arguing that it "signified a kind of physical or chemical union of two substances—and therefore 'mixture' or 'confusion' in which the deity of Christ was altered or modified."[16] Indeed, as Norris points out, "'one hypostasis' and 'one nature' were phrases which, for Cyril, signified the fact that the humanity belonged so intimately to the Logos that there was

14. Justo Gonzalez, *The Story of Christianity: Vol. 1, The Early Church to the Dawn of the Reformation* (San Francisco: Harper, 1984), 174.
15. Pelikan, *The Christian Tradition*, citing Cyril, 234.
16. Norris, *The Christological Controversy*, 29.

125

TOWARD A BETTER WORLDLINESS

actually only one subject or subsistent reality in Jesus. The one hypostasis and the one nature are the Logos himself."[17]

By understanding Cyril's insistence on the communication of attributes as an expression of Athanasian soteriology, it becomes evident that Cyril's position relied on eucharistic doctrine and practice as union with Christ.[18] Cyril's interest was not necessarily the unity of Christ's person itself; he cared about the unity of Christ's person because of the implications for the Eucharist.[19] For Cyril, every Eucharist is a reincarnation of the Logos.[20] Just as the divine and human were united in Christ, so the believer is united with Christ, and Christ's benefits are communicated to us. Christ's body instills life into our body. If the Logos and his flesh were separable, our unity with Christ and his benefits would be in question as well.

In the end, Pope Leo proposed a compromise position that Christ be understood as "one 'person' having two natures, each of which was the principle of a distinct mode of activity."[21] Thus the Council of Chalcedon affirmed Christ had two natures in one person. One nature was consubstantial with God and one with humanity, but the natures were united in one hypostasis. The *communicatio idiomatum* then was a way of articulating the relationship between humanity and divinity in Christ that maintained both union and difference.

The communication of properties was an integral part of Cyril's and Athanasius's soteriology and sacramentology, both of which depended on a profound union between God and humanity. With the nominalist influence of a strict separation between creator and creation, the soteriological importance of this union and even sharing of God's divinity was seemingly lost in late medieval, Reformation, and modern thought. However, as I will demonstrate, although it has been only marginally articulated, the patristic and biblical witness to this soteriological union was retained by Luther. In fact, the *communicatio*

---

17. Ibid., 28.
18. See Pelikan and Henry Chadwick, "Eucharist and Christology in the Nestorian Controversy," *Journal of Theological Studies* 2, no. 2 (1951): 145–64.
19. Chadwick, "Eucharist and Christology in the Nestorian Controversy," 153.
20. Ibid., 155.
21. Norris, *The Christological Controversy*, 29.

idiomatum became a touchstone of the scope of his theology linking everything from the sacraments, justification, and economic and social ethics.

Contemporary Debates about Luther's Interpretation of the *communicatio idiomatum*

To argue, as Hamm has, that Luther's concept of gift was unprecedented outside of biblical witness and signifies a break with earlier Christian concepts of gift that rely on exchange, fails to recognize the constructive ways Luther was reinterpreting, repeating, and extending early church thinkers. Rather than rejecting early church models of exchange in favor of a new concept of a pure gift, Luther's theology may be interpreted as a continuation and expansion of these models of soteriological and christological exchange and union.

The importance of the *communicatio idiomatum* for Luther cannot be overestimated. French Reformation historian Marc Lienhard explains that it is a key concept of Luther's Christology.[22] In a recent essay included in the provocatively titled collection on Luther's interpretation of the *communicatio idiomatum*, *Creator est Creatura*, Oswald Bayer argues that Luther's "Christology is really the doctrine of the *communicatio idiomatum*."[23] More than just Christology, though, K. O. Nilson argues it is the very heart of his theology because it articulates the relationship between God and creation. "It is the *communicatio idiomatum* by which Luther's whole system of theological thought stands or falls. The *communicatio idiomatum* is not merely a consequence of the unity in Christ, but an expansion of this unity itself and the whole basis on which, according to Luther, life and happiness rests."[24] Johann Anselm Steiger similarly emphasizes the pervasive influence of this doctrine on Luther's thought, arguing it is the

---

22. Marc Lienhard, *Luther: Witness to Jesus Christ, Stages and Themes of the Reformer's Christology*, trans. Edwin H. Robertson (Minneapolis: Augsburg Fortress, 1982), 335.
23. Oswald Bayer and Benjamin Gleede, *Creator est Creatura: Luthers Christologie als Lehre von der Idiomenkommunikation* (Berlin: Walter de Gruyter), 23.
24. Nilsson, cited in Lienhard, *Luther*, 355n100.

"hermeneutical motor of his whole theology . . . the axle around which many other theological themes now begin to turn."[25] As Lienhard explains, "In the sense that Luther intends it, it becomes a kind of touchstone of true theology."[26]

But how does Luther intend it? Debate of this question reemerges today, just as the question of the role of the *communicatio idiomatum* and the proper articulation of it became a locus of debate among the German and Swiss Reformers because of the ways it was employed in eucharistic theologies. Just as Steiger demonstrated how Luther expands the doctrine even beyond Christology and sacramentology to his theology of justification, I will argue he expands it again in his ethics. Interpreted in this way, his Christology, sacramentology, justification, and ethics are unified, a repetition of an exchangist (Steiger even suggests a *perichoretic*[27]) christological theme emphasizing God's entwined relationship with and commitment to the world.

Typically, Luther's ethics or horizontal, worldly, and exchangist relations are seen as a secondary consequence of the primary (pure gift) of relation with God. This is a pattern we have repeatedly witnessed from Sittler to Holm and others. Prioritizing a pure gift that gives way to exchange inevitably gives ethics and worldly relations a place of secondary importance, behind individual relations with God. However, in light of the central place of the *communicatio idiomatum* (especially in the particular way Luther understands it) in Luther's thought, I suggest that we might see the entire scope of the Christian life and experience as a repetition of a christological theme of indwelling and relational exchange.

---

25. Steiger, 125. In *Beyond Christology*, he argues this doctrine was key for "Luther's doctrine of the Lord's Supper, anthropology, the doctrine of justification, scriptural hermeneutics, rhetoric, the theology of pastoral care . . . theology of creation . . . [and] the cornerstone of Luther's humor" (ibid.).

26. Lienhard, *Luther*, 335.

27. Steiger, "The *communicatio idiomatum*," 125.

Communicating the Body of Christ

[B]y means of this sacrament, all self-seeking love is voided out
and gives place to that which seeks the common good of all.
When you have partaken of this sacrament . . .
your heart must go out in love and learn that this
is a sacrament of love. As love and support are given you,
you in turn must render love and support to Christ
in his needy ones. . . . The sacrament has no blessing
and significance unless love grows daily and so changes a person
that he is made one with the others. In times past this sacrament was
so properly used, and the people were taught to understand this
fellowship so well, that they even gathered food and
material goods in the church, and . . . distributed
them among those who were in need.
—Luther, "The Blessed Sacrament"

Some of the questions and concerns Cyril and Nestorius expressed remained with the church at least through the Reformation. In the fifth century, christological debates drew on and were influenced by eucharistic and liturgical practice. Conversely, in the sixteenth century, proposed shifts in eucharistic and liturgical practices by the Reformers reignited many of the christological questions and concerns raised by Cyril and Nestorius. In both contexts, controversy intensified around the *communicatio idiomatum*. While Luther famously rejected the interpretation of the mass as sacrifice in the "Babylonian Captivity of the Church" (1520), Reformation scholars note that, by comparison, the Eucharist and Christology were not a locus of controversy and debate between the Lutheran reformers and Roman Catholic representatives.[28] Even the doctrine of transubstantiation was not a point of particularly strong contention. Although Luther rejected it, his main objection was merely that it was an inappropriate attempt to explain something that is truly a mystery.

His alternative description of the union between the sacramental elements and the body of Christ is the first place we can see Luther's

---

28. For example, Article Ten of the Apology to the Augsburg Confession on the presence of Christ in the Eucharist (the Reformers'—mainly Melanchthon's—response to the Catholic reply to the Augsburg Confession) is very short since it mainly expresses agreement between the Lutheran, Roman, and Orthodox positions.

extension of the *communicatio idiomatum* beyond the bounds of Christology. Instead of Christ being bodily present by transubstantiation, Luther extends the *communicatio idiomatum*, arguing that the bread, wine, and water are united to Christ's body through a hypostatic union.[29] Although he expands the doctrine beyond the relation between the two natures as outlined in the Chalcedonian creed, there was precedent for this eucharistic extension in Cyril's thought. Where Cyril based his Christology on eucharistic practice and thought, Luther based his eucharistic thought on Christology. Cyril held that every Eucharist was a reincarnation of the Logos so that by taking Christ's body in the supper, the Logos implants itself in us and makes us incorruptible and immortal. In this way, Cyril's soteriology and sacramentology depended on the unity and exchange of the *communicatio idiomatum*, shared with the believer by taking in the body of Christ so that in the supper Christ's properties are communicated to the believer. Since the elements uniting with Christ's body are not transformed, they remain bread, wine, and water. Christ's body does not take their place but is present "in, with, and under" them.[30] We might say then, that where transubstantiation removes difference to create unity, the hypostatic union preserves it.

While Luther placed a great deal of importance on the sacramental union with Christ's body, the unity of the reformation movement paid dearly for it. While Luther's Christology had not been in question in his debates with the Roman Catholic Church,[31] after several attempts to unite, the German and Swiss reform movements efforts fell apart by the mid-1500s, mainly because of divergent views on the Eucharist and

---

29. For example, in his "Confession Concerning the Lord's Supper," Luther writes, "In the Eucharist, the body and blood of our Lord Jesus Christ are present, but at the same time the substance of the bread and wine that is, not through transubstantiation, but in a hypostatic union of Christ's humanity and the substances of the bread and wine." Cited in Lee Palmer Wandel, *The Eucharist in the Reformation: Incarnation and Liturgy* (Cambridge: Cambridge University Press, 2005), 217. See also Paul Althaus, *The Theology of Martin Luther*, trans. Robert C. Schultz (Minneapolis: Fortress Press, 1966), 179, on the Eucharist as an extension of the *communicatio idiomatum* and Lienhard on the parallel of the hypostatic union with the sacramental union (Lienhard, *Luther*, 220).

30. "In, with, and under" became the standard Lutheran position following *The Formula of Concord Solid Declaration*.

31. Lienhard, *Luther*, 23.

COMMUNICATING GRACE

Christology. At the root of this conflict were different positions with regard to the *communicatio idiomatum.*

Echoing Athanasius's and Cyril's earlier arguments, Luther insisted that by putting in question sacramental union, one also put in question the saving union between the human and divine natures in Christ.[32] For Swiss reformer Ulrich Zwingli, however, the preservation of the sacramental union was a confused mix of spiritual and material realms, attributing spiritual effect to a material act. Zwingli held that the sacraments were a sign of grace, of what was taking place in the soul of the believer, and thus were not a means or communication of grace as Luther held. Luther and Zwingli could never agree to join their reform movements together because Zwingli ultimately rejected the doctrine of the *communicatio idiomatum* altogether as a confusion or mixture of what should be kept completely distinct.

Contemporary theologians and historians point out that Calvin's Christology and sacramentology were much closer to Luther's than Zwingli's.[33] However, when an agreement of unity was signed between the Swiss Calvinist and Zwinglian reform movements, the German Lutherans declared any promise of an agreement between the Calvinist and Lutheran movements poisoned. Luther and Calvin agreed that Christ was present in the sacrament, and Calvin, like Luther, was concerned that the Eucharist create unity between the believer and Christ. The disagreement arose, however, around the question of Christ's bodily presence, and again, the interpretation of the *communicatio idiomatum,* which both reformers maintained but interpreted differently.

While Luther would not affirm the sacredness of the flesh in and of itself, his insistence on the believer's participation in and union with the flesh of Christ emerges as a surprising contrast to common modern misperceptions of Luther as someone who shifted Western Christian thought away from a rootedness in material life on account of his emphasis on an immaterial Word of God.[34] In fact, Luther's

---

32. See Lienhard, *Luther,* 220.
33. Davis, for example. Thomas J. Davis, *This Is My Body: The Presence of Christ in Reformation Thought* (Grand Rapids, MI: Baker Academic, 2008).

131

TOWARD A BETTER WORLDLINESS

understanding of the Word of God is always a fleshly, material, incarnated word. The believer's encounter with Christ is not merely intellectual, psychological, emotional, or spiritual (where spiritual is defined as a rejection of matter), but always with a material, fleshly Christ. As we will see, this emphasis on the bodily encounter with Christ, across both time and space, is a particular consequence of Luther's interpretation of the communication of properties.

Union with the past, historical flesh of Christ was not enough for Luther. He felt that although the historical Christ and his acts remain essential, they must be communicated—both verbally and materially—to the believer in every time and place.[35] In this sense, the Word and sacraments had to be for Luther, as they were for Cyril, a continuation of the incarnation, a prolongation of the body of Christ. Marc Lienhard notes, for example, that "One can say, as Luther does, that the incarnation continues in the sense that God continues to offer himself to us by the physical elements that are the bread and the wine of the Eucharist. . . . These physical elements have certainly not supplanted the humanity of Christ as such, but prolong it in some way, constituting his current way of being present."[36] Similarly, Hermann Sasse explains that, for Luther, the sacrament of the altar is "an extension of the incarnation into our time and into our lives,"[37] while Dawn DeVries notes that the "preached Word not only conveys Christ but continues Christ's living presence in the world."[38] Again, this communication is not just limited to an oral message because, like

---

34. For example, Wandel, a noted Reformation scholar, continues this misinterpretation in *The Eucharist in the Reformation: Incarnation and Liturgy*.

35. "For Luther, the salvation of believers is and remains linked to the flesh of Christ. It is necessary that this be given to them, because in it alone they find their justification. It is not enough for us to see that it is attested that God saves us, or that we can be content to receive only the benefits of the redemptive work of Christ accomplished in the past. We must receive Christ himself, Christ with his flesh because it was in his flesh that he accomplished redemption. Everything depends then on the identity between the historic Christ and Christ present, between Christ dead on the cross and Christ who now constitutes my righteousness before God" (Lienhard, *Luther*, 222).

36. Lienhard, *Luther*, 200.

37. Hermann Sasse, *This Is My Body: Luther's Contention for the Real Presence in the Sacrament of the Altar* (Minneapolis: Augsburg Fortress, 1959), 153.

38. Dawn DeVries, "The Incarnation and the Sacramental Word: Calvin's and Schleiermacher's Sermons on Luke 2," in *Toward the Future of Reformed Theology: Tasks, Topics, Traditions*, ed. David Willis-Watkins and Michael Welker (Grand Rapids, MI: Eerdmans, 1999), 392.

COMMUNICATING GRACE

preaching, Luther considered the sacraments a fleshly, "incarnational event."[39] In such articulations of an extended and prolonged body of Christ, we begin to see the particular relevance of the gift that resists linear time-and-space causality.

Calvin also emphasized union with Christ, but could not accept the bodily, fleshly presence of Christ in the Eucharist. In order for Christ's body to be present in every celebration of the sacrament, as well as, according to Scripture, ascended to the right hand of God, Luther insisted that Christ's body—even his *human* body—shared in the omnipresence of God through the communication of attributes.[40] To Calvin, the ubiquitous or omnipresent body of Christ was unacceptable because it sacrificed that which united Christ's body (made it *homoousious*) with the human body because he understood that the human body was, by definition, limited to the constrictions of time and space.

The key difference between the two reformers' views on the *communicatio idiomatum* lies in whether there is an exchange of properties between *natures* or an exchange of properties in the *person* of Christ. For Calvin, the *communicatio idiomatum* expressed a unity between the divine and human in the *person* of Christ. He maintained the difference between them by insisting that while there was unity in the person, Christ's divine nature and his human nature remained completely distinct. He rejected, as Joseph Tylenda explains, "any real ontological exchange of properties of one nature to the other."[41] For Calvin, the communication happens only on the level of "a *person*, a *subject* having that nature," but not the "nature itself."[42]

For the sake of clarity, the first generation of theologians after Luther articulated different levels of exchange in Luther's interpretation of the *communicatio idiomatum*. These are useful in explaining Calvin's acceptance of the ancient doctrine and the ways his

---

39. Ibid., 393.
40. I am using *communicatio idiomatum*, communication of attributes, and communication of properties interchangeably throughout this chapter.
41. Joseph N. Tylenda, "Calvin's Understanding of the Communication of Properties," *Westminster Theological Journal* 38, no. 1 (Fall 1975): 61.
42. Ibid., 59.

views diverged from Luther's particular articulation.[43] The first level of exchange, the *genus apostelesmaticum*, was shared by Luther and Calvin. This genus "attributes all the activities of Christ not to only one of the two natures, but to the unique person of the Savior."[44]

A second level the Lutheran tradition named the *genus majestaticum* because Christ's human nature is here considered to have become "majestic" as it is permeated with properties of the divine nature such as omnipresence. This is how, for Luther, the Christian could be united with the true body and blood of Christ across time and space. Lutheran orthodoxy affirmed this genus in the *Formula of Concord*, but Calvin and his followers could not accept it because they believed it resulted in lost unity with the defining characteristics of a human body.

It is not well known, Lienhard points out, that Luther himself goes one step further than Lutheran orthodoxy was willing to go in the communication of properties. Where the *genus majestaticum* accepts a communication of attributes from God to human nature, Luther's insistence on what later theologians called the *genus tapeinoticum* (or genus of humility) suggested a communication of *creaturely properties to the divine*. In other words, while Lutheran orthodoxy limited the exchange between God and creation to God's active gift to passive creatures, Luther emphasized the reverse as well: that God is so united with creaturely life that God cannot be but profoundly affected and moved by it. Lienhard, for example, explains that "one of the characteristic traits of Luther's christology is to envisage a kind of participation in Jesus Christ of the divine nature in human weakness."[45] Luther writes of the sufferings of the human nature being "communicated, attributed, and given to the divine nature." So, Luther does not hesitate to insist that "God is born, suckled and bred, sleeps in the cradle, is cold, walks, falls, wanders, wakes up, eats, drinks, suffers, dies, etc."[46] This profound and crucial aspect of Luther's Christology

43. These are articulated in the Formula of Concord.
44. Lienhard, *Luther*, 339.
45. Ibid., 340.
46. Luther, *Table Talk*, in Lienhard, *Luther*, 340–41. See also Thesis four of Luther's "Disputation on the Humanity and Divinity of Christ": "it is true to say: This man created the world, and this

COMMUNICATING GRACE

and soteriology was thus essentially cut off from the later Lutheran tradition and remains a key point of debate today.

Where most others (Calvinists as well as Lutherans in the tradition of Lutheran orthodoxy that followed) would want to clarify that God *in Christ* is born, and so on, implying that these events are attributed solely to the person of Christ and not human nature in general, Luther insisted that where God is, God is fully. This is no divine toe-dip into the pool of creature-hood, but a full and permanent baptismal emersion into the vicissitudes of life in the world. As Piotr Malysz explains, "underlying Luther's variegated Christological reflection was a fundamental and uncompromised insistence on the concreteness of the exchange of properties between Christ's two natures. As Luther saw it, only when taken as concrete—that is, reciprocally holding nothing back—can the togetherness of the natures in Christ's person give adequate expression to his identity as Saviour."[47] The parallels with Athanasius's soteriological exchange whereby God becomes fully human so that humans might become God comes to be entirely evident at this point, along with a clear indication that Luther's joyous exchange is merely a soteriological application of a much more pervasive christological theme in his theology.[48]

From Historical and Contemporary Concerns to New Possibilities?

The extent to which Luther allows the world to move God in the *communicatio idiomatum* has been an uncomfortable problem for many theologians over the ages.[49] In the *Formula of Concord*, Luther's followers rejected the *genus tapeinoticum* on the grounds that it limited the divine

---

God suffered, died, was buried, etc." cited in Paul Hinlicky, "Luther's Anti-Docetism" (Oswald and Gleede, eds., *Creator est Creatura*, 154).

47. Malysz, "Review of *Creator Est Creatura: Luthers Christologie als Lehre von der Idiomenkommunikation*, ed. Oswald Bayer and Benjamin Gleede," *Reviews in Religion & Theology* 16 (2009): 618.

48. Lienhard notes this connection.

49. A common critique of Luther is that he is promoting patripassianism or modalism. Marc Lienhard defends Luther's position against claims of patripassianism characteristic of modalism: "In order to distinguish Luther's position from modalism, Marc Lienhard suggests the term diepassianism to indicate that, in Luther's case, instead of the Father's suffering in Christ, it is God who suffers" (cited in Arnfridur Gudmundsdottir, *Meeting God on the Cross: Christ, the Cross, and the Feminist Critique* [New York: Oxford University Press, 2010], 82).

TOWARD A BETTER WORLDLINESS

nature and was inconsistent with God's unchangeability. More recently, David J. Luy has argued that modern theologians' (including Steiger, Nilsson, and Lienhard) embrace of Luther's *genus tapeinoticum* is misplaced—casting doubt on whether this is an accurate articulation of Luther's position at all. In *Dominus Mortis*, Luy argues that what modern theologians have highlighted as a unique turn in Luther's theology—an embrace of human characteristics such as suffering and death received by God—is "hardly a major innovation." Comparing Luther's statements to those of others in the same time period, Luy concludes that, "by insisting that God suffers or dies Luther is, in fact, taking up a long and distinguished history" since late medieval theologians regularly commented on human properties being given to God in the hypostatic union.[50] Ultimately, Luy is concerned that modern theologians have mistaken Luther's uniqueness on this matter and thus interpret Luther as a kind of "hinge point" for the rejection of divine impassibility. In modern theologies, a rejection of divine impassibility has led to a shift from soteriologies where Christ condescends to the human situation, only to rescue us from it, to an emphasis on the soteriological effect of Christ's (and thus God's) solidarity with humanity. Luy argues that although Luther makes statements seeming to imply God forgoes divine impassibility in order to embrace the whole of the human condition, Luther also repeatedly makes clear that he upholds God's impassibility. Therefore, Luy argues that Luther clearly understands that when he says things such as "God dies, suffers, etc.," he refers to suffering in the person of Christ and not the divine nature. Consequently, he concludes that it is inaccurate to suggest, as Lienhard, Steiger, myself, and others have, that Luther holds to a "bidirectional" doctrine of the *communicatio idiomatum* where a mutual exchange between God and humanity is affirmed.

Although Luy's argument is well researched and methodically argued, I believe there are compelling reasons to continue to interpret Luther's doctrine of the *communicatio idiomatum* as mutually reciprocal.

---

50. David J. Luy, *Dominus Mortis: Martin Luther on the Incorruptibility of God in Christ* (Minneapolis: Fortress Press, 2014), 118.

COMMUNICATING GRACE

As I will demonstrate, there are significant economic implications for this particular reading. What's more, I believe some of the most influential modern theologians in the Lutheran tradition, like Dietrich Bonhoeffer and various theologians of the cross, have read Luther in this way to fruitfully and profoundly address their contemporary contexts.

I do agree that it seems historically unlikely Luther would consciously have rejected divine impassibility. Rather than either assuming Luther is consciously making a radical break with the orthodox tradition of God's impassibility or simply not making an innovative statement in this regard at all as Luy argues, it seems more likely that in statements suggesting God receives from the world, Luther is reveling in his common and repeated affirmation of paradox. Luy argues that where Luther suggests God assumes human vulnerabilities and then, also, insists that the divine nature retains its proper characteristics (like impassibility), it would be illogical and self-contradictory for Luther to hold that "the divinity of Christ is impassible by nature, and retains this property even in the event of the incarnation" while also insisting that "Christ's divinity shares in the sufferings of humanity."[51] Luy highlights the logical tension remaining between these positions and suggests that Luther is relying on deeper logic that, much like Calvin's position, maintains strict separation between God's impassibility and human passibility. But isn't such holding of opposites in tension a basic characteristic of Luther's thought? Would he not argue, as he does with other paradoxical beliefs, that in such logical tension, God confuses our logic so that we cannot work our way to God through reason? Isn't this also the case with Luther's insistence that a person is simultaneously saint and sinner? So, while I too find it improbable from a historical perspective that Luther would have intentionally done away with the impassibility of God, I also find it improbable that he would have felt the need to resolve this tension logically. Given how often he relies on this il/logic, it seems Luther would have reveled in it, rather than felt compelled to

51. Luy, *Dominus Mortis*, 122.

137

TOWARD A BETTER WORLDLINESS

resolve it. Therefore, I think it more likely that by retaining the tension between God's traditionally held properties and the full embrace of human frailty, Luther cracked open a door that later theologians walked through.

Luy's argument is not all that different from consistent Calvinist concerns. Jürgen Moltmann, for example, explains that in the *genus majestaticum* and *tapeinoticum,* Luther went beyond the boundaries allowed by scholastic theology. He then indicates his own discomfort with Luther's articulation by reiterating Calvin's concerns:

> With the help of the notion of the *communicatio idiomatum* one can attribute the human characteristics of suffering and death to the whole person of Christ. One cannot say: Therefore the divine nature can suffer and die, it is only possible to say: Therefore the person of Christ is mortal. One cannot say: Therefore the body of the risen Christ is omnipresent, but only: Therefore the person of Christ is omnipresent.[52]

In Calvin's case, his main concern was to maintain the soteriological unity between Christ's humanity and human flesh. He describes his view of Luther's *genus majestaticum* and *tapeinoticum* in his *Institutes:*

> [For the Lutherans, Christ's] body was swallowed up by his divinity. I do not say that they think so. But if to fill all things in an invisible manner is numbered among the gifts of the glorified body, it is plain that the substance of the body is wiped out, and that no difference between deity and human nature is left. Then, if Christ's body is so multiform and varied that it shows itself in one place but is invisible in another, where is the very nature of a body, which exists in its own dimensions, and where is its unity?[53]

Calvin's concern remains a legitimate question, particularly for those of us with current concerns to emphasize embodiment with relation to divinity. However, in a context where "simple location" is questioned along with linear causality, might we be able to affirm that Luther's extendable, repeated, prolonged, even ubiquitous body of Christ suggests not so much an opposition to human bodily existence as a

---

52. Jürgen Moltmann, *The Crucified God: The Cross of Christ as the Foundation and Criticism of Christian Theology* (San Francisco: HarperCollins, 1974), 232.
53. Calvin, *Institutes,* Book IV, ch. 17, cited in Wandel, *Eucharist in the Reformation,* 162.

138

revelation about our own bodies of flesh and their relation to nonhuman elements? Might Luther's "majestic" body of Christ also suggest that the boundaries of our bodies, like Christ's, are perhaps not what they seem? Might it reveal that our bodies, like Christ's—while not unlimited—are composed of the stuff of stars as much as microbes? Might it disclose that to be fundamentally human we rely as much on nonhuman matter and organisms as we do on matter that shares human DNA?[54] Does this ubiquitous body reveal something simultaneously humbling and majestic about our selves that cannot be cleanly cut off from "outsiders"—that they dwell within us and that the line between what is inside and outside, self and alien, is not so much blurred as it is multiplied?[55]

By extending the *communicatio idiomatum* beyond Christology to sacramentology Luther emphasized the importance of God's communication of properties not just within the person of Christ, but to created material elements—water, wine, bread, human words. These material elements do not communicate the mere ethereal or psychic presence of Christ but, as Luther insisted, they communicate Christ's physical bodily presence to the sacramental elements. For Luther, the aim was, of course, human centered—the communication of God's saving properties to humans. For such a move to be truly salvific a further extension of the *communicatio idiomatum* to Luther's doctrine of justification was required.

Communicating Justification

In emphasizing Luther's reliance on the *communicatio idiomatum* in his sacramentology, we have already begun to address the impact of these exchanges on Luther's soteriology. Just as with the *genus tapeinoticum*, union has not been a majority position in Lutheran orthodoxy. Melanchthon, Luther's right-hand reformer, for example, did not accept the extent to which Luther understood the *communicatio*

---

54. See earlier references (introduction, etc.) to the microbiome.
55. This is Derrida's alternative to the single Cartesian line between the human and animal in *The Animal That Therefore I Am*.

TOWARD A BETTER WORLDLINESS

idiomatum as an exchange from humanity to God, and furthermore, resolutely rejected a sense of union or God's presence *intra nos* in justification.[56] For Melanchthon and the Lutheran orthodoxy that followed him, God's work is not primarily in union with the Christian *intra nos* but in God's active work on the passive human, *extra nos*. Increasingly, justification became separated from union and deification so that unity with Christ and the community of believers, along with ethics and sanctification, became a secondary effect of forensic justification articulated exclusively as a unilateral or free gift of grace.

Two historically separate minority movements in the Lutheran tradition have emphasized union with God in justification. In their own ways, they have disrupted any assumed break from early soteriologies of union with God and consequently disrupt the Protestant orientation toward increasing individualism with alternative understandings of God's gift. Both Andreas Osiander (sixteenth century) and the recent Finnish interpretation of Luther take issue with the interpretation of justification where any emphasis on God's indwelling presence or union with the human is rejected.

The first movement took place shortly after Luther's death. Andreas Osiander was an important early and active supporter of Luther, present at the Marburg Colloquy where Luther and Zwingli tried to find common theological ground, at the defense of the Reformation before the Roman Catholic Church at Augsburg, and in Smalcald with other reformers. After Luther's death, however, colleagues began to notice what they considered to be significant differences between Osiander's doctrine of justification and Luther's.

Emphasizing Luther's happy exchange as articulated in *The Freedom of a Christian,* Osiander taught that justification "occurs in the marriage of Christ and the believer, the unifying of the believer's soul with the indwelling divine righteousness."[57] However, Melanchthon and his

---

56. Melanchthon and his followers understood the *communicatio idiomatum* primarily in terms of preaching or proclamation rather than ontological union (see Moltmann, *The Crucified God,* 232).

57. Charles P. Arand, James A. Nestingen, and Robert Kolb, *The Lutheran Confessions: History and Theology of the Book of Concord* (Minneapolis: Fortress Press, 2012), 219.

supporters objected to Osiander's emphasis on indwelling grace, and instead, they exclusively emphasized the alien nature of Christ's righteousness outside the human communicated by the verbal word of God. Current supporters of Melanchthon's interpretation and Lutheran orthodoxy Robert Kolb, James Nestingen, and Charles Arand explain that "Melanchthon believed that Osiander's placement of saving righteousness within the sinner destroyed Luther's position that salvation comes from *extra nos* ('outside and apart from ourselves'), the dependence of faith upon God's external Word of promise, and its saving, life-restoring action in the forgiveness of sins."[58] Concerns were also raised by Osiander's contemporaries that he had been too much influenced by his study of Kabbalah and neo-Platonism and thus misinterpreted Christ's presence in the sinner substantially, where Luther understood Christ's work as merit from submitting to the will of God.[59] Furthermore, Kolb, Arand, and Nestingen explain that concerns with Osiander's views arose because his interpretation of grace was not limited to the forgiveness of sins.[60]

Kolb and Arand describe the response to Osiander's views as a resounding and unified rejection by Luther's closest and most ardent supporters. Only Osiander's prince, Duke Albrecht (whom he himself had converted) and pastor, reformer, and theologian Johannes Brenz supported him. Brenz argued the conflict was an un-Christian war of words and pointed out that Osiander himself denied he held the positions his antagonists condemned.[61] The controversy grew to the point that a church council was necessary. The resulting *Formula of Concord* addressed the Osiandrian controversy, deciding against Osiander and affirming Melanchthon's insistence on forensic

---

58. Ibid., 221.
59. Ibid., 217.
60. Ibid., 219. "He did little with the central Lutheran concept of the forgiveness of sins since in his view humanity is completed through this indwelling divine righteousness—in contrast to Luther's concept of the restoration of the proper relationship between God and human creatures through the remission of this sin that separates sinners from God."
61. For example, "He denied that he had ever taught that Christ's sufferings and death were not a part of the sinner's righteousness and minimized the substantial theological difference between him and his opponents" (ibid., 223).

TOWARD A BETTER WORLDLINESS

justification to the exclusion of an ontological indwelling union with Christ.

In the twentieth and twenty-first centuries, concerns similar to Osiander's have been voiced by Finnish Lutheran scholars. Like Osiander, those aligning with the Finnish interpretation of Luther suggest that Luther "before Lutheranism" understood that grace was not simply limited to forensic justification and the forgiveness of sins, but also encompassed a sense of indwelling communion with Christ present in faith.[62]

The Finnish interpretation is the fruit of ecumenical dialogue between the Finnish Lutheran Church and the Russian Orthodox Church beginning in the 1970s. Finnish scholar Tuomo Mannermaa was deeply involved in this dialogue, and as a result of this interdenominational exchange, came to question the dominant German interpretation of Luther's theology of justification and grace. In reading Luther alongside Orthodox understandings of *theosis* or deification, he came to see a different side of Luther, a side that did not fully depart from or reject patristic notions of salvation as deification. The implications of this shift are significant for current Lutheran thought, particularly in articulating an alternative concept of gift and strengthening the connection between justification and justice, faith and love.

The Finns are particularly critical of two significant shifts in the history of Lutheran orthodoxy. Unsurprisingly, they are critical of the positions the *Formula of Concord* took on justification and Osiander's emphasis on Christ's presence *intra nos*. They are also critical of the post-Kantian move away from ontology in Lutheran thought. After Kant, reference to ontology in Luther's writings became ignored or explained away. Any sense of union was constrained to an external

---

62. The "medium of spiritual existence was not the event of 'forensic justification' but the divine person of Christ" (Carl E. Braaten and Robert W. Jenson, eds., *Union with Christ: The New Finnish Interpretation of Luther* [Grand Rapids, MI: Eerdmans, 1998], 105). Milbank addresses the Finnish interpretation, but only in a footnote in *Being Reconciled*. While this interpretation would go a long way, addressing many of his critiques, Milbank explains he chose not to seriously address this interpretation because he finds it historically implausible that Luther would have agreed to their interpretation. What he does not make clear, though, is the distinction between Luther's work and the expression of Lutheranism in Lutheran orthodoxy as has been emphasized here.

union with the will of God, rather than the being of God, so that faith becomes "volitional obedience rather than [an] ontological participation."[63] Where the German-Kantian interpretation suggests Christ's presence is "just a subjective experience or God's 'effect' on the believer," the Finns would like to reemphasize the "real-ontic unity between Christ and the Christian."[64]

One of Mannermaa's first clues that a sense of union had been lost in the Lutheran tradition occurred to him while retranslating Luther's phrase from his lectures on Galatians, "'in ipsa fide Christus adest,'" which Mannermaa translates as "in faith itself Christ is really present."[65] He points out that in a traditional Lutheran forensic interpretation, the Christ pro nobis (Christ for us) of grace and forgiveness is emphasized while a sense of Christus in nobis (Christ within us) is all but lost. As North American scholar Carl Braaten explains in the text that introduced the Finnish interpretation to an American audience, "according to the forensic model of justification, it is as though we are righteous, while in reality we are not. But if through faith we really participate in Christ, we participate in the whole of Christ, who in his divine person communicates the righteousness of God." Recalling the ecumenical and patristic roots of this interpretation highlighted above with regard to Athanasius's soteriology, he then adds, "Here lies the bridge to the Orthodox idea of salvation as deification or theosis."[66]

One of the strengths of the Finnish interpretation is that it addresses a consistent area of weakness in the tradition. With such a strong emphasis on forensic justification as God's work outside of us to the exclusion of any works of our own, the Lutheran tradition has struggled to maintain a robust emphasis on sanctification, becoming holy, and acting with justice. Later reformers, especially Calvin and Melanchthon, distinguish sharply between justification and

63. Braaten and Jenson, Union with Christ, ix.
64. Veli-Matti Kärkkäinen, One with God: Salvation as Deification and Justification (Collegeville, MN: Unitas Books, 2004), 46.
65. Braaten and Jenson, Union with Christ, viii, citing Mannermaa, Der im Glauben gegenwärtige Christus (Hannover: Lutherisches Verlagshaus, 1989).
66. Braaten and Jenson, Union with Christ, viii.

TOWARD A BETTER WORLDLINESS

sanctification. Thwarting a deep presumption of theological history, Mannermaa argues that "at least on the level of terminology, the distinction, drawn in later Lutheranism, between justification as forgiveness and sanctification as divine indwelling, is alien to the Reformer."[67] Rather than separating justification from sanctification and placing them in a hierarchy, Mannermaa and others argue that, for Luther, justification itself encompasses these two aspects: forensic (favor or forgiveness) and effective (gift or participation in the divine life through union with Christ—what is typically considered sanctification).[68] In forensic justification, we are declared righteous by God on account of Christ's work (*extra nos*), and in effective justification, we become righteous in our lives through Christ's indwelling (*intra nos*) presence. It is no longer merely "as though" we were righteous on account of Christ, but we really *become* righteous because justification is no longer just about forgiveness of sins, but participation in divine reality. Consequently, rather than ignoring or deemphasizing sanctification, the Finns argue that Luther fully incorporated it into his concept of justification as the gift of Christ's presence.

In articulating justification in terms of union with Christ, the Finns shift the primary concept of gift from alienable to inalienable. The emphasis on union is a key accessory to exchange that differentiates this mode from a transaction. Rather than a transaction, the inalienable gift is a relational, community-forming exchange. The effect of this shift is demonstrated by Finnish Lutheran Veli-Matti Kärkkäinen, who notes the change from the Lutheran orthodox position which artificially delineates between the person and work (gift) of Christ: "It is highly significant that Luther himself—in contradistinction to later Lutheranism—does not differentiate between the person and work of Christ. Christ himself, his person and his work is the righteousness of man. In the language of the doctrine of justification it means that Christ is both *donum* and favor (not only

---

67. Mannermaa, "Justification and *Theosis* in Lutheran-Orthodox Perspective," in Braaten and Jenson, *Union with Christ*, 38.
68. Ibid.

COMMUNICATING GRACE

favor as subsequent Lutheranism teaches)."[69] Where the person and the work are so separated, this is merely a sign of an alienated gift. For the Finns, grace is no longer just God's favor as alienable gift declared on the sinner from pure exteriority. Rather, Christ both gives and *is* the saving gift because, as Mannermaa continually explains, Christ is truly present in faith: "The favor of God (i.e. the forgiveness of sins and the removal of God's wrath) and His 'gift' (*donum*; God himself, present in the fullness of his essence) unite in the person of Christ."[70] The shift we see here moves from idealizing the alienable gift indicating transaction and commodification to the inalienable gift as Christ, who both gives and is the content of the gift.[71]

The Finnish interpretation continues to gain in influence among Lutheran theologians and laypeople. Unfortunately, in spite of what might be promising insights applicable to contemporary concerns about the (often gendered) power dynamics in models of justification or the important shift we have been tracking toward relations where an internal/external boundary is disrupted in all relations (divine, human, other-than-human), it quickly becomes clear that, for the most part, they are not aiming for constructive and creative applications of the tradition for some of the world's most pressing contemporary concerns. Instead, the Finns are limited by their tone of recovering and reclaiming the "true" or "original" Luther. Consequently, they have been drawn into antagonistic relations with the majority of Luther scholars who are primarily influenced by a history of German scholarship. As a result, the gift of their interpretation gets distracted by arguments over who has claim to the true and original Luther.

I suggest that such minority interpretations of Luther emphasizing union would be more productively framed as creative, constructive Lutheran proposals for contemporary thought than as discoveries of

---

69. Kärkkäinen, "'Christian as Christ to the Neighbor': On Luther's Theology of Love," *International Journal of Systematic Theology* 6, no. 2 (2004): 107.

70. Tuomo Mannermaa, *Christ Present in Faith: Luther's View of Justification* (Minneapolis: Fortress Press, 2005), 5.

71. "Identifying the gifts from God with something unidentical with God emphasizes the forensic aspects of justification and the quadrille of sacrifice. On the contrary, when the gifts from God are understood as aspects of God's self-giving, the ontological aspects of justification are similarly strengthened" (Holm, *Word—Being—Gift*, 109).

145

TOWARD A BETTER WORLDLINESS

the "true" Luther. In doing so, we would find that the gift of reformation theology, like the unconditioned gift, is itself an extended communication with the tradition, dispersing through many trajectories, rather than a gift that must return to its origin. Such constructive proposals might be aimed at addressing current contextually significant religious, societal, and ecological desires for connection, rather than an overwhelming concern for one's personal and individual standing before God.

In my opinion, the Finns are not so much wrong in their historical arguments as missing a profound opportunity to connect with current gender and eco/nomic concerns. Luther's ubiquitous body of Christ and the *genus tapeinoticum* have been—and for some, continue to be—somewhat of a Lutheran orthodox embarrassment. Similarly, the emphasis on union has also been relegated to the margins because it calls into question some of the most rigidly maintained marks of later Lutheran orthodoxy: dualisms between inside and outside, self and other, God and creation, activity and passivity. Luther's ubiquitous body, the *genus tapeinoticum* and an emphasis on union, have generally been dismissed and filed under "Luther's excesses." But might these margins of Luther's thought and Lutheran orthodoxy now be creative and vivifying resources for contemporary constructive theologies?

Going even beyond Luther, building off his insights, might we let the *genus tapeinoticum* reveal a deeper and more reciprocal sense of exchange between creator and created than Lutheran orthodoxy generally accepts? Might the ubiquitous body of Christ reveal something majestic about creaturely bodies—not in and of themselves, but in their *perichoretic* interconnectedness and interdependence with God and all things?[72] Might the prolonged and repeated body of Christ shift our understanding to see that the incarnation of God continues in its extended trajectory and is ever new, fresh, and enfleshed for

---

72. This is a conclusion, it would seem, that goes beyond Luther's thought. I do not argue that he would maintain any majesty of the flesh apart from God. Nor does my constructive proposal maintain any majesty apart from God. The constructive shift I'm arguing for is that the majesty of the flesh would be found with its graced nature, in the ways it is given us through the multiplicity of gifts and exchanges with others, both divine and creaturely.

the world? Instead of rigorously maintaining a duality between *intra nos* and *extra nos*, could we not also say that the limit between self and other, inside and outside must be held in tension with Luther's prolongation of the fleshly body of Christ through time and space, his insistence on difference preserving union between Christ's body and the sacramental elements, and a scandalous sense of community-forming exchange between creation and creator?

Finally, what seems most provocative in the Finnish interpretation is an as-yet untapped possibility to disrupt old assumptions about the kind of self Luther's theology constructs. I see potential to trouble patriarchal, separatist, heterosexist, and static understandings of the self and God.[73] Rather than being defined by what we are not and who we are separated from, there is opportunity here to articulate the self according to who or what we are in relation with. Rather than allowing us to trace the modern sovereign subject from Augustinian interiority through Lutheran individualism to Descartes's *ego cogito*, I think the rhetoric of participation in and union with Christ can cause us to pause and look again at the kind of self Protestant theology could invigorate. Instead of a precursor of *ego cogito*, I think what we may find is this selfsame, self-knowing, self-controlled ego radically put in question by constitutive relationship. Such an intuition of a disrupted rather than a fortified modern sovereign subjectivity is further reinforced by examining the influence of the *communicatio idiomatum* on Luther's social and economic ethics.

---

73. For other, related, feminist engagements with the Finnish interpretation see Kathryn Kleinhans and Kirsi Stjerna. Regarding the Finnish interpretation Kleinhans notes: "The imputation of righteousness effects regeneration in the believer. I find in this recovered insight a useful image not only for talking about Christian faith and life but also for developing a more robust christology that is both Lutheran and feminist," in "Christ as Bride/Groom: A Lutheran Feminist Relational Christology," *Transformative Lutheran Theologies: Feminist, Womanist, and Mujerista Perspectives*, ed. Mary J. Streufert (Minneapolis: Fortress Press, 2010), 126. See also Kirsi Stjerna, "Ongoing Reformation of Language and Spirituality: Intersections with the Finnish Interpretation of Luther and Feminist Scholarship," *Currents in Theology and Mission* 43, no. 3 (2016): 17–21.

Communicating with Christ as Neighbor

This is what it means to change into one another through love,
to lose one's own form and take on that which is common to all.
—Luther, "The Blessed Sacrament of the Holy
and True Body and Blood of Christ (1519)"[74]

Luther's economic ethics and his eucharistic theology are inseparable.
—Cynthia Moe-Lobeda[75]

A case for one final extension of the *communicatio idiomatum* in Luther's thought is both possible and particularly significant. This may be the most applicable extension for current concerns, and yet, it also seems to be the most unfamiliar. With others, I have highlighted the ways that Luther has extended the divine human union from Christology to the sacraments to justification as union as well as forgiveness. In this section, I will demonstrate that Luther expands this doctrine still further to the social and economic ethical relations that revolve around an exchange of possessions or properties between Christ, the Christian, and the neighbor.

As mentioned earlier, a consistent concern in the Lutheran tradition has been the secondary or underemphasized place of ethics in relation to justification. Finnish scholar Veli-Matti Kärkkäinen articulates the kind of integration of Christology, sacramentology, and ethics we are aiming for: "As Christ has given himself to the Christian in the bread and wine, so also do Christians form a single bread and drink as they participate in the Eucharist. The Christian is bread to feed the hungry neighbor and drink to quench their thirst."[76] While not explicitly aligned with the Finnish interpretation of Luther, Marc Lienhard also recognizes the role of deification in Luther's thought, yet argues that the reformer reoriented this ancient theme toward worldly concerns.

---

74. Luther, "The Blessed Sacrament of the Holy and True Body and Blood of Christ (1519)," *Luther's Works, Vol. 35: Word and Sacrament,* ed. E. Theodore Bachmann (Minneapolis: Fortress Press, 1960), 48–73. Emphasis added.
75. Cynthia Moe-Lobeda, "Globalization in Light of Luther's Eucharistic Economic Ethics," *Dialog* 42, no. 3 (2003): 252.
76. Kärkkäinen, "'Christian as Christ to the Neighbour': On Luther's Theology of Love," 114.

> One is not able to exclude entirely the idea that the theme of divinization was present to a certain extent in the mind of Luther. The contrary would have been astonishing when one remembers how familiar he was with the patristic writings. However, it is certain that this theme takes a new turn with him. . . . [O]ne can effectively speak of man's becoming the Word, but for Luther it is less a question of envisaging a communication of the divine life than it is of seeing conformity of human beings with God on the ethical plane. . . . What is important to Luther is less a participation in the divine life than the personification of human beings, their humanization when they again become the image of God by faith.[77]

While Lienhard does not appear to see that "communication of the divine life" or "participation" might actually be a form of "conformity of human beings with God on the ethical plane," Luther himself makes such a connection.

In *The Freedom of a Christian*, Luther writes, "Surely we are named after Christ not because he is absent from us but because he dwells in us, that is because we believe in him and are Christs one to another and do to our neighbors as Christ does to us. . . . We conclude, therefore, that a Christian lives not in himself but in Christ and in his neighbor. . . . He lives in Christ through faith and his neighbor through love."[78] Here, Luther clearly connects union between Christ and the Christian to indwelling union between neighbors. As in the incarnation and the sacraments, Christ is present, bodily prolonged or extended in the works of Christians toward those they encounter.[79]

The reverse is also true; Christ not only becomes embodied in the Christian, but in the neighbor one meets as well. Luther explains, "There [in the suffering and needy neighbor] we should find and love God; that is, we should serve the neighbor and do good to him, whenever we want to do good to God and serve him."[80] Note here that the gift of the ethical act to the neighbor is simultaneously affirmed as a gift to God. Remarkably, this is a reversal of Saarinen's and

77. Lienhard, *Luther*, 54.
78. Luther, "Freedom of the Christian," *Luther's Works, Volume 31: Career of the Reformer I*, ed. Harold J. Grimm and Helmut T. Lehmann (Minneapolis: Fortress Press, 1957), 371.
79. See Mannermaa, *Christ Present in Faith*, "Luther argues that Christ . . . becomes, as it were, incarnate in Christians' works," 50.
80. Luther, *WA*, 17, 99, cited in Althaus, *The Theology of Martin Luther*, 133.

Gregersen's nonlinear beneficiary. In their example, the Christian is the beneficiary of Christ's gift of sacrifice, but here, God is the indirect beneficiary of gifts between creatures. This multilateral gifting structure would not be possible without the *genus tapeinoticum* and its profound sense of the bilateral communicability of divine and creaturely properties.

In this social and economic encounter with another, the incarnational communication of attributes between God, Christ, Christian, and neighbor is fully extended. Luther aligns traditionally held vertical relations to God with horizontal relations to creaturely neighbors. He explains, the "commandment to love God is fully and completely subsumed in the commandment to love our neighbor. . . . It was for this reason that he laid aside his divine form and took on the form of a servant so that he might draw our love for him down to earth and attach it to our neighbor."[81] Elsewhere, he condenses this collapse of the commandments, stating simply, "To love God is to love the neighbor."[82]

In his Galatians lectures, he writes of a noteworthy exchange between Christ, the Christian, and the neighbor. Remarkably, here, the exchange with Christ is not free, but creates a particular kind of debt. The gift turns out to be unconditioned or noncircular because repayment of the debt is not directed back to the donor, but disseminated to the neighbor. Luther encourages the Christian to be so united with Christ that they *are* Christ, not holding individual claim to any divine gifts as personal possessions, but ensuring these gifts continue to disperse. Explaining why Christians should not differentiate themselves from those in need, but meet the need with their own properties, Luther writes,

> Furthermore, if there is anything in us, it is not our own; it is a gift of God. But if it is a gift of God, then it is entirely a debt one owes to love, that is, to the law of Christ. And if it is a debt owed to love, then I must serve others with it, not myself. Thus my learning is not my own; it belongs to the unlearned and is the debt I owe to them. My chastity is

81. Ibid.
82. Luther, WA, TR 5, 5906, cited in Althaus, *The Theology of Martin Luther*, 133.

not my own; it belongs to those who commit sins of the flesh. . . . Thus my wisdom belongs to the foolish, my power to the oppressed. Thus my wealth belongs to the poor, my righteousness to the sinners.[83]

Gifts, even and especially those given by Christ, are meant to continue being exchanged. Christ's benefits can—and if properly used, must be—communicated to ourselves and to our neighbors. What seems to be wholly and most personally "my possessions"—my righteousness, my morality, my learning—are only proper gifts when communicated from me to another. Just as in Christ's communication of properties, where seemingly essential characteristics of God and human are actually communicated one to another, so also one's property, that which is "proper" to oneself (like learning, morality, etc.), is actually communicated from others and can be shared with others. Here, it becomes clear that Luther's interpretation of the *communicatio idiomatum* shapes his view of service and ethics, both personal and economic.

Such an articulation of ethics is inextricable from the celebration of communion: "You must take to heart the infirmities and needs of others as if they were your own. Then offer to others your strength, as if it were their own, just as Christ does for you in the sacrament. *This is what it means to change into one another through love, to lose one's own form and take on that which is common to all.*"[84] No love or work for God exists apart from love or work for the created other. God, self, and neighbor here communicate their attributes—even "change into one another"—so that love of God can only be properly expressed *as* love of neighbor and any act of love for neighbor is an act of love for self and God. From this perspective, it is entirely fitting that Luther insisted, as Torvend and Lindberg have suggested, on liturgically connecting the distribution from the community chest with the Eucharist since both enact and express the communication of divine, human, and neighborly properties for the good of the community.

In a similar spirit, Vitor Westhelle argues that Luther's two kingdom

---

83. Luther, "Lectures on Galatians—1519," *Luther's Works, Vol. 27: Lectures on Galatians Chapters 5-6*, ed. Jaroslav Pelikan (St. Louis: Concordia, 2007), 393.
84. Luther, *LW* 35:61, cited in Torvend, *Luther and the Hungry Poor*, 126. Emphasis added.

TOWARD A BETTER WORLDLINESS

teaching (discussed more fully in chapter one) was influenced by Luther's interpretation of the *communicatio idiomatum*. What have been interpreted as dualistic and separative realms—God's right-hand realm concerned with the spiritual, justification, and the gospel and God's left-hand realm concerned with the world, laws, society, and politics—are actually intricately interconnected and related. Difference between them is maintained, but without absolute separation. Westhelle explains that while the two realms should not be confused,

> they do overlap with each other without one displacing the other. . . . The genius of the Reformer was to sustain, through and through, a communication between presence and representation, between event and institution, between heaven and earth, between passivity and activity, justification and justice. But the trick lies in the irreducible mystery of the communication between the two.[85]

When we see Luther's interpretation of the communication of properties extended from Christology to sacramentology and ethics, Luther's interest in the Leisnig community chest no longer seems surprising.

By demonstrating a communicating relation between what are usually held as dualistic opposites for Luther—vertical relations with the horizontal, worship of God with right relation to neighbor, left- and right-hand kingdoms—this interpretation undermines all assumptions of Luther's theology as assuming or creating a separative individual self with alienable possessions. This is a crucial rereading of Luther where common interpretations easily align his purported individualist soteriology and the free, alienable gift with currently destructive economic systems.[86] The economics of modern subjectivity depends

---

85. Vitor Westhelle, *Transfiguring Luther: The Planetary Promise of Luther's Theology* (Eugene, OR: Cascade, 2016), 11–12.

86. Feminist philosopher of religion, Grace Jantzen, is a prime example. Jantzen critiques the idea of individual salvation, that "a particular individual can be saved, singled out for rescue, though all others around her perish. A combined influence of Luther and Calvin on Protestant theology has made this individualized aspect of salvation central to much subsequent theological thought." Jantzen continues, articulating commonly associated economic implications: "There have been many studies which have discussed the convoluted connections between these Protestant conceptions of personal salvation and the rise of capitalism and individualistic liberalism" (Grace

152

on and assumes the absolute self; the participant in modern society and economics is self-sufficient, independent, self-possessed, and self-conscious. In modern thought, alienable possessions have everything to do with subjectivity. From René Descartes to John Locke, self-possession (i.e., self-consciousness) is the key to the right to property. In order to be a human subject with the rights and privileges to participate fully in society, politics, and economics, one must be in full possession of oneself, without significant debts or dependencies on others. In early modernity, for example, only those who were fully self-possessed (property-owning males) were full human subjects who could therefore be trusted with the responsibility of a political voice (the vote). All who depended on others or were in debt to others (women, children, slaves, indentured servants) lacked full possession of themselves, and were thus restricted from full public participation.

Where Luther's soteriological individualism is typically seen as a neat precursor to the modern self defined as self-conscious, self-aware, and self-possessed, his emphasis on union and his exchangist interpretation of the *communicatio idiomatum* fundamentally disrupt this common narrative. Rather than self-possession (the return of the gift of consciousness to the self), for Luther, a person's justification (their ultimate worthiness) arises through an encounter with others —specifically, an exchange of their most fundamental, constitutive, and value-laden properties with Christ and neighbors. In so doing, Luther gives witness to profound biblical and patristic alternatives to modern subjectivity and economics.

Communicating Grace: Luther's Unconditioned and Multilateral Gift

A free, unilateral gift of forgiveness by forensic justification alone simply cannot account for the fluidity and porosity Luther describes between selves, their gifts or possessions, Christ, and created others. For that matter, a bilateral reciprocal gifting structure would not

Jantzen, *Becoming Divine: Towards a Feminist Philosophy of Religion* [Bloomington: Indiana University Press, 1999], 164).

TOWARD A BETTER WORLDLINESS

account for it any better. Where God and neighbor "change into" one another so that a gift given to the neighbor is also an indirect gift to God, we witness a multilateral and nonlinear gifting structure emerge. Here, the gift is given in and through a network of relations between God, self, and neighbor. Where this is the case, the multilateral gift facilitates a wider circulation of gifts. Where love of God can only be properly expressed as love of neighbor and acts of love for neighbor are also acts of love for self and God, the gifting structure is not directly or linearly causal, but multilateral. This is no disruption of exchange from pure exteriority, nor is it a capitalizing circular gift that must return to its origin with (self)interest. The circular gift consolidates goods in the hands of those who already have, restricting to capitalizing, growth-based economics. The noncircular, multilateral gift of this eco/nomy of grace, by contrast, is communicated, disseminated, and scattered broadly with a disregard for efficiency, profit, or gain and an aim toward continual redistribution, flow, and exchange of gifts. As such, Luther's grace emerges as an alternate eco/ nomy, one that protests a growth-based circulation of goods that can only affirm good investments bringing a return to the donor.

Rather than a free gift, such a spirituality would be better aligned with an economy for and of the common good and an ecology of mutual interdependence and shared resources that fundamentally calls into question a model of the separative self and fixed binaries between you and me, self and other, God and creation, inside and outside. In this worldly divine eco/nomy, goods exchange and dependence—even debt in the form of commitment to others—is acknowledged. Consequently, in addition to grace declared to the sinner, I argue that it is vital to express a model of "communicating grace." Instead of the purely unilateral gesture commonly associated with Luther's articulation of grace, Luther's rendition of the communication of Christ's divine and human properties affirms communication (or mutual sharing) of *property* as profoundly Christomorphic and graced. Here, grace, that most transforming and sustaining resource, must be communicated, not just declared.

COMMUNICATING GRACE

As Lienhard suggests, the theme of divinization does indeed seem to take a new turn with Luther. However, despite Lienhard's reading, it seems clear that, for Luther, "conformity of human beings with God on the ethical plane" remains intimately related to the "communication of divine life." Indeed, I would argue that Luther's understanding of deification does not mean a departure from the world to be with God, but is found and properly expressed, on account of Luther's particular interpretation and extension of the *communicatio idiomatum*, as a profound commitment to the world. On this account, any love piously expressed to God apart from the world is false. "It was for this reason," Luther explains, "that [Christ] laid aside his divine form and took on the form of a servant so that he might draw our love for him down to earth and attach it to our neighbor. But we let our neighbor lie here and meanwhile stare into heaven and pretend to have great love for God and serve [God] greatly."[87] This trajectory of divine and worldly communication of properties finds itself extended once more in Dietrich Bonhoeffer's provocative proposal of a "better worldliness."

---

87. Luther, *WA*, 17, 99, cited in Althaus, *The Theology of Martin Luther*, 133. Similarly, "God 'teaches us to understand this deed of Christ which has been manifested to us, helps us receive and preserve it, use it to our advantage, and impart it to others, increase, and extend it" (*LW*, vol 36, 366, in Saarinen, *God and the Gift*, 46).

6

————

Toward a "Better Worldliness"

As reality is one in Christ so the person who belongs to this Christ-reality
is also whole. Worldliness does not separate one from Christ, and being
Christian does not separate one from the world. Belonging completely to
Christ, one stands at the same time completely in the world.
—Dietrich Bonhoeffer, *Ethics*

"Belong, body and soul." When I want to describe what swimming in the
ocean feels like, this phrase comes to me. It is from the Heidelberg
Catechism. As a child, when I felt scared, I'd repeat the first question
—What is your only comfort in life and in death?—and answer to myself,
"That I am not my own, but belong—body and soul, in life and in death—
to my faithful Savior, Jesus Christ."
—Kristin Dombeck, "Swimming Against the Rising Tide"

Christians, it seems, are in critical need of a better worldliness. Perhaps
it is more to the point to say the *world* needs this economically and
politically influential group of human beings to be able to passionately,
unreservedly, and inextricably embrace the connection between their
faith and the world. This is not a challenge to take lightly. Centuries
of Christian ways of "belonging not to the world"—a spirit infused
in predominant models of grace and its interconnected modes of
selfhood—must be revised or differently embodied.[1] Rather than being

157

TOWARD A BETTER WORLDLINESS

pressed to decide whether they belong, body and soul, to Jesus or to the vast contingency of the world, we might foster a sense of belonging body and soul to the world *and* God. So, what particular resources can faith offer as we begin to face the frightening contingencies of climate change?

The twentieth century brought unprecedented challenges to the Protestant view of God, the world, and humanity. In the midst of WWII in Germany, Dietrich Bonhoeffer addressed what he called the "failure" of Western ethics that had allowed the Nazi regime to rise virtually uncontested in the land of the Reformation.[2] In particular, he was critical of the interpretation of Lutheran ethics that divided reality into two realms, and consequently, handed over the public or civic realm to Hitler: God and world, sacred and secular, personal and public, ecclesial and civic. However, Bonhoeffer also recognized this dualistic tendency among theologians who protested Nazi Germany. Consequently, he diagnosed that theology "had arrived at an impasse, oriented either to the world or to the Word."[3] Recently published research on Bonhoeffer's theology and ethics demonstrates that in order to overcome this impasse Bonhoeffer relied on his reading of Luther.

Scholars have long noted the christological orientation of Bonhoeffer's theology. Even more than his often-cited contemporary influences—Barth on the one side and the German liberal theological tradition on the other—H. Gaylon Barker's recent work extensively outlines how Bonhoeffer's theology is permeated by Luther's Christology. In constructing an alternative to the impasse theology faced in dualistic choices between God and world, Bonhoeffer relied on

---

1. John 17. See Jürgen Moltmann's interpretation of what John's Jesus is referring to with regard to the world: "The people who would like to see [God's kingdom] as belonging to the next world always point to Jesus' saying that 'my kingdom is not of this world' (John 18:36). But in doing so they are overlooking the fact that this is a statement about the origin of the kingdom, not its place. . . . If it is the kingdom of the creator God, then it embraces the whole of creation, heaven and earth, the invisible side of the world and the visible side too" (Moltmann, *Jesus Christ for Today's World* [Minneapolis: Fortress Press, 1995], 20).

2. See Bonhoeffer's letter, "After Ten Years," in *Letters and Papers from Prison*, ed. Eberhard Bethge (New York: Macmillan, 1971).

3. H. Gaylon Barker, *The Cross of Reality: Luther's Theologia Crucis and Bonhoeffer's Christology* (Minneapolis: Fortress Press, 2015), 38, citing DeJonge, 3–5. Barker notes that "a central task of Bonhoeffer's early theology, from 1927-1933 is the negotiation of this impasse."

Luther's interpretation of the *communicatio idiomatum* because in it he saw that Luther was not constrained by choosing either God or world, dogmatics or ethics.[4] Barker notes, "It was Luther's understanding of the *communicatio idiomatum* that enabled him to see God as participating in the life of the world."[5] The alternative Bonhoeffer proposes is a unified reality, a "better worldliness."[6] Consequently, in Bonhoeffer's unified conception of reality—with God's profound engagement with and commitment to the world—a better worldliness can be seen as the logical conclusion of a Christology shaped by the *communicatio idiomatum*.[7] In this final chapter, I will demonstrate that Bonhoeffer unfolds Luther's extension of the communication of properties as a "better worldliness"—a relational doctrine of God and ontology of "being-with-others."

Reconciled in Faith

In Bonhoeffer's early works, *Sanctorum Communio* and *Act and Being*, he demonstrates a commitment to articulating Christian doctrine in relational terms. The significance of these early works remains under-recognized in Lutheran theology, in spite of persuasive studies from Bonhoeffer scholars demonstrating their importance.[8] In particular, Bonhoeffer's work in *Act and Being* seems an important contribution to contemporary Protestant unease with the tradition's emphasis on passive grace and the world's calls for active justice.

For Bonhoeffer, what scholars describe as a relational or social ontology becomes key for reconciling a Western philosophical opposition between act and being. This opposition is clearly at work in the Protestant tradition, as can be discerned from Moltmann's particular framing of the liberating potential of Luther's theology of

4. Barker, *Cross of Reality*, 38.
5. Ibid., 103.
6. Bonhoeffer, *Dietrich Bonhoeffer Works, Volume 6: Ethics*, ed. Clifford J. Green, trans. Reinhard Krauss, Charles C. West, and Douglas W. Stott (Minneapolis: Augsburg Fortress, 2005), 60.
7. Barker, *Cross of Reality*, 373n28.
8. Marsh, Green, and Frei all emphasize the significance of Bonhoeffer's two dissertations (*Act and Being* and *Sanctorum Communio*) for the development of his later, more recognized work in *The Cost of Discipleship, Letters and Papers from Prison*, and *Ethics*.

grace. In *Theology of Play*, Moltmann summarizes Luther's intervention in theology as a rejection of Aristotelian metaphysics where doing (acts, *habitus*, practice) can lead to being. Where Luther's argument is summarized as an emphasis on (passive) Being that cannot be attained through activity or practice, this interpretation suggests the reformer supports a radical distinction between act and being and a unique emphasis on being over action.[9] Binaries between justification and justice and even grace and exchange follow along this same divide. Therefore, a thesis such as Bonhoeffer offers where act and being are reconciled *from a Lutheran perspective* would be a feat worthy of note and replication.

In *Act and Being*, Bonhoeffer seeks to make an intervention in dialectical theology. Bonhoeffer notes this school's overemphasis on God's act of revelation as an act over and against the world, suggesting God's freedom is freedom *from* the constraints of the world: a unilateral action par excellence. Bonhoeffer argues that key insights from both transcendental philosophy (emphasizing act) and ontological philosophy (emphasizing being) must be integrated in our theologies. Following Heidegger's integration of act and being, Bonhoeffer argues that being in the abstract is meaningless and can only be articulated concretely as "being in." He argues for an interdependent relationship between act and being, where there is "never being without act and never act without being."[10]

The key to this interdependence is the social category Bonhoeffer introduced in his first dissertation, *Sanctorum Communio*, whereby all theological aspects are reinterpreted assuming a social or communal ontology.[11] A fundamentally social or relational nature of his ontology becomes clear in the following quote: "The individual exists only in relation to an 'other'; individual does not mean solitary. On the contrary, for the individual to exist, 'others' must necessarily be there."[12] For Bonhoeffer, there is no existence that is not in relation

9. Moltmann, *Theology of Play*, trans. Reinhard Ulrich (New York: Harper & Row, 1972), 45–46.
10. Bonhoeffer, *Act and Being*, 159.
11. "By introducing the sociological category, the problematic of act and being—and with it the problem of knowledge—is stated for theology in an entirely new manner" (ibid., 113).

TOWARD A "BETTER WORLDLINESS"

to others. In the preface to *Sanctorum Communio*, he writes, "The more this investigation has considered the significance of the sociological category for theology, the more clearly has emerged the social intention of all the basic Christian concepts. 'Person,' 'primal state,' 'sin,' and 'revelation' can be fully comprehended only in reference to sociality."[13] For example, he takes Luther's insight into the nature of human sinfulness, articulated as the heart turned in on itself—*cor curvum in se*—and interprets it, as Joseph Sittler later would, as separative individualism.[14]

Bonhoeffer constructs a view of reality wherein he can argue that when one sees oneself as self-reliant and fundamentally autonomous or disconnected from relationship with others, one is in a state of sinfulness—not merely as a matter of improper behavior, but because one is in denial of reality.[15] Charles Marsh notes that here Bonhoeffer offers a "christological description of life with others [that] offers a compelling and unexpectedly rich alternative to post-Kantian models of selfhood—to conceptions of the self as the center of all relations to others."[16] A social description of reality allows Bonhoeffer to disturb Protestant active/passive binaries when he reinterprets faith—typically seen as passive and psychological or emotional, rather than physical—in terms of the social category as an *act* of turning out from the individualist self toward Christ and the other. The proper sense of act, then, is always "'in relation to' that never comes to rest."[17] Such a

---

12. Bonhoeffer, *Dietrich Bonhoeffer Works, Volume 1: Sanctorum Communio: A Theological Study of the Sociology of the Church*, ed. Clifford J. Green, trans. Reinhard Krauss and Nancy Lukens (Minneapolis: Fortress Press, 2009), 32, cited in Green, "Human Sociality and Christian Community," 115.

13. Bonhoeffer, *Sanctorum Communio*, 13.

14. On Sittler, see chapter three. Clifford Green describes Bonhoeffer's interpretation of the *cor curvum in se* with ample reference to *Act and Being* in the following way: "The man with the 'autonomous self-understanding' who considers himself capable, by his own knowing, of finding the truth about human existence and placing himself in that truth, has the following characteristics. His is an autonomous I, understanding himself from himself and by his own power. His existence, consequently, is isolated and individualistic. His being and thinking are imprisoned, caught in his own system, closed in upon himself; his fundamental orientation is that of the *cor curvum in se*" (Green, *Bonhoeffer: A Theology of Sociality*, 78).

15. For Bonhoeffer, especially as articulated in *Ethics*, Christ is the nature of reality.

16. Marsh, *Reclaiming Dietrich Bonhoeffer: The Promise of His Theology* (New York: Oxford University Press, 1994), vii.

17. Bonhoeffer, *Act and Being*, 42f., cited in Green, *Bonhoeffer: A Theology of Sociality*, 81–82.

definition presupposes a proper sense of human being, which is always "in relation to something beyond themselves."[18] Rather than opposites, act and being are reconciled in faith when defined as the act of being in relation to others that never comes to rest.

From *Pro me* to the "One for Others"

Rather than emphasizing religious transcendence as otherworldliness, Bonhoeffer reinterprets religious experience in terms of his interpretation of the incurved self. He argues that when we talk of transcendence, what we transcend is not the world, or material relations, or even just the self, but the *incurved* self. Consequently, encounters with those the self would identify as "other" become not only ethical, but sacred since it is through such encounters that we meet the limits of our self-will and are forced to turn out from ourselves and our own desires. The transcendence of self-orientation becomes a mark of divinity—a characteristic of God reflected in creation. Bonhoeffer scholar Clifford Green explains, "God's transcendence is not remote otherness or absence, God's otherness is embodied precisely in the other person who is real and present, encountering me in the heart of my existence."[19] Consequently, Bonhoeffer can confidently declare that the "Thou of the other man is the divine Thou. So the way to the other is also the way to the divine Thou, a way of recognition or rejection."[20] Here, we see a direct application of Luther's insistence that God and neighbor change into one another so that our acts of love to neighbor are the proper expression of love for God. Rather than otherworldliness, divinity is experienced in and through our worldly encounters; only in the midst of our worldly relationships do we encounter God.

In encountering the other, turning out from our isolated selves, we experience divine transcendence because "the God we meet is 'the one-for-others,' the one 'for us' (*pro nobis*)."[21] Bonhoeffer takes Luther's

18. Green, *Bonhoeffer: A Theology of Sociality*, 81.
19. Green, "Human Sociality and Christian Community," 124.
20. Bonhoeffer, *Communio Sanctorum*, 47 cited in Larry Rasmussen, *Dietrich Bonhoeffer: Reality and Resistance* (Louisville: John Knox, 2005), 19.

TOWARD A "BETTER WORLDLINESS"

christological orientation around the *communicatio* and argues that God's very "essence" or mode of divinity is in the act of communication, in giving, *pro me*. Remarkably, though, Bonhoeffer takes the *pro me*—one of the most individualizing doctrines of the Reformation tradition—and turns (or curves) it inside out.[22] He articulates this shift in his Christology lectures, which he gave shortly after writing *Act and Being*. Luther and the reformers insisted that Christ and the incarnation reveals that God is not against us, but for us. This life-giving message ultimately became individualizing, though, as it shifted the focus away from a grand cosmological creator God to God's acts as they impact me, my life, my salvation—how God feels about *me*.[23] Bonhoeffer's interpretation of this *pro me* shifts the emphasis back to an ontological statement about not just me and my relationship with God, but who God and Christ are and what this means for the world, our perception of reality, and how we are to ethically respond to reality.

For Bonhoeffer, the "essence" of Christ is a relational *pro me* only possible in an encounter with an other: "Christ is Christ not as Christ in himself, but in his relation to me. His being Christ is his being *pro me*."[24] Bonhoeffer continues, explaining that Christ's being *pro me* is not an aspect or mere description of Christ's behavior. Christ's being *pro me*, he says, is an *ontological* statement. Therefore, to think of Christ in Christ's self, apart from any other reality or relationship, is impossible as Christ *pro me* can only be thought of "in the community" as the one-for-others. He concludes, "it is not only useless to meditate on Christ in himself, but even godless."[25] Consequently, Christ "the center" can be no stable solid center since it is continually and multiply de-centered in relationship, in being-for-the-other.[26] Larry Rasmussen explains that

---

21. Larry Rasmussen, "The Ethics of Responsible Action," in *The Cambridge Companion to Dietrich Bonhoeffer*, ed. John W. de Gruchy (New York: Cambridge University Press, 1999), 218.
22. Paul Santmire says the anthropocentric readings of Scripture are mainly a result of the Reformation focus on *pro me* (*Nature Reborn: The Ecological and Cosmic Promise of Christian Theology* [Minneapolis: Augsburg Fortress, 2000], 31).
23. See Paul Althaus, *The Theology of Martin Luther*, trans. Robert C. Schultz (Minneapolis: Fortress Press, 1966), 18.
24. Bonhoeffer, *Christ the Center*, trans. Edwin H. Robertson (San Francisco: Harper, 1978), 47–48.
25. Rasmussen, *Reality and Resistance*, 18, citing *Christ the Center*, 47–48.

for Bonhoeffer, "Christ can be thought of only in relational terms. 'Being-there-with-and-for' is the manner of his existence and presence. Bonhoeffer can thus say that Christ exists 'as community' . . . which is to say, God's very being, too, is relational."[27] By interpreting the central Reformation insight that God is *pro me* in relational, interdependent, and interpenetrating (*perichoretic*) terms, Bonhoeffer transforms the insight, preserving it from isolating individualism through a communicating relationality.

Here again, act and being are reconciled—not just in faith, but in God. Where God emerges as no stable Being, neither can God appear as pure act since God's only being is in the act of being-for-others.[28] Describing Bonhoeffer's shift Clifford Green explains,

> God is revealed as present to us in the world—God's being is being-in-relation-to-us. This is the meaning of the incarnation: God with us, and God for us. If this is so, it follows that human existence is also fundamentally relational. To be a human is to be a person before God, and in relation to God. The relation of individual persons to each other, and relations between human communities of persons, has this theological understanding of God and human existence at its core.[29]

This view of God is a profound statement about God's mode of gifting since God's being, God's divinity, and God's "essence" are only properly divine in the act of being given. God embodies the out-turned heart in God's relation to the world and in Christ as the person-for-others. God is only truly Godself in the act of giving divine being to the other, to the world. Consequently, God is only God outside of Godself, beside Godself, in relation to the other. Giving is not just something God does. God gives (act) because this is who God is (being); reciprocally, God's being can only be maintained in the act of giving God's being.

---

26. John F. Hoffmeyer offers this insight of the de-centered nature of Bonhoeffer's Christocentrism. Hoffmeyer, "Multiplicity and Christocentric Theology," in *Divine Multiplicities: Trinities, Diversities, and the Nature of Relation,* ed. Chris Boesel and S. Wesley Ariarajah (New York: Fordham University Press, 2014).

27. Rasmussen, "The Ethics of Responsible Action," 216.

28. This is one of the findings of *Act and Being.* Only later, in the writings collected in what would be *Letters and Papers from Prison,* does he fully apply this as God Being-for-others.

29. Green, "Human Sociality and Christian Community," in *The Cambridge Companion to Dietrich Bonhoeffer,* ed. John W. de Gruchy (New York: Cambridge University Press, 1999), 114–15.

Communicating a "Better Worldliness"

In his later work, when his life has taken a more worldly turn, Bonhoeffer develops this divine communication as "worldliness," thus voiding any sense that as a Christian one must make a choice between God and world. Countering the predominant dualistic interpretation of Luther's "two kingdoms," he insists that there are not two kingdoms or realms of reality, but, on account of the reconciliation of the incarnation, there is only one realm, one reality in which the world and God cohere. For example, Bonhoeffer writes, "As reality is one in Christ so the person who belongs to this Christ-reality is also whole. Worldliness does not separate one from Christ, and being Christian does not separate one from the world. Belonging completely to Christ, one stands at the same time completely in the world."[30] The communicating nature of this Christ/world relation becomes ever more clear when Bonhoeffer exhorts, "It is a denial of God's revelation in Jesus Christ to wish to be 'Christian' without being 'worldly' or to wish to be worldly without seeing and recognizing the world in Christ."[31]

Bonhoeffer articulates a relation between God and the world where the two are neither wholly identified, nor dualistically detached. He saw that differences, such as those between God and world, do not separate so much as enhance one another. He compares this to the role of polyphony in music: undivided, yet distinct, entangled, the differences do not blur or blend together but enrich one another. He notes the beauty with which Christ and community, Christ and peace, Christ and David, "divine and human nature," love of "God and [God's] eternity" and "earthy, erotic love" "communicate with consummate ease in a Christological interplay."[32]

"Worldliness," Bonhoeffer insists, does not mean accepting the

---

30. *Ethics*, 62.
31. Ibid., 57.
32. Bonhoeffer, *Christ the Center*, 151. The reference here is subtle, but in including "Christ and David" Bonhoeffer indicates here that he would also include interreligious difference—a potent expression for him during a time of Jewish oppression and injustice at the hands of those who claimed to be followers of Christ.

world as it is, but striving for a "better worldliness."[33] He explains, "This is what I mean by worldliness, taking life in one's stride, with all its duties and problems, its successes and failures, its experiences and helplessness. It is in such a life that we throw ourselves utterly in the arms of God and participate in his sufferings in the world and watch with Christ in Gethsemane."[34] Worldliness is participation in the suffering of God in the world. As the suffering of the world is communicated to God, so also the suffering of God may be communicated to the Christian.

The extension of the *genus tapeinoticum* is noteworthy here. While the *genus majestaticum* holds for the communication of Godself with creation—expressed by Bonhoeffer as God's giving *pro me*—the *genus tapeinoticum* suggests that the world communicates itself—including suffering, weakness, loss, and so on—to God. Bonhoeffer's God, like Luther's, is a "suffering God"[35] whose very mode of being is in giving, *pro me*. God suffers not because God has evacuated Godself, but because God's being is in relation to the world where God gives Godself and where the sufferings of the world are communicated to God.

Here, we find the possibility for an alternative articulation of Moltmann's *ex se*. Recall that for Moltmann (chapter three) there was the one exception to the *perichoretic* relations within God and the ecological relations of the world. In spite of affirming remarkable interdependent relations, Moltmann reverts to the unilateral gift in insisting that the Spirit alone exists *ex se*. Where the Spirit alone exists out of itself, this is the one exception to all other exchangist relations

---

33. "In the name of a better Christianity Luther used the worldly to protest against a type of Christianity that was making itself independent by separating itself from the reality of Christ. Similarly, Christianity must be used polemically today against the worldly in the name of a better worldliness; this polemical use of Christianity must not end up again in a static and self-serving sacred realm" (ibid., 60).

34. Bonhoeffer, *Prisoner of God* (later republished as *Letters and Papers from Prison*), 166–67, 169, cited in Ronald A. Carson, "The Motifs of *Kenosis* and *Imitatio* in the Work of Dietrich Bonhoeffer, with an Excursus on the *Communicatio Idiomatum*," *Journal of the American Academy of Religion* 43, no. 3 (1975): 551.

35. Rasmussen, *Reality and Resistance*, 17. Emphasizing the suffering of God should not be taken as a glorification of suffering, but an echo of Luther's particular understanding of the *communicatio idiomatum* whereby God not only gives to the world, but receives from it as well. That God participates in the suffering of the world should not exclude the possibility that God also participates in the joys of the world.

TOWARD A "BETTER WORLDLINESS"

ab alio et in aliis, the other from another. In Bonhoeffer's work, inspired by Luther's communicating relations between God and creation, God out of Godself ceases to be a measure of self-sufficiency and independence but becomes profound and transcending relationality: the spirit exists out of itself, always outside itself, or beside itself in relation with an other. While Bonhoeffer may not explicitly articulate this, a clear logical consequence of his articulation of God's mode of gifting is that without an other who is the gifting partner, God could not be properly Godself.[36] Here, God's mode of being out of God's self fundamentally depends—as McFague's critique of Moltmann called for—on a profound encounter with difference, an other. Here, God's only essence emerges as an in/essential mode of relationality.

Both Bonhoeffer and the Finns emphasize that a defining characteristic of divinity is in a particular mode of gifting. In Bonhoeffer's emphasis on God's mode of gifting, we find resonance with the Finnish emphasis that God both *gives* and *is* the gift. Recall that the Finns argue that "according to Luther the divinity of the triune God consists in that '[God] gives' and what [God] gives is ultimately [Godself]."[37] That God *gives* and *is* the gift suggests an inalienable gift between two or more parties united in the midst of their preserved differences. Where the Finns argue that Christ's work cannot be separated from Christ's person, that in faith Christ is present, and that Christ is and gives the gift, Bonhoeffer makes a parallel argument in emphasizing that God's act and being must be reconciled. Bonhoeffer reconciles these in terms of giving: God's being is in giving and what God gives (act) is God's being. God's gifting mode of being is in being-with.

Yet, while Bonhoeffer does not explicitly articulate Christ-in-me, as the Finns do, this indwelling presence emerges as a necessary consequence of his reconciliation between act and being where God's being is in giving and what God gives is God's being. We would note, then, that if being-*with* is truly *being*-with and not holding something

---

36. Malysz suggests something similar in "Exchange and Ecstasy."
37. Carl Braaten and Robert W. Jenson, eds., *Union with Christ: The New Finnish Interpretation of Luther* (Grand Rapids, MI: Eerdmans, 1998), 10.

167

back that would put this in question, then being-with also implies being-in. In such communicating interplay of act and being, justification can no longer be opposed to justice, just as grace cannot be the antithesis of exchange because the gift God gives is no alienable object, but the communication of Godself to creation.

What neither Bonhoeffer nor the Finns emphasize is that where God's divinity is in God's giving Godself in relation, then a defining characteristic of divinity depends on something other than God. God is utterly intra-dependent in communicating relation, rendering the world thoroughly indispensable, even for God. This sense of God's being dependent on something outside Godself does not account for an unstable or annihilation of being, but an alternate mode of being-in-relation. Milbank is critical of "other-oriented ontologies" because he argues they are self-depleting, leading to nihilism and the loss of self, God, and meaning. However, I would argue that a relational or other-oriented ontology such as Bonhoeffer articulates is only a self-depleting nihilism if it is trapped in an individualist ontology. Just as Bonhoeffer found that act and being are only opposing concepts in an individualist ontology, so also the self being-with-the-other is only self-depleting in an individualist ontology with unilateral or bilateral gift-exchange relations. Where the self is not an isolated individual but a self located and constituted through a web of multilateral gifts, there is no isolated selfsame bottom to deplete to. Rather than a pure isolated self or loss of self, what emerges is an alternative mode of being, a transcendent, sacramental, Christomorphic, being-in-with-and-through relation with others.

This relational mode of being suggests an understanding of grace that emerges from within entangled relations with the world, not apart from them. Moving toward this "better worldliness," Protestant insights about the nature of grace may again find new life and relevance in a world of eco/nomic beauty, uncertainty, and conflict. When we consider that we are ourselves only in, with, and through others in a web of multilateral divine and creaturely gifts, then this

TOWARD A "BETTER WORLDLINESS"

relational mode of being and giving may open toward a worldliness that is simultaneously ecological and profoundly graced.

Conclusions: Graceful Gratitude

I had actually wanted to say something more, to express wider gratitude for the meal we were about to eat but I was afraid that to offer words of thanks for the pig and the mushrooms and the forest and the garden would come off sounding corny and worse, might ruin some appetites. The words I was reaching for, of course, were the words of grace.
—Michael Pollan, *The Omnivore's Dilemma*[38]

To stand nearly naked and heavy from winter on the water's edge, wade awkwardly into the shallows, dive under the first cold wave, taste first salt, surface and dive again to reach the calmer waters beyond, floating there until water and skin become the same temperature— this is the best way I know to belong again, body and soul, to some larger part of the planet.
—Kristin Dombeck, "Swimming Against the Rising Tide"

Even in our least confessional moments, we seem to desire the means to account for the ways that we have and continue to be sustained —even constituted—by the gifts of others. Perhaps there is a way to give thanks to the creatures who gave their work and lives for our sustenance as a way of also giving thanks to the divine. Perhaps our gratitude need not be addressed to either God or not-God. Perhaps it could signal an awareness that there is something sacred in, with, and under the digestive-like exchanges of the world in the entanglement of seeming opposites: creator and creature, human and nonhuman, inside and outside.

We call the table blessing Michael Pollan refers to, as he does, *grace*, which seems intuitively fitting but doctrinally unclear. This is at least the case from a Protestant perspective where, in "proper" and "serious" theological discourse, grace is nearly exclusively aligned with forensic justification. For a tradition known for its distinctive emphasis on grace, it seems remarkable that in its doctrinal expressions it is not

---

38. Michael Pollan, *The Omnivore's Dilemma: A Natural History of Four Meals* (New York: Penguin, 2006), 407.

TOWARD A BETTER WORLDLINESS

able to account for grace in the world radically enough. However, when taken seriously, the mundane table blessing might just account for a pervasive sense of grace that ties together creation and redemption more properly. Where God and world are not opposed but commune and communicate in a Christomorphic play of unity and difference, this mode emerges as sacramental as much as ecological in a turn toward a better worldliness. As such, this expression of grace emerges as proper for a blessing of an interspecies communing table as much as for "serious" theology within the walls of the church.

When asked why he consistently returned to a focus on the doctrine of grace, Joseph Sittler replied that his motives were both strategic and theological.[39] He understood that grace and its corollary, justification, were the doctrines on which the church stands or falls. This is how the Reformers referred to it, at least, and due in great part to Karl Holl's work, it remains true today. Sittler understood that the church and its leaders would simply not be swayed by anything not deemed as central as the doctrine of justification. So it seems that our basic interconnectedness will not sink in, swaying changes in lifestyle and perspective, unless it can be shown that in this particular doctrine, we are basically interconnected and not mere separative individuals.

In examining the Protestant tradition and its broad and compelling influence on Western modern culture and economies, we have come to see that the doctrine of grace and the gifting models thereby implied present a particularly important locus of analysis. What might grace look like in the midst of the challenge of altering vast economic systems and ecological relations? I suggest that grace might take the form of a profound sense of gratitude. Like Michael Pollan's desire to say table grace, gratitude acknowledges the ways we are indebted to the many creaturely and divine others who make our life and actions—even our being human—possible. I would also suggest, as Dombek intuited, that this sense of gratitude—inasmuch as it acknowledges our part in a vast and humbling contingency—might not

---

39. Sittler, *Gravity and Grace*, ed. Thomas S. Hanson (Minneapolis: Augsburg Fortress, 2005), 2–3.

TOWARD A "BETTER WORLDLINESS"

merely comfort or reconcile, but also kindle a sense of responsibility for vast communities who simultaneously are "me" and exceed "me."

We are learning to float on a rising tide within an ocean of interdependent relations, and so, have begun to articulate a different way of relating to the world and an alternate way of envisioning grace in relation to the world. We have explored the challenges such an articulation of grace might face, particularly from a Protestant theological perspective. Noting, in particular, the ways a definition of grace as free, nonreciprocal, and opposed to exchange exceeds its theological bounds to impact economic systems, we have seen how it affects our relation to the exchanges that sustain the world.

We have noted the heightened predicament that grace as free gift finds itself in when we consider the conditions of climate change. Even when well-intended protests of an oppressive economic system logically oppose grace to economic exchange, they unwittingly align grace with an interruption or even annihilation of the eco/nomic exchanges that sustain the world. So, we have insisted on resisting the continual recurrence and idealization of the original unilateral divine gift. Rather than accepting this as an essential characteristic of Protestant thought, we have articulated an alternative: the gift of grace as unconditioned and multilateral in the sense that it may refuse a capitalizing return to its origin and, instead, continue to disperse, sparking a wider exchange of gifts rather than an opposition to exchange.

Where a gift emerges as free of reciprocal returns, it remains alienable, isolated and individualistic, cut off from the ties that create human and other-than-human communities. Early on, therefore, we wondered if a yoked ontology of being-with would be able to find root in Reformation soil. In tracing the trajectories of marginal voices in the tradition, we have noted strains from Luther to Osiander to the Finns and Bonhoeffer ready to sustain a robust relational ontology of being-with-others. In the process, grace models and gifting ideals significantly shift from an alienable gift—the commodified object, free to shuttle between separative subjects—to a communing Christo-

171

TOWARD A BETTER WORLDLINESS

morphic gift, given in, with, and under the vast multilateral ecological web of continual gift-exchange.

Grace, here, is not some gift object passed between discrete parties, nor does it depend on preconditions. It does, however, presume relationship, a connection that counts. Where the gift might not return to its origin, grace is the occasion—no state suggesting simple location—that allows for a different kind of encounter, a kind of love given with the understanding that it may not be a good, capitalizing investment for the giver. Even as one always hopes for the return of relationship, grace is not given with the condition of a return to its origin.

Grace emerges as a possibility *within* an entangled relationality rather than opposed to it when see ourselves as gifts to others and from others—as fully embedded in a multilateral web of continual gift-exchange. Grace, though, is not the same as interconnection. Where interconnection is a given, rather than a goal, it may just as easily effect our undoing as our salvation. For better or worse, we humans are part of the nature we seek to know and, too often, to control, and use:[40] climate change presses the reality of this fact upon us. As awe-inspiring as our interdependence may be, it can turn on a dime to poison. Entangled reality leaves us incredibly vulnerable to short-sighted and self-interested acts—vulnerable, that is, to the consequences of a maintained illusion of separative individualism.

Where grace emerges as embedded in an eco/nomic web of multilateral gift-exchange, so too does the self. In classical Christian thought from Augustine through Luther and Calvin, grace has been articulated as an opening of the self curved in on itself. As the remedy for a human tendency toward self-absorption and ego-centricity, grace has been aligned with an opening and emptying out of the self. However, as we noted through feminist engagements with the tradition in the introduction, this mode of selfhood has tended toward a dangerous self-evacuation. In addition, the strong and exclusive

---

40. Barad, "Posthumanist Performativity: Toward an Understanding of How Matter Comes to Matter," *Signs: Journal of Women in Culture and Society* 28, no. 3 (2003): 828.

TOWARD A "BETTER WORLDLINESS"

emphasis on God's grace *extra nos* has encouraged a rigid inside/outside dualism corresponding to an equally rigid passive/active binary. Given rising awareness of an ecologically interdependent reality, can people today still imagine that their selves are contained in an interior opposing an exterior? More to the point: Should they be persuaded of this when such dichotomies continue to support a view of a separative, individualistic self?

Milbank and others aligning with Radical Orthodoxy also critique the self-negating other-orientation of Protestant grace and ethics. Clearly, a more relational ontology of continual gift-exchange is necessary to counter the separative individualism and commodification of the free gift, but Milbank's self-affirming ethic exposes the vulnerability of his gift-exchange to growth-dependent economics. In order to interrupt the economic ideologies fueling climate change, both the purely other-interested, unilateral, alienable gift *and* Milbank's circular gift that must return to its origin need to be challenged. This is precisely why the unconditioned and multilateral gift emerges as key.

We should also note, however, that only an isolated, self-contained individual is in danger of pouring her whole self out. Such self-negation can only function if the self is an isolated, selfsame island in the first place. For the self to be negated, there must be a self-contained, isolated bottom to scrape. If the self is always already multilaterally embedded in an ocean of otherness, there is no self-contained bottom to the self because the opening and other orientation only pours out as it lets in. Therefore, what if the Protestant spirituality that problematically praised and desired the no-self could be constructively articulated as a shift away from the self/no-self dualism to a multiplied self embedded in a web of relations and riddled with otherness? In other words, as Catherine Keller intuits, reflecting on the mysterious overflow of our planetary relations, what if "the no-thingness appears to be the very site of the intricately interconnected whole"?[41] With

---

41. Catherine Keller, *Cloud of the Impossible: Negative Theology and Planetary Entanglement* (New York: Columbia University Press, 2015), 145. Also: "The nothingness of the 'knowing nothing' is not a neat nihil of names but a chaotic multiplicity, an overflow in excess" (ibid., 75).

TOWARD A BETTER WORLDLINESS

communicating grace, the out-turning of the self is not only a force for emptying by giving or losing ourselves; it can also be something that opens up the self to more profoundly realize and acknowledge dependence on the other in order to be a unique and particular self in the first place. Would this not be a posture of gratitude?

Embedding the self in a relational ontology or ecology suggests that the opening of grace is not merely for pouring out, but for filling up as well—allowing the other in, so to speak. Taking the shape of the *communicatio idiomatum*, the drama of grace in the life of the sinner emerges not just as the opening of the incurved self toward others in service, but as mutual receptivity as well. Being-for-others, in other words, does not merely mean turning away from self or emptying the self but turning to interdependence and, in gratitude, acknowledging the ways we are entangled with the world and others. Rather than erased, would not this self emerge as multiply figured, multiply sourced, multiply gifted, prolonged, and extended? In other words, would this not be a Christomorphic eco/nomic self? Refusing the persistent lure of the sovereign, individualist self—*incurvatus in se*—the opening of grace transforms us into gifts for others by taking in, not refusing, the multiplicity and exchangist nature of the gift, meeting it with courage, love, and the similarly given ability to respond with love.

When grace does not circle back to the giver, it becomes an opening event, simultaneously turning the self outward to the others who have always already been there and initiating our readiness to respond with care. The possibility for grace-filled relations emerges through "withness itself," an ontology of being-with. Never outside entangled relations, but always within them, grace gives space for others to be more than extensions of my own interests. Where grace is the experience of being opened by gratitude to the multitude of others (divine, human, and other-than-human alike) who are gifts to us, we are freed through Christomorphic relations. Freed to "change into" or be "little Christs" to one another, we may be sacramentally inspired toward right response (not just any response) for the flourishing of all.[42] When grace is recognized as a grateful opening to, with, and

TOWARD A "BETTER WORLDLINESS"

through the divine and creaturely gifts that continue to constitute my self, we can affirm the reformer's key insight that the possibility of responsibility opens only through grace.

In rejecting a view of the human defined by conscious self-possession transcending the world's exchanges, the modern ethical individual whose relational dependencies are only liabilities must also be challenged. As biologist Donna Haraway notes, "response and respect are possible only in those knots"[43] between self and other, human and other-than-human, and we might add, God and creature. Being responsible is not a matter of removing oneself to make decisions from above the world. We can neither know nor be responsible by removing ourselves to stand outside the world—these are only possible in, with, and through the world. As Barad reminds us, "in our sensibility we are exposed to the outside, to the world's being, in such a way that we are bound to answer for it."[44] Not everyone who is entangled will be responsible. But our ability to respond with care and grace to one another is only possible through our entangled and interdependent relations and not apart from them. Where gracious gratitude deepens a sensibility of the outside, inside, it may indeed be a revelatory gift as we muster the courage to address the vortex of factors contributing to climate change.

In addition to responsibility for our worldly eco/nomic relations, we have also addressed responsibility for the gifts we inherit in the form of traditions. How best do we accept the gift of an inheritance in the form of a tradition? Do we respond most gratefully by preserving and protecting it in its "original" form? What then is the original form? These are the kinds of unending arguments and unanswerable questions Finnish theologians invite by insisting they have discovered an authentic or original Luther. I suggest that in accepting the gift of

---

42. These are Luther's terms in "The Freedom of a Christian": "change into" and being "little Christs" to one another. See chapter five.

43. Donna Haraway, *When Species Meet* (Minneapolis: University of Minnesota Press, 2008), 42.

44. Karen Barad, "On Touching—The Inhuman That Therefore I Am," *Differences: A Journal of Feminist Cultural Studies* 23, no. 3 (2012): 226.

TOWARD A BETTER WORLDLINESS

our inheritance, we must not only be accountable *to* the Protestant tradition, but also responsible *for* it.

Derrida's interpretive insight is key here. In *Of Grammatology*, Derrida notes that in traditional criticism, commentary on a text has only ever protected it. In embracing Nietzsche's embrace of play rather than Rousseau's mourning of the loss of certain and centered meaning, Derrida invites us to open a text—or in this case, a body of texts—for new interpretations, rather than protecting them by digging for an original meaning or intention.[45] If we lay claim to or self-identify with a tradition, protecting it then becomes a matter of self-preservation. But if we are claimed by a tradition and sometimes feel we have no compelling rational reason to continue to claim it, save for a presumably grace-filled experience of continuing to be claimed by it, then we must dare to approach readings playfully and not just preserve and protect them. In other words, I'm suggesting we might receive a tradition like any other gift that follows an economy of grace: just as we resist gift economies where the gift must return to the donor, so we should also resist interpretations of the Protestant tradition that *must* return to an origin. They certainly *may* return with some playfulness, but in a spirit of grace, it seems the tradition would be most faithfully continued if our interpretations themselves resisted incurved, self-preserving tendencies. This is not intended to indicate a departure from or erasure of texts and voices that have been and continue to be meaningful. Nor does it imply a disregard for history or responsible scholarship. It would, however, seem a fitting contribution to the tradition and its communicating economy of grace to open texts more creatively, constructively, and critically to address some of the most pressing issues we as humans—not just people of faith—face today.

The Reformation inspired massive social, economic, political, and religious shifts five hundred years ago. Today, it appears that the climate-challenged world needs shifts of this same scale and broader.

---

45. Jacques Derrida, *Of Grammatology*, trans. Gayatri Chakravorty Spivak (Baltimore: Johns Hopkins University Press, 1997), 158.

TOWARD A "BETTER WORLDLINESS"

The practical implications of this articulation of gift are significant and widely untapped in contemporary American expressions of the churches inspired by these events. If God's mode of saving and life-giving activity emerges primarily in exchanges that create community in communion with Christ's body, then our churches can no longer theologically or ethically afford to limit grace to the forgiveness of human sins. If God's work appears not as anti-exchange but in community-building exchanges, then our congregations are not called primarily to self-preservation, nor to engage their communities with mere acts of philanthropy and charity. In a spirit of grace-filled gratitude for the very gift of creation, communities of faith are called to engage global economic systems, and on a local level, envision alternative economies that work toward practices to build up community rather than exclude, alienate, or degrade the natural world—including other humans. As we look to the next five hundred years, my hope is that we might communicate a message of grace that disseminates inspiration for reimagining social, economic, political, divine, and ecological relations for a better worldliness.

Bibliography

Althaus, Paul. *The Theology of Martin Luther.* Translated by Robert C. Schultz. Minneapolis: Fortress Press, 1966.

American Natural History Museum. "The Secret World Inside You," http://www.amnh.org/exhibitions/the-secret-world-inside-you.

Arand, Charles P., James A. Nestingen, and Robert Kolb. *The Lutheran Confessions: History and Theology of the Book of Concord.* Minneapolis: Fortress Press, 2012.

Aristotle. "The History of Animals." In *The Animals Reader: The Essential Classical and Contemporary Writings,* edited by Linda Kalof and Amy Fitzgerald, 5–7. New York: Berg, 2007.

Barad, Karen. "Deep Calls unto Deep: Queer Inhumanism and Matters of Justice-to-Come." Paper presented at the Drew University Transdisciplinary Theological Colloquium, Madison, NJ, 2014.

——. *Meeting the Universe Halfway: Quantum Physics and the Entanglement of Matter and Meaning.* Durham, NC: Duke University Press, 2007.

——. "Nature's Queer Performativity." *Kvinder & Køn Forskning* 12 (2012): 25–53.

——."On Touching—The Inhuman That Therefore I Am." *differences: A Journal of Feminist Cultural Studies* 23, no. 3 (2012): 206–23.

——. "Posthumanist Performativity: Toward an Understanding of How Matter Comes to Matter." *Signs: Journal of Women in Culture and Society* 28, no. 3 (2003): 801–31.

——. "Quantum Entanglements and Hauntological Relations of Inheritance:

TOWARD A BETTER WORLDLINESS

Dis/continuities, SpaceTime Enfoldings, and Justice-to-Come." *Derrida Today* 3, no. 2 (2010): 240–68.

Barker, H. Gaylon. *The Cross of Reality: Luther's Theologia Crucis and Bonhoeffer's Christology*. Minneapolis: Fortress Press, 2015.

Braaten, Carl E., and Robert W. Jenson, eds. *Union with Christ: The New Finnish Interpretation of Luther*. Grand Rapids, MI: Eerdmans, 1998.

Bakken, Peter. "Introduction: Nature as a Theater of Grace: The Ecological Theology of Joseph Sittler." In *Evocations of Grace: The Writings of Joseph Sittler on Ecology, Theology, and Ethics*, edited by Steven Bouma-Prediger and Peter Bakken, 1–19. Grand Rapids, MI: Eerdmans, 2000.

Bataille, Georges. "The Meaning of General Economy." In *The Accursed Share: An Essay on General Economy, Vol. 1: Consumption*. Translated by Robert Hurley, 19–41. Brooklyn, NY: Zone Books, 1991.

Bauman, Whitney. *Religion and Ecology: Developing a Planetary Ethic*. New York: Columbia University Press, 2014.

Bayer, Oswald, and Benjamin Gleede, *Creator est Creatura: Luthers Christologie als Lehre von der Idiomenkommunikation*. Berlin: Walter de Gruyter.

Belsey, Catherine. *Poststructuralism: A Very Short Introduction*. New York: Oxford University Press, 2002.

Bennett, Jane. *Vibrant Matter: A Political Ecology of Things*. Durham, NC: Duke University Press, 2010.

Billings, J. Todd. "John Milbank's Theology of the 'Gift' and Calvin's Theology of Grace: A Critical Comparison." *Modern Theology* 21 (2005): 87–105.

Bonhoeffer, Dietrich. "After Ten Years." In *Letters and Papers from Prison*, edited by Eberhard Bethge. New York: Macmillan, 1971.

_____. *Christ the Center*. Translated by Edwin H. Robertson. San Francisco: Harper, 1978.

_____. *Dietrich Bonhoeffer Works, Volume 1: Sanctorum Communio: A Theology Study of the Sociology of the Church*, edited by Clifford J. Green. Translated by Reinhard Krauss and Nancy Lukens. Minneapolis: Fortress Press, 2009.

_____. *Dietrich Bonhoeffer Works, Volume 2: Act and Being*, edited by Wayne Whitson Floyd Jr. Translated by H. Martin Rumscheidt. Minneapolis: Fortress Press, 1996.

_____. *Dietrich Bonhoeffer Works, Volume 6: Ethics*. Edited by Clifford J. Green.

180

Translated by Reinhard Krauss, Charles C. West, and Douglas W. Stott. Minneapolis: Augsburg Fortress, 2005.

Calvin, John. *Institutes of the Christian Religion.* Edited by John McNeill. Translated by Ford Lewis Battles. Philadelphia: Westminster, 1960.

Caputo, John. *The Prayers and Tears of Jacques Derrida.* Bloomington: Indiana University Press, 1997.

Carson, Ronald A. "The Motifs of *Kenosis* and *Imitatio* in the Work of Dietrich Bonhoeffer, with an Excursus on the *Communicatio Idiomatum.*" *Journal of the American Academy of Religion* 43, no. 3 (1975): 542–53.

Cavanaugh, William. "Eucharistic Sacrifice and the Social Imagination in Early Modern Europe." *Journal of Medieval and Early Modern Studies* 31, no. 3 (2001): 585–605.

Chadwick, Henry. "Eucharist and Christology in the Nestorian Controversy." *Journal of Theological Studies* 2, no. 2 (1951): 145–64.

Chapman, Mark D. *Ernst Troeltsch and Liberal Theology: Religion and Cultural Synthesis in Wilhelmine Germany.* New York: Oxford University Press, 2001.

Chung, Paul. *Church and Ethical Responsibility in the Midst of World Economy: Greed, Dominion, and Justice.* Eugene, OR: Cascade, 2013.

_____, Ulrich Duchrow, and Craig L. Nessan. *Liberating Lutheran Theology: Freedom for Justice and Solidarity with Others in a Global Context.* Minneapolis: Fortress Press, 2011.

Cobb Jr., John B. *Sustaining the Common Good: A Christian Perspective on the Global Economy.* Cleveland: Pilgrim Press, 1994.

Connolly, William E. *Capitalism and Christianity, American Style.* Durham, NC: Duke University Press, 2008.

_____. "The Evangelical-Capitalist Resonance Machine." *Political Theory* 33, no. 6 (2005): 869–86.

Coole, Diana, and Samantha Frost, eds. *New Materialisms: Ontology, Agency, and Politics.* Durham, NC: Duke University Press, 2010.

Crompton, Rosemary. *Class and Stratification.* Malden, MA: Polity Press, 2008.

Daly, Herman E., and John B. Cobb Jr., *For the Common Good: Redirecting the Economy Toward Community, the Environment, and a Sustainable Future.* Boston: Beacon, 1994.

Davis, Thomas J. *This Is My Body: The Presence of Christ in Reformation Thought.* Grand Rapids, MI: Baker Academic, 2008.

Derrida, Jacques. *The Animal That Therefore I Am.* Edited by Marie-Louise Mallet. Translated by David Wood. New York: Fordham University Press, 2008.

_____. "A Certain Impossible Possibility of Saying the Event." In *The Late Derrida.* Edited by W. J. T. Mitchell and Arnold I. Davidson. Translated by Gila Walker, 223–43. Chicago: University of Chicago Press, 2007.

_____. *Given Time: I. Counterfeit Money.* Translated by Peggy Kamuf. Chicago: University of Chicago Press, 1994.

_____. *Of Grammatology.* Translated by Gayatri Chakravorty Spivak. Baltimore: Johns Hopkins University Press, 1997.

_____. *Writing and Difference.* Translated by Alan Bass. Chicago: University of Chicago Press, 1978.

_____, and Geoffrey Bennington. *Circumfession.* Translated by Geoffrey Bennington. Chicago: University of Chicago Press, 1993.

DeSalle, Rob, and Susan Perkins. *Welcome to the Microbiome: Getting to Know the Trillions of Bacteria and Other Microbes In, On, and Around You.* New Haven: Yale University Press, 2015.

DeVries, Dawn. "The Incarnation and the Sacramental Word: Calvin's and Schleiermacher's Sermons on Luke 2." In *Toward the Future of Reformed Theology: Tasks, Topics, Traditions,* edited by David Willis-Watkins and Michael Welker, 386–405. Grand Rapids, MI: Eerdmans, 1999.

Dombek, Kristin. "Swimming Against the Rising Tide: Secular Climate-Change Activist Can Learn from Evangelical Christians." *New York Times,* August 9, 2014.

Douglas, Mary. Foreword to *The Gift: The Form and Reason for Exchange in Archaic Societies,* by Marcel Mauss, vii–xviii. New York: W. W. Norton, 1990.

Duchrow, Ulrich. *Alternatives to Global Capitalism: Drawn from Biblical History, Designed for Political Action.* Translated by Elizabeth Hickes et al. Utrecht, The Netherlands: International Books, 1995.

Emerson, Ralph Waldo. "Gifts," in *Essays and Lectures.* New York: Penguin Putnam, 1983.

EPA. "Overview of Greenhouse Gases." http://www3.epa.gov/climatechange/ghgemissions/gases/n2o.html.

BIBLIOGRAPHY

French, William C. "Review: Returning to Creation: Moltmann's Eschatology Naturalized." *The Journal of Religion* 68, no. 1 (1988): 78–86.

Gerle, Elisabeth. *Passionate Embrace: Luther on Love, Body and the Sensual.* Eugene, OR: Cascade, 2017

Godabout, Jacques T., and Alain Caillé. *The World of the Gift.* Translated by Donald Winkler. Montreal: McGill-Queen's University Press, 1998.

Gonzalez, Justo. *The Story of Christianity: Vol. 1, The Early Church to the Dawn of the Reformation.* San Francisco: Harper, 1984.

Grau, Marion. "Erasing 'Economy': Derrida and the Construction of Divine Economies." *Cross Currents* 52, no. 3 (2002): 360–70.

_____. *Of Divine Economy: Refinancing Redemption.* New York: T&T Clark International, 2004.

_____. "'We Must Give Ourselves to Voyaging': Regifting the Theological Present." In *Interpreting the Postmodern: Responses to 'Radical Orthodoxy,'* edited by Rosemary Radford Ruether and Marion Grau, 141-60. New York: Bloomsbury T&T Clark, 2006.

Green, Clifford. *Bonhoeffer: A Theology of Sociality.* Grand Rapids, MI: Eerdmans, 1999.

_____. "Human Sociality and Christian Community." In *The Cambridge Companion to Dietrich Bonhoeffer,* edited by John W. de Gruchy, 113-33. New York: Cambridge University Press, 1999.

Gregersen, Niels Henrik. "Radical Generosity and the Flow of Grace." In *Word - Gift - Being: Justification - Economy - Ontology,* edited by Bo Holm and Peter Widmann, 117-44. Tübingen: Mohr Siebeck, 2009.

_____, Bo Holm, Ted Peters, and Peter Widmann, eds. *The Gift of Grace: The Future of Lutheran Theology.* Minneapolis: Augsburg Fortress, 2005.

Gregory, C. A. *Gifts and Commodities.* London: Academic, 1982.

Grim, John, and Mary Evelyn Tucker. *Religion and Ecology.* Washington, DC: Island Press, 2014.

Gudmundsdottir, Arnfridur. *Meeting God on the Cross: Christ, the Cross, and the Feminist Critique.* New York: Oxford University Press, 2010.

Gustafson, Scott W. *At the Altar of Wall Street: The Rituals, Myths, Theologies, Sacraments, and Mission of the Religion Known as the Modern Global Economy.* Grand Rapids, MI: Eerdmans, 2015.

Hamann, Johann Georg. *Hamann: Writings on Philosophy and Language.* Edited by Kenneth Haynes. New York: Cambridge University Press, 2007.

Hamm, Berndt. "Martin Luther's Revolutionary Theology of Pure gift without Reciprocation." Translated by Timothy J. Wengert. *Lutheran Quarterly* 29 (2015): 125–61.

Hampson, Daphne. "Luther on the Self: A Feminist Critique." *Word and World* 8 (1988): 334–43.

Haraway, Donna J. *When Species Meet.* Minneapolis: University of Minnesota Press, 2008.

Haroutunian, Joseph. *God With Us.* Philadelphia: Westminster, 1965.

Hessel, Dieter T., and Rosemary Radford Ruether, eds. *Christianity and Ecology: Seeking the Well-Being of Earth and Humans.* Cambridge: Harvard University Press, 2000.

Hoffmeyer, John F. "Multiplicity and Christocentric Theology." In *Divine Multiplicities: Trinities, Diversities, and the Nature of Relation,* edited by Chris Boesel and S. Wesley Ariarajah, 234–51. New York: Fordham, 2014.

Holm, Bo Kristian and Peter Widmann, eds. *Word - Gift - Being: Justification - Economy - Ontology.* Tubingen, Germany: Mohr Siebeck, 2009.

Irenaeus. *Against the Heresies.* Translated by Dominic J. Unger. Paulist, 2012.

Jackson, Wes. "The Land Institute," "Issues." Accessed, July 5, 2015. http://www.landinstitute.org/our-work/issues/#.

Jantzen, Grace M. *Becoming Divine: Towards a Feminist Philosophy of Religion.* Bloomington: Indiana University Press, 1999.

Kärkkäinen, Veli-Matti. "'Christian as Christ to the Neighbor': On Luther's Theology of Love." *International Journal of Systematic Theology* 6, no. 2 (2004): 101–17.

_____. *One with God: Salvation as Deification and Justification.* Collegeville, MN: Unitas Books, 2004.

Keller, Catherine. *Apocalypse Now and Then: A Feminist Guide to the End of the World.* Minneapolis: Augsburg Fortress, 2006.

_____. "Be a Multiplicity: Ancestral Anticipations." In *Polydoxy: Theology of Multiplicity and Relation,* edited by Catherine Keller and Laurel Schneider, 81–102. New York: Routledge, 2011.

BIBLIOGRAPHY

_____. *Cloud of the Impossible: Negative Theology and Planetary Entanglement.* New York: Columbia University Press, 2015.

_____. *From a Broken Web: Separation, Sexism and Self.* Boston: Beacon, 1988.

_____. "Is That All?: Gift and Reciprocity in Milbank's *Being Reconciled*." In *Interpreting the Postmodern: Responses to 'Radical Orthodoxy,'* ed. Rosemary Radford Ruether and Marion Grau, 18–35. New York: Bloomsbury T&T Clark, 2006.

_____. "Talking Dirty: Ground Is Not Foundation." In *Ecospirit: Religions and Philosophies for the Earth,* edited by Laurel Kearns and Catherine Keller, 63–76. New York: Fordham University Press, 2007.

_____, and Stephen D. Moore. "Derridapocalypse." In *Derrida and Religion: Other Testaments,* edited by Yvonne Sherwood and Kevin Hart, 189–208. New York: Routledge, 2005.

Kelly, J. N. D. *Early Christian Doctrines.* New York: HarperCollins, 1978.

Klein, Naomi. "A Radical Vatican?," *The New Yorker,* July 10, 2015, http://www.newyorker.com/news/news-desk/a-visit-to-the-vatican.

_____. *This Changes Everything: Capitalism vs. the Climate.* New York: Simon & Schuster, 2014.

Kleinhans, Kathryn A. "Christ as Bride/Groom: A Lutheran Feminist Relational Christology." In *Transformative Lutheran Theologies: Feminist, Womanist, and Mujerista Perspectives,* edited by Mary J. Streufert, 123–34. Minneapolis: Fortress Press, 2010.

Lathrop, Gordon. *Holy Ground: A Liturgical Cosmology.* Minneapolis: Fortress Press, 2003.

Lazareth, William. *Christians in Society: Luther, the Bible and Social Ethics.* Minneapolis: Augsburg Fortress, 2001.

Lienhard, Marc. *Luther: Witness to Jesus Christ, Stages and Themes of the Reformer's Christology.* Translated by Edwin H. Robertson. Minneapolis: Augsburg, 1982.

Lindberg, Carter. *Beyond Charity: Reformation Initiatives for the Poor.* Minneapolis: Fortress Press, 1993.

Lüdemann, Susanne. *Politics of Deconstruction: A New Introduction to Jacques Derrida.* Stanford, CA: Stanford University Press, 2014.

Luther, Martin. "The Blessed Sacrament of the Holy and True Body and Blood of Christ (1519)." *Luther's Works, Vol. 35: Word and Sacrament*, edited by E. Theodore Bachmann. Minneapolis: Fortress Press, 1960.

———. "The Bondage of the Will." In *The Annotated Luther, Volume 2: Word and Faith*, edited by Kirsi I. Stjerna, 153–258. Minneapolis: Fortress Press, 2015.

———. "Confession Concerning Christ's Supper." In *Martin Luther's Basic Theological Writings*, edited by Timothy Lull, 26–32. Minneapolis: Fortress Press, 2012.

———. "The Freedom of a Christian." In *Martin Luther's Basic Theological Writings*, edited by Timothy Lull, 386–411. Minneapolis: Fortress Press, 2005.

———. "Freedom of the Christian," *Luther's Works, Volume 31: Career of the Reformer I*, edited by Harold J. Grimm and Helmut T. Lehmann. Minneapolis: Fortress Press, 1957.

———. "The Large Catechism." In *The Book of Concord: The Confessions of the Evangelical Lutheran Church.* Edited by Robert Kolb and Timothy J. Wengert. Translated by Charles Arand et al. Minneapolis: Fortress Press, 2000.

———. "Lectures on Galatians—1519." *Luther's Works, Vol. 27: Lectures on Galatians Chapters 5-6*, edited by Jaroslav Pelikan. St. Louis: Concordia, 2007.

Lutz, Kaelber. "Max Weber's Protestant Ethic in the 21st Century." *International Journal of Politics, Culture, and Society* 16, no. 1 (2002): 133–46.

Luy, David J. *Dominus Mortis: Martin Luther on the Incorruptibility of God in Christ.* Minneapolis: Fortress Press, 2014.

Mannermaa, Tuomo. *Christ Present in Faith: Luther's View of Justification.* Minneapolis: Fortress Press, 2005.

———. "Justification and *Theosis* in Lutheran-Orthodox Perspective." In *Union with Christ*, edited by Carl Braaten and Robert Jenson, 25–41. Grand Rapids, MI: Eerdmans, 1998.

Malysz, Piotr J. "Exchange and Ecstasy: Luther's Eucharistic Theology in Light of Radical Orthodoxy's Critique of Gift and Sacrifice." *Scottish Journal of Theology* 60 (2007): 294–308.

———. "Review of *Creator Est Creatura: Luthers Christologie als Lehre von der Idiomenkommunikation*, edited by Oswald Bayer and Benjamin Gleede." *Reviews in Religion & Theology* 16 (2009): 618–22.

Marsh, Charles. *Reclaiming Dietrich Bonhoeffer: The Promise of His Theology.* New York: Oxford University Press, 1994.

BIBLIOGRAPHY

Mauss, Marcel. *The Gift: The Form and Reason for Exchange in Archaic Societies.* Translated by W. D. Halls. New York: W. W. Norton, 1990.

McDougall, Joy Ann. *Pilgrimage of Love: Moltmann on the Trinity and Christian Life.* New York: Oxford University Press, 2005.

McFague, Sallie. *Life Abundant: Theology and Economy for a Planet in Peril.* Minneapolis: Fortress Press, 2001.

_____. *Models of God: Theology for an Ecological, Nuclear Age.* Minneapolis: Fortress Press, 1987.

McKibben, Bill. *The Comforting Whirlwind: God, Job, and the Scale of Creation.* Cambridge, MA: Cowley, 2005.

_____. "Global Warming's Terrifying New Math." *Rolling Stone,* July 19, 2012.

Meeks, Douglas. *God the Economist: The Doctrine of God and Political Economy.* Minneapolis: Augsburg Fortress, 1989.

Milbank, John. *Being Reconciled: Ontology and Pardon.* New York: Routledge, 2003.

_____. *Beyond Secular Order: The Representation of Being and the Representation of the People.* Malden, MA: Wiley-Blackwell, 2013.

_____. "Can a Gift Be Given?: Prolegomena to a Future Trinitarian Metaphysic." *Modern Theology* 11 (1995): 119–61.

_____. "The Gift and the Given." In *Theory, Culture & Society* 23 (2006): 444–47.

_____ and Slavoj Žižek, *The Monstrosity of Christ: Paradox or Dialectic?* Edited by Preston Davis. Cambridge, MA: MIT Press, 2009.

Moe-Lobeda, Cynthia D. "Climate Change as Climate Debt: Forging a Just Future." *Journal of the Society of Christian Ethics* 36, no. 1 (Spring/Summer 2016): 27–49.

_____. "Globalization in Light of Luther's Eucharistic Economic Ethics." *Dialog* 42, no. 3 (2003): 250–56.

_____. *Resisting Structural Evil: Love as Ecological-Economic Vocation.* Minneapolis: Fortress Press, 2013.

Moltmann, Jürgen. *The Crucified God: The Cross of Christ as the Foundation and Criticism of Christian Theology.* New York: HarperCollins, 1974.

_____. *God in Creation.* Minneapolis: Fortress Press, 1991.

_____. *Jesus Christ for Today's World.* Minneapolis: Fortress Press, 1995.

_____. "The Resurrection of Christ and the New Earth." In *Resurrection and Responsibility: Essays on Theology, Scripture, and Ethics in Honor of Thorwald*

Lorenzen, edited by Keith D. Dyer and David J. Neville, 51–58. Eugene, OR: Pickwick, 2009.

_____. *Theology of Play.* Translated by Reinhard Ulrich. New York: Harper & Row, 1972.

Montag, John. "Revelation: The False Legacy of Suárez." In *Radical Orthodoxy: A New Theology,* edited by John Milbank, Catherine Pickstock, and Graham Ward. New York: Routledge, 1999.

Moore, Stephen. *Mark and Luke in Poststructuralist Perspectives: Jesus Begins to Write.* New Haven: Yale University Press, 1992.

_____. "Why There Are No Humans or Animals in the Gospel of Mark." In *Mark as Story: Retrospect and Prospect,* edited by Kelly R. Iverson and Christopher W. Skinner, 71–94. Atlanta: Society of Biblical Literature, 2011.

Nessan, Craig. "Reappropriating Luther's Two Kingdoms." *Lutheran Quarterly,* 29 (2005): 302–11.

Niebuhr, Reinhold. *The Nature and Destiny of Man: A Christian Interpretation,* vol. 2. New York: Scribner's, 1964.

Norris, Richard A. Jr., ed. and trans. *The Christological Controversy.* Minneapolis: Fortress Press, 1980.

Northcott, Michael. *A Political Theology of Climate Change.* Grand Rapids, MI: Eerdmans, 2013.

Oberman, Heiko A. *The Dawn of the Reformation: Essays in Late Medieval and Early Reformation Thought.* Edinburgh: T&T Clark, 1992.

_____. *Luther: Man Between God and the Devil.* Translated by Eileen Walliser-Schwarzbart. New York: Doubleday, 1992.

Ozment, Steven. *The Age of Reform, 1250-1550: An Intellectual and Religious History of Late Medieval and Reformation Europe.* New Haven: Yale University Press, 1980.

Pedersen, Else Marie Wiberg. "This Is Not About Sex?: A Discussion of the Understanding of Love and Grace in Bernard of Clairvaux's and Martin Luther's Theologies," *Dialog* 50, no. 1 (2011): 15–25.

Pelikan, Jaroslav. *The Christian Tradition: A History of the Development of Doctrine, Vol. 1: The Emergence of the Catholic Tradition: (100-600).* Chicago: University of Chicago Press, 1971.

BIBLIOGRAPHY

Peters, Ted. *Sin Boldly!: Justifying Faith for Fragile and Broken Souls.* Minneapolis: Fortress Press, 2015.

Plotnitsky, Arkady. *Complementarity: Anti-Epistemology After Bohr and Derrida.* Durham, NC: Duke University Press, 1994.

_____. "Re: Re-Flecting, Re-Membering, Re-Collecting, Re-Selecting, Re-Warding, Re-Wording, Re-Iterating, Re-et-Cetra-ing . . . (in) Hegel." *Postmodern Culture* 5, no. 2 (1995).

Poggi, Gianfranco. *Weber: A Short Introduction.* Malden, MA: Polity Press, 2006.

Pollan, Michael. *The Omnivore's Dilemma: A Natural History of Four Meals.* New York: Penguin, 2006.

Pope Francis, *Laudato Si': On Care for Our Common Home.* Vatican City: Libreria Editrice Vaticana, 2015.

Primavesi, Anne. *Gaia's Gift: Earth, Ourselves and God after Copernicus.* New York: Routledge, 2004.

_____. "The Preoriginal Gift—and Our Response to It." In *Ecospirit: Religions and Philosophies for the Earth,* edited by Laurel Kerns and Catherine Keller, 217–32. New York: Fordham University Press, 2007.

Radicalizing Reformation. "Radicalizing Reformation: A Critical Research and Action Project Towards 2017." http://radicalizing-reformation.com/index.php/en/.

Rasmussen, Larry L. *Dietrich Bonhoeffer: Reality and Resistance.* Louisville: John Knox, 2005.

_____. *Earth-Honoring Faith: Religious Ethics in a New Key.* New York: Oxford University Press, 2013.

_____. "The Ethics of Responsible Action." In *The Cambridge Companion to Dietrich Bonhoeffer,* edited by John W. de Gruchy, 206–25. New York: Cambridge University Press, 1999.

Rowe, Terra S. "Communicating Grace." *Currents in Theology and Mission* 43, no. 4 (2016): 22–26.

_____. "Grace and Climate Change: The Free Gift in Capitalism and Protestantism." In *Eco-Reformation: Grace and Hope for a Planet in Peril,* ed. Jim Martin-Schramm and Lisa Dahill, 253–71. Eugene, OR: Wipf & Stock, 2016.

_____. "Grace in Intra-action." In *Entangled Worlds: Science, Religion, Materiality.*

Edited by Mary-Jane Rubenstein and Catherine Keller. New York: Fordham University Press, 2017.

———. "Protestant Ghosts and Spirits of Capitalism: Ecology, Economy, and the Reformation Tradition." *Dialog: A Journal of Theology* 55 (2016): 50–61.

Rubenstein, Mary-Jane. "Capital Shares: The Way Back Into the With of Christianity." *Political Theology* 11, no. 1 (2010): 103–19.

Saarinen, Risto. *God and the Gift: An Ecumenical Theology of Giving.* Collegeville, MN: Liturgical, 2005.

Santmire, H. Paul. *Nature Reborn: The Ecological and Cosmic Promise of Christian Theology.* Minneapolis: Augsburg Fortress, 2000.

———. *The Travail of Nature: The Ambiguous Ecological Promise of Christian Theology.* Minneapolis: Fortress Press, 1985.

Sasse, Hermann. *This Is My Body: Luther's Contention for the Real Presence in the Sacrament of the Altar.* Minneapolis: Augsburg, 1959.

Sherwood, Yvonne. *The Prostitute and the Prophet: Reading Hosea in the Late Twentieth Century.* New York: T&T Clark, 2004.

Shiva, Vandana. *Soil Not Oil: Environmental Justice in an Age of Climate Crisis.* Brooklyn, NY: South End Press, 2008.

———. "Soil Papered Over," Speech give at the Seizing the Alternative Conference, Claremont, CA, June, 2015.

Sittler, Joseph. "Called to Unity." *Ecumenical Review* 14, no. 2 (1962): 177–87.

———. *The Care of the Earth.* Minneapolis: Fortress Press Facets, 2004.

———. *Essays on Nature and Grace.* Philadelphia: Fortress Press, 1972.

———. *Evocations of Grace: The Writings of Joseph Sittler on Ecology, Theology, and Ethics.* Edited by Steven Bouma-Prediger and Peter Bakken. Grand Rapids, MI: Eerdmans, 2000.

———. *Gravity and Grace.* Edited by Thomas S. Hanson. Minneapolis: Augsburg Fortress, 2005.

Smith, Adam. *The Wealth of Nations.* Edited by Kathryn Sutherland. New York: Oxford University Press, 2008.

Steiger, Johann Anselm. "The *communicatio idiomatum* as the Axle and Motor of Luther's Theology." *Lutheran Quarterly* 14 (2000): 125–58.

Stjerna, Kirsi. "Ongoing Reformation of Language and Spirituality:

BIBLIOGRAPHY

Intersections with the Finnish Interpretation of Luther and Feminist Scholarship." *Currents in Theology and Mission* 43, no. 3 (2016): 17–21.

Szelenyi, Ivan. "Weber on Protestantism and Capitalism." Yale University Open Courses, SOCY-151: Foundations of Modern Social Theory, Lecture 16 (Oct. 27, 2009), http://oyc.yale.edu/sociology/socy-151/lecture-16.

Tanner, Kathryn. *Economy of Grace.* Minneapolis: Fortress Press, 2005.

_____. *Politics of God: Christian Theologies and Social Justice.* Minneapolis: Augsburg Fortress, 1992.

Taylor, Mark C. "Capitalizing (on) Gifting." In *The Enigma of Gift and Sacrifice,* edited by Edith Wyschogrod, Jean-Joseph Goux, and Eric Boynton, 50–74. New York: Fordham University Press, 2002.

Thompson, Deanna. *Crossing the Divide: Luther, Feminism, and the Cross.* Minneapolis: Fortress Press, 2004.

Torvend, Samuel. "Those Little Pieces of White Bread: Early Lutheran Initiatives among the Hungry Poor." *Dialog* 52, no. 1 (2003): 19–28.

Tylenda, Joseph N. "Calvin's Understanding of the Communication of Properties." *Westminster Theological Journal* 38, no. 1 (1975): 54–65.

Volf, Miroslav. *Free of Charge: Giving and Forgiving in a Culture Stripped of Grace.* Grand Rapids, MI: Zondervan, 2005.

Walter, Gregory. *Being Promised: Theology, Gift, and Practice.* Grand Rapids, MI: Eerdmans, 2013.

Wandel, Lee Palmer. *The Eucharist in the Reformation: Incarnation and Liturgy.* New York: Cambridge University Press, 2005.

Weber, Marianne. *Max Weber: A Biography by Marianne Weber.* Translated by Harry Zohn. New York: John Wiley & Sons, 1975.

Weber, Max. *The Protestant Ethic and the 'Spirit' of Capitalism and Other Writings.* Translated and edited by Peter Baehr and Gordon C. Wells. New York: Penguin, 2002.

_____. *The Protestant Ethic and the Spirit of Capitalism.* Translated by Talcott Parsons. New York: Charles Scribner's Sons, 1958.

Weiner, Annette. *Inalienable Possessions: The Paradox of Keeping-While-Giving.* Berkeley: University of California Press, 1992.

Westhelle, Vitor. "God and Justice: The Word and the Mask," *Journal of Lutheran Ethics* 3, no. 1 (2003).

TOWARD A BETTER WORLDLINESS

Whitehead, Alfred North. *Process and Reality*. Edited by David Ray Griffin and Donald W. Sherburne. New York: Free Press, 1978.

_____. *Science and The Modern World*. New York: Free Press, 1967.

Zemon Davis, Natalie, *The Gift in Sixteenth-Century France*. New York: Oxford University Press, 2000.

Index

agency, xvii, xxv, xxvii, xxx, xxxv,
 10, 112, 116, 181
agriculture, xxxix, 84
alienable, xlv, 43, 50, 51, 83, 101,
 121, 144, 152, 168, 171, 173
Althaus, Paul, xv, 130, 149, 150, 155,
 163
American Natural History Museum,
 xxix
Animals, xxii, xxiii, xxiv, 42
anti-semitism, 18
Apollinarius, 124
Arand, Charles P., 18, 140, 141
Aristotle, xxii, xxiii
Arius, 124
Athanasius, 123–26, 130, 135, 143
Augustine, 15, 52, 71, 102, 103, 123,
 172

Barad, Karen, xxv–xxvii, 1, 3, 7, 92,
 113–17, 172, 175
Barker, H., Gaylon xvii, 158, 159
Barth, Karl, 57, 81, 158
Braaten, Carl E., 141–43, 167

Bakken, Peter, 67, 70–72, 111
Bataille, Georges, 57, 58, 59, 61, 111
Bauman, Whitney, xxix
Bayer, Oswald, xlv, 127, 135
Being, being–with, xxiii, xlvi, 31, 32,
 54, 75, 108, 120, 122, 159, 160,
 162–64, 166–68, 171, 174
Belsey, Catherine, 55
Bennett, Jane, xxviii, 90
bilateral gifting, xliv, 92, 96, 103,
 102, 109–12, 117, 149, 153, 168
Billings, J. Todd, xxxvi
Boesel, Chris, xi, 164
Bohr, Niels, xxvii, 111, 113
Bonhoeffer, Dietrich, xlvi, 15, 19,
 122, 136, 155, 157–68, 171
Bouma–Prediger, Stephen, 67, 71,
 111

Caillé, Alain, 50
Calvin, John, xxxvi, xli, xlii, 3, 9, 10,
 12, 13, 17, 18, 27, 28, 30, 31, 38,
 52, 76, 131–34, 137, 138, 143, 152,
 172

capitalism, xix, xx, xxii, xxv, xxxi, xxxii, xxxvi, xxxvii, xl, xli, xlii, 1–32, 33–35, 40, 42, 49, 51, 52–54, 61, 63, 64, 93, 94, 152

Caputo, John, 49, 55, 56

Carson, Rachel, xlii

Carson, Ronald A., 166

Cavanaugh, William, xxxvii, 34, 51, 97, 98

Chadwick, Henry, 126

Chalcedon, Council of, 124, 126, 130

Chapman, Mark D., 13

Chung, Paul, xxxi, 13, 19, 20, 40

Christ, xv, xvi, xliv, xlv, 24, 39, 72, 81, 98, 99, 120, 122–55, 157, 161, 163–67, 174, 177

Christianity, xxi, 18, 31, 37, 50–53, 63, 93, 125, 166

Christology, 70, 120, 124–34, 139, 148, 152, 158, 159

Church, xxxi, 13–28, 37, 38, 46, 53, 70, 83, 97, 123, 125, 127, 129, 130, 140–42, 161, 170, 176, 177

climate, climate change, xiii, xv, xvi, xix, xxv, xxvi, xxxii, xxxiii, xxxiv, xxxv, xxxviii, xxxix, 2, 4, 12, 26, 27, 32, 33, 45, 48, 64, 83–86, 90, 158, 171–73, 175, 176

Cobb, John B. Jr., xix, xx, xxi, xxii, xxxii, xxxiii, xl, xli, 12, 18, 40

Connolly, William E., 28, 29

consumption, xli, 12, 28, 30, 57

commodification, xlii, 32, 49, 50, 51, 83, 145

common good, xx, xxi, xxii, xxxii, xxxiii, xl, xli, 12, 17, 18, 21–24, 44, 48, 49, 56, 83, 98, 128, 151, 153, 154

communicatio idiomatum, communication of properties, communication of attributes, xlv, xlvi, 47, 83, 86, 117, 119, 120, 121–39, 147, 148–55, 159, 162, 163, 165, 166, 168, 174

communion, 23, 24, 67, 74, 75, 78, 83, 122, 141, 151, 177

community, xxi, xxviii, xxix, xxxiii, xxxix, xlv, 2, 7, 21–25, 51, 78, 82, 85, 86, 99, 105, 122, 139, 144, 146, 151, 152, 163–65, 176, 177

complementarity, xxvi, 111

Coole, Diana, xxv, xxvi, 112

creation, xxi, xxxii, xliii, xlv, 17, 38, 40, 41, 44, 45, 51, 62–65, 68, 69–71, 75, 76, 77, 79–86, 96, 97, 100, 116, 117, 121–27, 134, 146, 154, 158, 162, 166–69, 177

Crompton, Rosemary, 6

Cyril of Alexandria, 124–26, 129–30, 132

Daly, Herman E., xx, xxii, xxxii, xxxiii, xl, xli, 12, 18

Davis, Thomas J., 131

deconstruction, 31, 54, 55, 111

de-creators, 45, 64

debt, climate debt, xxxiv, xxxvii, 2,

INDEX

37, 48–50, 87, 94, 95, 98, 103, 115,
125, 150, 152, 154, 170
Derrida, Jacques, xxiii, xxxvii,
xxxviii, xliv, 35, 36, 48, 49, 54,
55–62, 92, 105–13, 120, 139, 175,
176
DeSalle, Rob, xxix
Descartes, Rene, xxii–xxiv, 44, 45,
112, 147, 152
DeVries, Dawn, 132
difference, 28, 38, 58–61, 82, 86, 96,
105–9, 112, 117, 122–26, 130, 133,
138, 146, 151, 165, 167, 170
divinity, 77, 97, 121, 124–26, 137,
138, 162–68
divinization, 148, 154
Dombek, Kristin, xiii–xv, 170
Douglas, Mary, xxxvi, 43
Duchrow, Ulrich, xxxi, 13, 16–20,
27, 40, 93

earth, xxii, xxviii, xxix, xxxix, 39,
45, 53, 74, 120, 150, 154, 165
Emerson, Ralph Waldo, 89, 101, 102,
105
ecology, ecological, xix, xxv, xxvi,
xxviii, xxix–xlvi, 11, 26–32, 35,
36, 41, 42, 44, 49, 51, 57, 63–65,
68–84, 110–12, 117, 120, 154, 166,
168, 170–72, 174, 177
economy, xx, xxv, xxx–xxxvii,
xxxix, xlvi, 15, 21, 22, 27, 32, 36,
39–42, 48, 53–64, 93–96, 110–12,
119, 154, 176

eco/nomy, xxx–xxxv, xxxviii, xl,
xlvi, 4, 29, 67, 91, 117, 145, 154,
168, 171, 172, 174, 175
ecotheology, xvi, 54, 68, 70, 86, 120
entanglement, xxvii, 1, 3, 113, 115,
116, 169
EPA, xxxix, 85
Eucharist, 24, 32, 51, 72, 97, 126,
128–32, 147, 148, 151
evangelical, xiii, 29
extra nos, xv, xvi, xvii, xxix, 139, 140,
143, 146, 172
exchange, exchangist, xv, xxi, xxx,
xlv, 32, 34–65, 68, 69, 73, 75, 82,
83, 85, 86, 91–118, 119–59, 166,
168–77

feminism, xvi–xxi, 57, 59, 61, 99,
113, 115, 135, 147, 152, 172, 175
Finnish interpretation of Luther,
xliv, xlv, 97, 99, 121, 140–48, 167,
175
forensic justification, xv, 139, 141,
143, 145, 153, 169
forgiveness, xliii, 9, 45, 63, 101, 102,
109, 140, 141, 143, 144, 148, 153,
177
The Formula of Concord, 130, 133–35,
141, 142
fossil fuel, xxv, xxxix, xli, 4, 11, 12,
26–28, 53, 84–86
freedom, Christian freedom, xvi, 19,
29, 33, 90, 91, 95, 98, 116, 140,
148, 149, 160, 174

195

French, William C., 80

Frost, Samantha, xxv, xxvi, 112

genus apostelesmaticum, 133

genus majestaticum, 133, 134, 137, 138, 166

genus tapeinoticum, 134, 135, 137, 139, 146, 149, 166

Gerle, Elisabeth, 99

gift, gift-exchange, xiv, xv, xxix, xxxv–xlvi, 33–65, 67–70, 73–76, 83–87, 89–118, 120–22, 127, 128, 132, 134, 138–46, 149–55, 164–77

Gleede, Benjamin, xlv, 127, 135

global warming, xxxiv, xxxix, 12

Godabout, Jacques T., 50

grace, xiii–xxii, xxix, xxxv, xxxvi, xxxviii–xlvi, 10, 20, 21, 24–27, 31–42, 45–49, 54, 56, 57, 61, 64, 65, 67–77, 83, 85, 86, 91–105, 109, 110, 113, 115, 117, 118, 119–24, 131, 139–44, 153, 154, 157, 159, 160, 168–77

Grau, Marion, xxxii, xl, 40, 48, 59, 61–64

Green, Clifford, 159, 161, 162, 164

greenhouse gases, xxxix, 84, 85

Gregersen, Niels Henrik, xliv, 35, 92, 96, 100–112, 120, 149

Gregory, C. A., 50

Grim, John, 120

Gudmundsdottir, Arnfridur, 135

Gustafson, Scott W., 18

Hamann, Johann Georg, 119

Hamm, Berndt, 35, 37–42, 44, 46, 54, 96, 112, 123, 127

Hampson, Daphne, xvi–xviii

Haraway, Donna J., xxviii, xxxii, 115, 175

Haroutunian, Joseph, 67, 75

Hegel, Georg Wilhelm Friedrich, 54, 58–61

Hessel, Dieter T., xxi, 67

Hoffmeyer, John F., xi, 163, 164

Holl, Karl, xvii, 14–26, 170

Holm, Bo Kristian, 35, 39, 96–100, 103, 105, 117, 120, 128, 145

Ignatius of Antioch, 123

impassibility, 121, 123, 136, 137

impossibility, 39, 49, 55

inalienable, 43, 50, 94, 98, 99, 121, 144, 145, 167

incarnation, xv, 64, 124–32

individualism, xx, xxxvi, xl, xlii, 25, 27, 32, 49, 51, 54, 62, 69, 71, 75, 114, 140, 147, 153, 161, 164, 172, 173

intra-action, xiii, xxvii, xxviii, 33, 113–16

intra nos, 139, 142, 144, 146

Irenaeus, 124

Jackson, Wes, 84

Jantzen, Grace M., 59, 152

Jenson, Robert W., 141–43, 167

INDEX

Jesus, 124, 125, 129, 134, 157, 158, 165

justice, xxxiii, xxxiv, xxxv, xlii, xliv, 2, 3, 17–27, 35, 36, 39–41, 45, 69, 142, 143, 152, 159, 160, 168

justification, xv, 21, 22, 25, 27, 29, 30, 33, 34, 38–41, 97, 98, 120, 121, 126, 127, 128, 139–45, 148, 151–53, 160, 169, 170

Kärkkäinen, Veli-Matti, 142, 144, 148

Keller, Catherine, xi, xii, xiii, xviii, xxi, xxii, xxiv, 31, 33, 56, 61–63, 65, 68, 90, 111, 117, 173

Kelly, J. N. D., 123

Klein, Naomi, xiii, xxxiv

Kolb, Robert, 18, 140, 141

Kleinhans, Kathryn A., 99, 147

Lathrop, Gordon, xxxi

Lazareth, William, 13, 14, 16, 20, 26, 28

liberal theology, 13, 16, 158

Lindberg, Carter, 13, 14, 20–25, 37, 39, 40, 93, 151

liturgy, xxxi, 20, 24, 25, 50, 83, 129, 130, 131, 151

love, xvii, xviii, 24, 25, 42, 74, 75, 79, 97–105, 119, 128, 129, 142, 144, 147–54, 162, 162, 172, 174

Lüdemann, Susanne, 54

Luria, Isaac, 81

Luther, Martin/Lutheran, xiii, xv, xvi–xviii, xli, xlii, xliv–xlvi, 3, 8–32, 35–41, 46, 47, 51, 52, 54, 71, 97–100, 104, 117, 120– 23, 126–55, 158–67, 171–75

Luther Renaissance, 14, 15

The Lutheran Confessions, 14, 18, 140

Lutz, Kaelber, 5

Luy, David J., xlv, 135–37

Mannermaa, Tuomo, 142–44, 149

Malysz, Piotr J., 39, 96–98, 117, 120, 135, 167

Marsh, Charles, 159, 161

Marx, Karl, xl, xli, 6, 8, 58

matter, materialism, xxii, xxiv–xxviii, xxxix, xli, 6, 13, 14, 19, 20, 22, 23, 45, 57, 59, 63, 72, 73, 76, 90, 92, 112–15, 118, 129, 131, 132, 138, 139, 162, 172

Mauss, Marcel, xxxv–xxxvii, xlii, xliv, 36, 37, 42–44, 48, 49, 51, 54, 55, 68, 75, 83, 98, 101–3, 108, 109

McDougall, Joy Ann, 124

McFague, Sallie, xix–xxii, 12, 82, 86, 167

McKibben, Bill, 12, 64

Meeks, Douglas, xxxi, 18

Melanchthon, Philip, 14, 38, 129, 139–43

metaphysics, 54, 73, 107, 108, 160

microbiome, xxix, 138

Milbank, John, xxxvi–xliv, 33–36, 42–64, 83, 91–105, 108, 109, 120, 141, 168, 173

modernity, xix, xxii–xxv, xxviii,
xxix, xxxvi, xlv, 2, 4, 6, 13, 20,
34, 35, 42–45, 47–53, 63, 72, 73,
77–79, 84, 85, 91, 102, 108, 114,
116, 117, 122, 131, 135, 136, 147,
152, 153, 170, 175
Moe-Lobeda, Cynthia D., xxxiii,
xxxiv, 2, 12, 147
Moltmann, Jürgen, xix, xlii, xliii, 29,
30, 33, 34, 40, 67, 69, 76–86, 91,
116, 120, 122, 137–39, 158–60,
166, 167
money, xxxvi, 8, 18, 21, 24, 93
Montag, John, 47
Moore, Stephen, xxiii, xxiv, 56, 106,
multilateral gifting, xv, xliv, xlv, 92,
96, 101–10, 113, 115, 117, 120,
149, 153, 168, 171–73
multiple, multiplicity, xxiv, xxix,
58, 73–75, 85, 106, 109, 111, 116,
139, 146, 163, 164, 173, 174

neighbor, xvi, xvii, xlv, 95, 104, 116,
144, 147–54, 162
Nessan, Craig L., xi, 13, 15–17, 19,
20, 40
Nestingen, James A., 140, 141
Niebuhr, Reinhold, 14
Nietzsche, Friedrich, 105, 106, 108,
109, 176
nominalism, 44–47, 53
nonlinear, xxvi, xliv, xlv, 29, 117,
149, 153
non-locality, 111

Norris, Richard A. Jr., 124–26
Northcott, Michael, 45, 53

Oberman, Heiko A., 46
occasion, 74, 75, 172
Ockham, William of, 44, 46, 47, 53
omnipotence, 56, 81, 104, 123
omnipresence, 81, 133, 134
ontology, xxv, xxvii, xxxvii, xl, xlvi,
35, 43, 49, 52, 62, 63, 73, 75, 92,
97, 112–14, 117, 122, 142, 159,
160, 168, 171, 173, 174
Osiander, Andres, 140–42
Ozment, Steven, 46, 47

Pedersen, Else Marie Wiberg, 99
Pelikan, Jaroslav, 122, 125, 126, 150
Performativity, xxv, 114, 117, 172
Perkins, Susan, xxix
Peters, Ted, 35
Plotnitsky, Arkady, 58, 59, 111–13
Poggi, Gianfranco, 6–9, 11
Pollan, Michael, xxviii, xxxix, 169,
170
Pope Francis, xxxiii, xxxiv
possessions, 4, 18, 43, 90, 148, 150,
152, 153
postmodern, 48
poststructuralism, 55
presence, bodily presence, xv, xxix,
xlv, 45, 47, 55, 71, 79, 81, 96,
106–8, 125, 129, 131–34, 139,
140–42, 144, 164, 167

INDEX

Primavesi, Anne, xxxviii, xxxix, xliii, xliv, 68, 69, 83, 110, 111, 113

pro me, xvi, xxix, 120, 162, 163, 164, 166

property, 18, 27, 43, 51, 94, 122, 137, 150, 152, 154

Protestantism, xvii, xli, 5, 6, 8, 12, 29, 33, 34, 47, 51

Protestant ethic, xli, 4-6, 8, 10-15, 25, 28, 39, 56, 92, 158, 173

Quantum Physics, xxv, xxvii, 73, 111, 113

Queer, 113, 114, 116, 117

Radical Orthodoxy, xxxvii, xlii, 34, 35, 47, 48, 53, 62, 91, 97, 173

Radicalizing Reformation, 40

Rasmussen, Larry L., 11, 12, 49, 120, 162, 163, 164, 166

reciprocal, reciprocal gift, reciprocation, xiv, xxi, xxxvi, xxxvii, xxxix, xl, xlii, 34-38, 41-45, 48, 49, 51, 52, 56, 62, 63, 65, 70, 79, 85-87, 92, 97-100, 104, 109, 112, 120, 121, 135, 136, 146, 164, 171

reconciliation, 5, 165, 167

Reformation, xiv, xv, xxi, xxii, xl, xli, xliv, 1, 3, 7, 8, 12-14, 16, 17, 20-22, 25, 27, 29, 30, 32-34, 36, 38-42, 45, 46, 48, 52, 54, 69, 77, 80, 91, 93, 97, 102, 117, 125-27,

129-31, 138, 140, 145, 147, 158, 163, 164, 171, 176

responsibility, xiv, xxxi, xxxv, xlii, xlvi, 1-4, 16, 19, 23, 24, 26, 27-30, 32, 81, 91, 116, 152, 170, 175

resurrection, 52, 57-59, 61, 62, 81

Roman Catholic, 9, 41, 129, 130, 140

Rubenstein, Mary-Jane, xiii, 30, 31, 32, 33

Ruether, Rosemary Radford, xxi, 48, 62, 67

Saarinen, Risto, xliv, 35, 92, 96, 97, 102, 103, 105, 109, 149, 155

sacrament, sacramental, 9, 18, 23, 24, 32, 50, 121, 126, 128-33, 139, 146-49, 151, 152, 168, 170, 174

sacrifice, 51, 58, 76, 97, 98, 103, 129, 133, 145, 149

sanctification, 139, 143, 144

Santmire, H. Paul, xix, 163

salvation, 9, 20, 38, 39, 40, 46, 47, 72, 81, 97, 98, 104, 122, 132, 140, 142, 143, 152, 163, 172

Sasse, Hermann, 132

Scotus, Duns, 38, 44, 46, 47

secularism, 35

separative self, xxi, xlii, 35, 54, 62, 69, 72, 73, 75, 78, 91, 92, 113, 114, 115, 117, 122, 151, 152, 154, 161, 171, 172, 173

sexism, xii, xviii, xxi, 90

Sherwood, Yvonne, 56, 106, 107

199

Shiva, Vandana, xxxii, xxxviii, xxxix, 84, 85
Sittler, Joseph, xix, xlii, xliii, xliv, 40, 65, 67, 68, 69, 70, 71, 72, 73, 74, 75, 76, 77, 79, 80, 83, 86, 91, 110, 111, 113, 116, 120, 122, 128, 161, 170
Smith, Adam, xx, xxi, 6, 58, 59
socialism, xl, xli, 15, 17, 77
soil, xxxii, xxxviii, xxxix, 83–86, 171
sustainability, xxx
Steiger, Johann Anselm, 121, 127, 128, 135, 136
Stjerna, Kirsi, xv, 147
Szelenyi, Ivan, 5, 6

Tanner, Kathryn, xl, 2, 3, 91–96, 103, 110
Taylor, Mark C., 58, 59
Tertullian, 123
theosis, 142, 143
Thompson, Deanna, xviii
Torvend, Samuel, 13, 20–25, 37, 151
transubstantiation, 129, 130
Trinity, 51–53, 77, 78, 82, 95, 122
Troeltsch, Ernst, 12–16, 19, 20, 25–28
Tucker, Mary Evelyn, 120
Two Kingdoms, 15, 16, 17, 20, 152, 165
Tylenda, Joseph N., 133

unconditioned gift, xv, xliv, 36, 64,

65, 89, 91, 92, 95, 103, 110, 120, 145, 150, 153, 171, 173
unilateral, xviii, xxi, xxxix, xliii, xliv, xlv, 42, 45, 46, 51, 52, 56, 63, 69, 76, 83, 85, 86, 87, 91, 92, 95, 97, 100, 102–4, 105, 109, 110–12, 117, 120, 122, 139, 153, 154, 160, 166, 168, 171, 173
unreciprocal, xxxix, xl, 42

Volf, Miroslav, xl, xli, 96

Walter, Gregory, 35, 41, 42, 57
Wandel, Lee Palmer, 130, 131, 138
Weber, Marrianne, 5
Weber, Max, xli, xlii, 3–17, 25 (Weber-Troelschian), 27, 28, 29, 30, 33, 34, 35, 47, 49
Weiner, Annette, 43
Westhelle, Vitor, 15, 151, 152
Whitehead, Alfred North, xxiv, 73, 74
Widmann, Peter, 35, 97, 98, 100, 103
Word, 47, 77, 83, 124, 131, 132, 140, 148, 158
worldly, worldliness, xv, xlvi, 4, 8, 9, 10, 57, 93, 101, 118, 122, 128, 148, 154, 155, 157, 159, 162, 165, 166, 168, 170, 175, 177

Žižek, Slavoj, 33, 51
Zwingli, Ulrich, 84, 130, 131, 140